Sustainable Retrofits

Presenting the state-of-the-art in sustainable retrofits in post-war residential towers, *Sustainable Retrofits* captures and re-informs the current intense refurbishing process that is taking place in Britain, which is part of a global phenomenon happening all over the world, as cities upgrade their building stock in an attempt to comply with governmental emission reduction targets. The authors present inspections of 20 sustainably retrofitted social housing towers, analysing their aesthetic and technical modifications, as well as the shifts occurring in their social structure. The authors use over 200 full colour plans, elevations, photographs, maps and illustrations to beautifully support the statistical and analytical information collected. Finally, they include interviews with some of the architects who designed the retrofits, residents and key stakeholders to inform the conclusions.

Asterios Agkathidis is an architect (ARB) and lecturer in digital architecture at the University of Liverpool, UK, where he is currently leading the MA in Architecture. He studied architecture in Thessaloniki and the RWTH Aachen, and completed his postgraduate studies in Advanced Architectural Design at the Städelschule Architecture Class in Frankfurt. His built work has been published, awarded and exhibited internationally. His seventh book, *Biomorphic Structures*, was published in 2017.

Rosa Urbano Gutiérrez is a Senior Lecturer at the Liverpool School of Architecture, UK, and founding director of the Environmental Ceramics for Architecture Laboratory (ECAlab). She is a registered architect, who studied and worked at the Massachusetts Institute of Technology, Harvard University, and the School of Architecture of Madrid. Her research revolves around documenting, analysing and pursuing the invention and implementation of pioneering sustainable materials and technologies for architecture.

Sustainable Retrofits
Post-War Residential Towers in Britain

Asterios Agkathidis and
Rosa Urbano Gutiérrez

First published 2018
by Routledge
2 Park Square, Milton Park, Abingdon, Oxon OX14 4RN

and by Routledge
711 Third Avenue, New York, NY 10017

Routledge is an imprint of the Taylor & Francis Group, an informa business

© 2018 Asterios Agkathidis and Rosa Urbano Gutiérrez

The right of Asterios Agkathidis and Rosa Urbano Gutiérrez to be identified as authors of this work has been asserted by them in accordance with sections 77 and 78 of the Copyright, Designs and Patents Act 1988.

All rights reserved. No part of this book may be reprinted or reproduced or utilised in any form or by any electronic, mechanical, or other means, now known or hereafter invented, including photocopying and recording, or in any information storage or retrieval system, without permission in writing from the publishers.

Trademark notice: Product or corporate names may be trademarks or registered trademarks, and are used only for identification and explanation without intent to infringe.

British Library Cataloguing-in-Publication Data
A catalogue record for this book is available from the British Library

Library of Congress Cataloging-in-Publication Data
Names: Agkathidis, Asterios, 1974- author. | Urbano Gutiérrez, Rosa, author.
Title: Sustainable retrofits : post war residential towers in Britain /
Asterios Agkathidis and Rosa Urbano Gutiérrez.
Description: New York : Routledge, 2018. | Includes bibliographical
references and index.
Identifiers: LCCN 2017045304| ISBN 9781138689886 (hb : alk. paper) | ISBN
9781138689893 (pb : alk. paper) | ISBN 9781315537344 (ebook)
Subjects: LCSH: High-rise apartment buildings--Environmental aspects--Great
Britain. | Buildings--Retrofitting--Great Britain. | Sustainable
architecture. | Sustainable buildings. | Public housing--Great
Britain--History--20th century.
Classification: LCC NA7863.G7 A39 | DDC 720.941/0904--dc23
LC record available at https://lccn.loc.gov/2017045304

ISBN: 978-1-138-68988-6 (hbk)
ISBN: 978-1-138-68989-3 (pbk)
ISBN: 978-1-315-53734-4 (ebk)

Typeset in Avenir LT STD by
Servis Filmsetting Ltd, Stockport, Cheshire

Contents

Acknowledgements	vi
Introduction	1
1 Public high-rise blocks in Britain: a brief review of their historic context	2
2 Carbon emissions reduction: the need for sustainable retrofits	22
3 Types and techniques: a retrofit manual	38
4 Tower block retrofits	101
5 Conversations with the architects	212
6 Final discussion	233
Figure credits	276
Index	281

Acknowledgements

We would like to express our deepest gratitude to the RIBA Research Trust Awards, for providing the funding that made it possible for us to initiate this research work. Many thanks also to the RIBA Research Grants Committee, and in particular, to John-Paul Nunes, RIBA Head of Education Projects, for their continuous feedback and support.

We are very grateful to the Liverpool School of Architecture, and specially to our Head of School, Professor Soumyen Bandyopadhyay, and our colleagues Professor Simon Pepper, Professor Neil Jackson and Professor Steve Sharples, for their time and dedication reading our manuscript, their inspiring insights and their always encouraging advice. We are also indebted to the University of Liverpool's School of the Arts Research Development Initiative Funding committee, for their funding and support.

We are immensely grateful also to the many second and third year students from our technology and environmental design courses, who during the academic year 2013/14 helped us with the first stage of our documenting process, producing invaluable drawings, photographs and surveys.

We would also like to offer our special thanks to all the people who have generously dedicated time to share with us instrumental information for our research:

- David Rudkin (Halsall Lloyd Partnership Architects), Charles Ellis, (John Robertson Architects), Andrew Mellor (PRP Architects), Roy Roberts (Falconer Chester Hall Architects), Jonathan Falkingham (Urban Splash) and Craig Bolton and Paul Swallow (MacHell Architects) for their critical comments, collected in the interviews that form Chapter 5.
- Sam Webb, for his insider knowledge and extensive experience on the technical assessment of towers, and particularly, on fire safety.
- John Claridge, Robert Blomfield's family, Simon Pepper, Lotte Grønkjær, the Liverpool Record Office and the British Library, for giving us permission to use their photographs, which we found crucial to illustrate our argument.
- All the scholars, architectural practices, housing associations and the different governmental and non-governmental organisations, who directly or indirectly, through their work, have helped us to shape the book, and whose contributions are acknowledged in the endnotes.

We would also like to extend our gratitude to the Routledge team, Fran Ford, Trudy Varcianna and Susan Dunsmore, for making the production of this book a very easy and enjoyable journey.

Finally, we would like to warmly thank our families, for bearing with us during this process. Rosa would like to dedicate this book to Eduardo and Arvo.

Introduction

This book is the report on our RIBA-funded research project presenting the state of the art of sustainable retrofits in post-war residential towers in Britain. The main aim in writing this book is to capture and re-inform the current intense refurbishing process that is taking place in this country, which is part of a global phenomenon happening all over Europe and the world, as cities are upgrading their building stock in an attempt to comply with governmental emission reduction targets. In the UK, greenhouse gas emissions must be drastically reduced by 80 per cent of the 1990 levels by 2050. High-rise concrete tower blocks offer some of the best candidates for an energy-efficient upgrade, presenting structural vulnerability to cold, draughts and damp, becoming unaffordable to heat, unattractive to view and undesirable to occupy.

Due to the magnitude of such a study, we will focus on two main regions: Northwest England and the Greater London areas, where we believe most representative samples can be found. The key objective is the compilation, analysis and categorization of intervention data for a paradigmatic selection of retrofitted social high-rise housing in these two areas. We have inspected 89 sustainably retrofitted social housing towers, analysing their aesthetic and technical modifications, as well as the shifts occurring in their social structure. The book includes a brief historical review of the towers; an evaluation of the socio-cultural and environmental context of their refurbishment for both the 'before' and 'after' situations; the analysis of the towers through drawings, photographs, maps and statistics in reference to the different types of refurbishing interventions; and interviews with some of the architects and developers who designed the retrofits. The final section reveals our conclusions and outlook, including a reflective criticism of fire regulations and safety, based on the tragic aftermath of the Lakanl House and Grenfell Tower disasters.

Chapter 1

Public high-rise blocks in Britain
A brief review of their historic context

The origins of public housing and high-rise estates

The post-war period represented a very distinctive situation in the history of public housing in Europe. Obviously, the Second World War had left the continent devastated, with many cities bombed or in ruins, involving a massive destruction of all kinds of buildings. There was indeed an overwhelming demand for buildings, and most urgently, people needed homes. How the reconstruction of Europe would take shape in those years was very much affected by different trends, some of them had in fact started their trajectory decades before.

An important part of this process is based upon one overarching concept – modernity – which was profoundly focused on the pursuit of health, well-being and progress of society. Important theoretical movements across Europe underpinned this positive thinking. The provision of decent homes for the low-income population was fundamentally connected to these currents of thought: the moral crusade to improve the extremely poor living standard conditions of the working class brought about by industrialisation was very much led by the urgent need to eradicate the epidemics that still haunted Europe at the turn of the twentieth century.

The pursuit of health and well-being consolidated new lines of experimentation. These years would see significant investigations into comfort and the environmental control of buildings that led to important developments, particularly in Britain and France. Numerous designs for walls, floors and ceilings emerged, as multi-layered assemblies with cavities that housed innovative heating, cooling and ventilation equipment of all kinds. The invention or optimisation of new non-porous, easy-to-clean materials (glass, concrete and steel), together with new construction techniques was critical for envisioning the modern *urbanscape*, with large expanses of smooth non-ornate surfaces. The pursuit of health would also bring new building typologies (e.g. sanatoria, spas) or new ideas about how to approach old ones (e.g. the open-air school movement). This line of thought was also influential in theories of the planning of cities, establishing a new relationship with nature in terms of ventilation, sun exposure, views and landscape, while firmly based on a new understanding of civilisation as closely related to technology. These principles, the essence of the Modern Movement, were vastly promoted through the seminal works of Le Corbusier (*Ville Radieuse*, 1929), or Lewis Mumford (*Technics and*

Civilization, 1934), which were highly influential in the following years.[1] In relation to housing in particular, modernity encouraged the generation of new social arrangements, proposing the concept of collective social housing and communal living, which is deeply rooted in the development of a critical concept: the modern welfare state.

The welfare state, as the proposal for an increasingly stronger role of governments in social matters, would definitely be a determining factor in the initiation of social housing. The industrialisation process that had taken place in the nineteenth century had attracted masses of people to the main cities, which were flourishing as industries were concentrated, beginning a depopulation of rural areas. Cities were ill suited to effectively absorb this massive and rapid growth, lacking not only the physical infrastructure to accommodate these huge flows of migrants, but also the regulatory and planning framework. There is abundant literature illustrating the extreme misery affecting the poor newcomers, stuck in overcrowded housing in tenements that could not cater to their hygiene and health needs, generating a breeding ground for the emergence and expansion of contagious diseases. The demand for housing was first of all provided by private initiatives in the form of high-density small dwellings for rent, that often failed to meet thermal and sanitary standards. Aggravating this situation, the commonest practice, as the quickest and cheapest solution for the poorest families, was to subdivide the existing conventional houses into 'rooms'. Later initiatives to improve these conditions were also privately managed by companies, factory owners and philanthropists (following the concepts of model villages, utopian communities, and garden cities), who felt compelled to cater for the accommodation and education of the urban poor all over Europe. Nonetheless very few of the urban poor actually benefitted from these early forms of social housing, which represented a very small percentage of the existing stock, with the majority still left to live in precarious conditions.

A combination of factors paved the way towards engaging civil authorities in the creation of public housing. Primarily, the threat to health and safety: cities were not only dirty and unhealthy, they were also hotbeds for social unrest. The fear of riots, epidemics, and loss of economic profit due to debilitated labour provided the conditions for the generation of Housing Acts in all the European countries. By 1914, the crucial principles and instruments of the regulatory housing policy had been basically established in nearly all the European countries, with the aim of offering a combination of private and public initiatives to solve the housing problem. Housing became a key element in British politics: the building of homes through public agencies was a clear objective, and the civil authorities were the only ones in a position strong enough to assume responsibility for tackling the problem in a comprehensive way.

Despite the provision of a legislative framework, results would not be substantial until after the First World War; in Britain, the effect would not be visible until 1919. To create the space for the implementation of a comprehensive rebuilding programme, the eradication of tenements, cellars and back-to-back terraces had to be conclusive,[2] and this meant a clear trend towards massive slum clearance. Despite the extensive governmental support, by 1931, there was still evidence of both housing shortage and excessive overcrowding

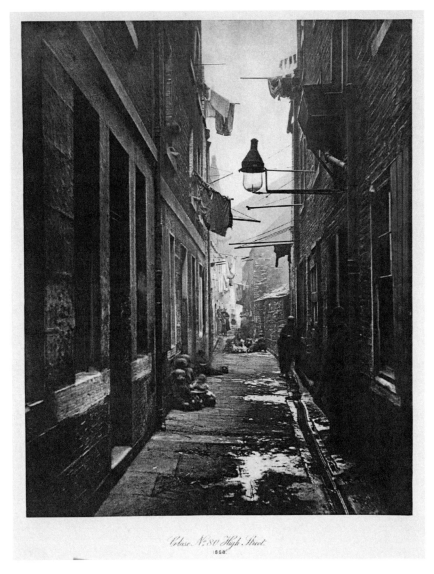

◀ Figure 1.1

Slum in Glasgow, Lanarkshire, 1868

(Figure 1.1). Over those years, the number of areas labelled as slums and potentially to be cleared kept rising, prioritising the quick production of new dwellings over quality and well-planned strategies to optimise the use of the available land.[3, 4] Of all the housing construction between 1919 and 1939 (nearly four million dwellings), over one million dwellings were supplied from public initiative (30 per cent of all new dwellings), and many of the rest had also benefitted from state subsidies.[5, 6] On the whole, basing the strategy on slum clearance generated problems of social imbalance, not only because it privileged those who lived in the designated areas, ignoring others who might be in equal or worse conditions, but also because the massive destruction and rehousing did not take into account an understanding of and protection of the existing communities.

This negligence would unfortunately continue in future interventions, and had a disastrous critical impact, as we will see in later discussions.

Regarding housing types, until 1930, both the public and the private sectors predominantly followed traditional typologies. In the British context, the government adopted the 'cottage' model in garden suburbs as the ideal home for the working class. However, after 1930, a new philosophy emerged, strongly promoting the ascendant progression in the design evolution of flats. Supporting this process, there was not only the pressing need to densely rehouse the slum population, but also, in some cities, the convenience of keeping the workers in the city centres. A critical influence in the creation of flats was the arrival of the new model of collective rental housing for workers promoted by the Modern Movement's ideology. Multi-storey flats seemed the immediate answer to house large numbers of slum dwellers following the new sanitary standards.[7] In 1930, the freestanding high-rise block was promoted at the third CIAM Congress[8] as the typology that would incarnate the Modernist building principles of the functionalist, standardised mass-produced city. In line with these principles, in the Housing Act of 1930, subsidies were related to the numbers of people rehoused rather than the dwellings supplied, giving an extra allowance to developments taking the shape of blocks of flats. Both the European modern vision and the economic affluence helped to establish the modern flat as an acceptable family home.

London, Liverpool, Leeds, Sheffield and Manchester presented the largest clearance programmes in the country. Two of these cities, Liverpool and the various London authorities, would be the only ones to build central flats as their primary strategy to rehouse the working classes. London's reasons for doing this were evident. The outer low-cost land was simply too far away to offer an affordable solution for these families, and in the case of the boroughs, they could not build outside their own boundaries. These reasons were not critical in the case of the main provincial cities, where the leading trend was to accommodate the slum families cheaply and comfortably in suburban cottage developments. The flats were effectively the opportunity for local politicians to experiment with modern European principles and the positive social value associated with this typology through the development of large central buildings, publicising a progressive approach to rehousing that would grant these municipalities (particularly exceptional in Liverpool and on a minor scale in Manchester, Sheffield and Leeds) and their architects a unique reputation.[9]

Rehousing in the original inner-city slum areas, where sites were small and highly priced, meant similar densities were achieved while allowing for the provision of open space and social amenities. Until 1935, the courtyard type of layout was the most successful in Britain, as a design that provided the highest and most economical density. The enclosing rings also provided a public front and a private more domestic back towards the courtyard, typical of most English houses.[10]

An early pioneering project was Ossulston Estate[11] between Euston and St. Pancras stations, built by the London County Council (LCC) between 1927 and 1931[12] (Figure 1.2). Other initiatives to explore the new typology followed, such as the experimental schemes developed for the Metropolitan Borough of

◀ Figure 1.2

View of Ossulston Estate, London, 1927–31

Stepney between 1925–37,[13] or the project for Bethnal Green and East London Housing Association flats at Brunswick Street, Hackney, from 1936 (Figure 1.3). Outside London, Liverpool's Central Redevelopment Area started with St. Andrew's Gardens, designed by John Hughes (1932–35), and followed by Gerard Gardens (1935–39), Myrtle Gardens (1936–37) (Figure 1.4), Caryl Gardens (1936–37), Warwick Gardens (1938), Sir Thomas White Gardens (1938–40) and the Corlett Street flats (1938–39). Quarry Hill, designed by Richard Alfred Hardwick Livett (1934–41), is another, although isolated, eminent example of the European vision in Leeds.

During 1935, the *Zeilenbau* layout, already tried in most European countries, started to appear in Britain. The German development was based on the optimisation of sunlight exposure for each flat, by arranging them in long strips running north to south and giving most habitable rooms a westward outlook receiving sunshine for the non-working part of the day. This arrangement was mostly thought suitable for suburban areas due to space and orientation demands, coupled with inferior capability to deliver high density. Therefore, the concept would not substantially develop until after 1945. Heights were still limited to five or six storeys in most of the cases because lifts were too expensive, but the schemes benefitted from generous floor areas, social communal amenities and some technical novelties, such as the provision of bathrooms and electric lighting. With the exception of London, the private sector showed little interest in building schemes of flats during the 1930s. Two

▲ Figure 1.3

View of the terraced balconies in Bethnal Green and East London Housing Association flats at Brunswick Street, Hackney, July 1936

6   CHAPTER 1 Public high-rise blocks in Britain

▶ Figure 1.4

Myrtle Gardens, Liverpool, 1937. (a) Planned layout; (b) view of the central courtyard facing Myrtle Street; (c) view of one of the internal courtyards showing the children's playground

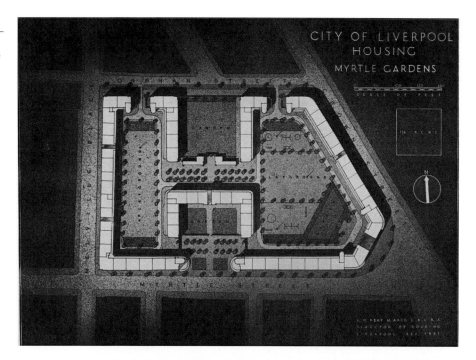

◀ Figure 1.4 (continued)

of the most renowned Modernist examples of that period emerging from private initiative are Highpoint One flats in Highgate (seven storeys), built by Berthold Lubetkin and Ove Arup between 1933 and 1935, and the Isokon Building on Lawn Road (five storeys) designed by Wells Coates, which opened in 1934.

1945–68: The ascent of high-rise social housing

After the Second World War, definite circumstances made the Modernist vision of the functionalist residential tower block a reality. During the 1950s, its production was still mostly characterised by low-rise blocks of flats (three to five storeys tall), and the construction of high-rise blocks would only reach relevant numbers between 1958 and 1968. Their emergence was obviously related to the urgent need to solve the long-standing problem of housing shortages, but this time it would be accompanied by the necessity to use new construction techniques to support cheaper and quicker production.[14] This necessity would offer the opportunity to explore this typology as a laboratory to finally provide 'homes for a fairer society', whose ultimate goal was to improve the overall quality of life, both in comfort and convenience terms. The post-war period is in fact regarded as providing the grounds for the emergence of the modern welfare state, social housing being a crucial instrument in local and national welfare policies.[15]

In that sense, the image of the new social housing had to be effectively new in every way: offering spacious rooms with high quality standards (maximising ceiling heights and window areas to optimise natural light and air ingress), in combination with the implementation of innovative technologies and social and leisure visions. Layouts and planning were driven by modern life in the flats: acknowledging new functions (e.g. the bathroom), but also new types of households, allowing for the first time flexible use of the spaces. The concept of the estate would take full meaning in these years, comprising communal functions such as playgrounds, shops, clubs, nurseries or schools, and new family-oriented uses such as a car parking space, or a garden that was no longer considered a means to provide food to the family, but an environment for leisure (Figures 1.5, 1.6, 1.7).

As in the past, high-rise blocks were not the preferred typology: the cottage model (the three-bedroom family house) was still the most favoured form of public housing, accounting for 64 per cent of the total output between 1945 and 1979 (Figure 1.8). But to all intents and purposes, high-rise blocks embodied the ideals of modernity, bringing the opportunity to create landmarks that represented the progressive attitude of cities. All the actors involved in the provision of social housing competed to offer their symbolic buildings. In the British context, this typology would receive the greatest subsidies from public housing programmes, including the much-needed 1946 lifts subsidy, which would allow higher flats to be built. It was centrally determined that subsidies would increase with height (more than six storeys),[16] which was particularly useful in inner city or landlocked areas where expanding the boundaries proved impossible. High density housing seemed the only effective way to deal with a housing problem that showed even worse conditions than in 1919, and factors such as the advances in prefabrication building techniques, or the introduction of the tower crane in the building construction process presented a more feasible way of meeting the targets.

▶ Figure 1.5
View of internal courtyard of Park Hill, Sheffield 1957–61, designed by Sheffield Corporation City Architect's Department, John Lewis Womersley

◀ Figure 1.6

Great Arthur House, Golden Lane Estate, Finsbury, London, 1957: detail of the roof terrace of the tower block

◀ Figure 1.7

Barbican Estate, City of London, 1961: full-scale mock-up of kitchen, built in the architect's studios

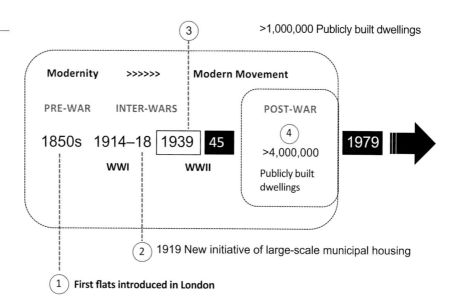

▶ Figure 1.8

Public high-rise housing construction between 1850 and 1945

All the progressive architects wanted to work for the local authorities and their active housing programmes, contributing to the general idealism of a better future for all. A good example of this is the LCC Architects Department, which by the end of the 1950s had more than 3,000 staff, including 503 qualified architects.[17] Central government established the National Building Agency in 1963 to support the local authorities design teams to embrace the emergent construction systems. These technologies were imported from more experienced countries, particularly from Scandinavia, in a variety of methods. The early developments using slab blocks and their scientific *Zeilenbau* arrangement soon gave way to other formal explorations, in search of the 'aesthetics of height'. Since the early 1950s, mixed heights, for instance, through the use of maisonettes and point blocks, would firmly define a new design trend, forming different configurations complemented by explorations in deck accesses, bridges, *piloti* and other topographical landscapes. Local housing policies also favoured point blocks over slabs, encouraging the production of progressively taller towers, which by the mid-1960s vertiginously increased to over 20 or even 30 storeys[18] (Figure 1.9).

All the countries in Europe launched programmes to meet symbolic production figures (typically one million dwellings), and all the legal processes were speeded up for that to happen. In many areas, the demolition of pre-war dwellings was a product of deliberate eradication of slums rather than the need to tackle war damage[19] (Figures 1.10 (a) and (b) and 1.11). Some countries envisioned the new typology as a 'modern village in which all classes would live in harmony'.[20] That certainly happened in all the Eastern European countries, and that aim was also included in the British Housing Act of 1949. Estates of flats remained of no interest to the private sector, and their construction was left in the hands of municipal authorities, as part of their target to build four-fifths of all new housing.[21] Despite extensive support, flats in blocks above six

CHAPTER 1 Public high-rise blocks in Britain

 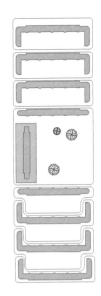 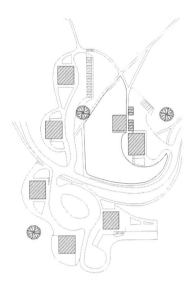

◀ Figure 1.9

Evolution of the social high-rise housing typology in England according to three layouts: enclosed courtyards (left), *Zeilenbau* slabs (centre) and point blocks (right)

◀ Figure 1.10

(a) and (b) Two views showing the emergence of high-rise housing blocks in slum clearance areas, East End, London in the 1960s.
(a) Odds against tomorrow.
(b) Another gloomy Sunday.

▶ Figure 1.11 (a–c)

Three views of the emergence of the Netherthorpe Estate in slum clearance areas of Sheffield, 1952–57

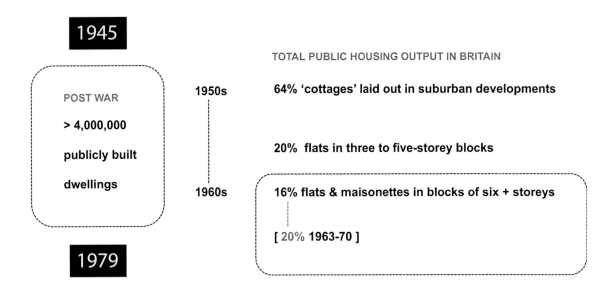

Figure 1.12

Public high-rise housing construction between 1945 and 1979

storeys represented a minor proportion: just accounting for over 2 per cent of all council housing in 1991[22, 23] (Figure 1.12).

In spite of the low numbers, high-rise estates were very visible. It was easier to produce them in cleared areas that needed redevelopment, or in greenfield sites in the peripheries of cities to allow tower cranes to systematise their erection following parallel rows to minimise cost and maximise sun exposure, which led to highly concentrated areas of tower blocks. Nationally, some regions accumulated the highest concentrations of high-rise flats, nearly 80 per cent of the total production in those years: Greater London and the North West again led this trend, this time also followed by the West Midlands and Glasgow.[24] Some developments effectively became real landmarks, in some cases even achieving protected status years later. Examples of these prominent estates are Golden Lane Estate, designed by Chamberlin Powell & Bon in 1957; the Trellick Tower, designed by Ernő Goldfinger in 1972; Robin Hood Gardens, designed by Alison and Peter Smithson in 1972; or Park Hill, designed by Jack Lynn and Ivor Smith in 1957. But the image that remains for the majority of the population is that of the hundreds of massive 'anonymous' interventions (designed by the municipal Housing Departments), which colonised the peripheral landscape of these cities: of the 6,544 post-war blocks built in the UK, 2,789 were built in Greater London, 458 in Birmingham, 692 in the North West, and 863 in Scotland (261 in Glasgow alone).[25]

1968 to the 1980s: The decline of high-rise housing

By the end of the 1960s, the perception of tower blocks, and their optimistic modernist connection to technology as a vehicle for social change, had shifted dramatically. Apart from a sudden general scepticism regarding the Modern Movement ideology by architects and planners, different realistic facts became apparent at that time, in relation to technical, social and financial issues, with a major impact on young families with children:

- The management of these big estates was a new responsibility for the municipal authorities, and proved to be very challenging, lacking a continuous approach in the provision of services (e.g. maintenance), and in many cases counting on insufficient resources, which seriously affected the estate's viability.
- Estates turned out to be technically dysfunctional for different reasons: deficient in acoustic and weather insulation, inefficient lifts (or even absence of them), structural problems connected with the use of new techniques, low quality materials, and inadequate building services equipment.
- Social and spatial problems in the environments outside and inside the blocks: lack of security, failure to favour communication between neighbours, lack of privacy, traffic and noise pollution, and a poor location (developments far from local facilities, aggravated when social and leisure amenities were not provided within the estate).
- Statistics showed that building high was actually more expensive,[26] running the estate involved high maintenance and large losses, and that actually people preferred to live at ground level.[27]
- Socio-economic issues related to the wider context: high unemployment, poverty, poor schooling, and new problems in relation to drug consumption and anti-social behaviour.[28]

▲ Figure 1.13

Linda Marshall on the balcony of her new home on the 19th floor flat of Ferrier Point in Canning Town, after being evacuated from Ronan Point

All these factors, together with the withdrawal of subsidies in 1967 and the fatal partial collapse of Ronan Point in 1968, marked the decline of the high-rise block venture in Britain. Major concerns about safety, along with the high operating costs, predisposed local authorities to support the development of structural surveys of the blocks, which soon would lead to decisions to demolish many of them, in some cases after only 18 years of existence. The first demolitions took place in Birkenhead in Merseyside in 1979: two 11-storey high-rise blocks. The actual Ronan Point would be demolished in 1984 together with another eight almost identical blocks, and many others came after them following reports commissioned by the Ministry of Housing[29] (Figure 1.13). The advice to authorities was to appraise all their blocks over six-storeys in height which were built of large pre-cast concrete panels to form load-bearing walls or floors or both in order to carry out dynamic and fire tests, and assess whether they were susceptible to progressive collapse.

Some of these studies led to interventions to strengthen the buildings; in other cases, to demolitions. In Liverpool, two-thirds of their 67 tower blocks were approved for demolition. The debate as to whether it is more appropriate to demolish or to refurbish these buildings is still current today across Europe

CHAPTER 1 Public high-rise blocks in Britain   15

◀ Figure 1.14

Demolition of AAB Afdeling 43 in Copenhagen. Photograph taken from the 11th floor of the opposite block within the estate, 13 May 2012.

(Figure 1.14). The high cost of demolitions in combination with a change of vision in the welfare activities of states since the mid-1980s changed attitudes towards this typology once more.

High-rise blocks: new visions

The Right-to-Buy law passed in the Housing Act of 1980 allowed council tenants in the UK to buy their properties for the first time, the majority of sales being of family houses (cottages) and with flats only accounting for 10 per cent of the sold high rise stock.[30] As a result, now most public housing in the UK is flats. The increasing demand for social housing, together with the fact that some of the flats are privately owned and that some of these buildings have been listed by Historic England, make many of these blocks unsuitable for demolition. These circumstances and evidence from surveys performed between 1980 and 1990s of the positive views of tenants[31,32] (who in many cases have been living in their flats for 30 years), have moved this part of the council housing stock back into the category of assets.

In these years, the initiative for intervention and management remained with the municipal housing authorities, and some started to develop refurbishment strategies for their high-rise stock. In the 1990s and the early 2000s many local authorities put their housing stock in the hands of housing associations through Large Scale Voluntary Transfers, as a way to provide managers with access to raise private funding to enable the modernisation of their properties. In 2001, local authorities owned 2.8 million homes (13 per cent of the housing stock), which by 2010 had decreased to 1.8 million (8 per cent of the stock). Over the same period, the number of housing association homes has increased from 1.4 million to 2 million.[33]

Refurbishment not only offers opportunities for technical upgrades, but also for social rearrangements to improve the social imbalance that occurred over the different periods, while providing for the new social demands. Social housing was not only an instrument to deliver accommodation to the working classes in the aftermath of the two wars; in some countries it was also an instrument for municipal authorities to 'organise' the poor (including 'persons considered unable to behave decently in a normal house'[34]) in a selective and controlled way.[35] In the past, working families with young children able to pay their rents and take care of their tenancies received the highest priority, but rehousing from slum clearance involved a diversity of social compositions, and in some cases this organisation could lead to blocks entirely accommodating 'residual' populations with extreme conditions of unemployment or poverty. When social conflict became palpable, those tenants with more options left, and high-rise blocks were occupied by those tenants with least choice: migrants, single people, and 'problem families'.[36]

Local strategies to regenerate the blocks during the 1990s included the specialisation of some blocks into 'sheltered housing' to accommodate the increasing numbers of older and ill people, as well as blocks for single people and students. Some of these blocks were comprehensively refurbished with successful results, although in limited numbers, and that has become the general practice nowadays. The current social profile of tower blocks varies according to locations and circumstances, as explained above. Where gentrification has not happened, the typical profile presents high proportions of retired or unemployed tenants, tenants whose income is at the level of state benefits, and households containing persons with a long-term illness. The latest demographic analysis of the English high-rise housing stock reveals that:

- only 7 per cent of owner-occupier households with people aged 60 years old or over live in flats compared with 20 per cent of such households in the private rented sector, and 45 per cent in the social rented sector;
- a high proportion of households in poverty[37] (52 per cent) rent flats from social landlords;
- ethnic minority households are much more likely to live in flats.[38]

The central government has not devised specific strategies to target the regeneration of the high-rise stock in particular. Although the typology could benefit from global refurbishment programmes, this route offers limited resources and hard competition from other models of housing.[39]

New trends support the refurbishment of high-rise housing as a demanded alternative for new urban lifestyles, which is attracting the interest of both the public and private sectors:

- Many of the towers are now considered 'well located' for populations and cities that keep growing, becoming in some cases (mostly in London) listed buildings in which their historic features are favourably appreciated, going not only through processes of specialisation (young/single population) but even of gentrification (liberal professionals).
- They are well suited to the increasing number of smaller and childless households.[40]

CHAPTER 1 Public high-rise blocks in Britain

- Retrofitting and reusing buildings also suit the environmental sensitivities of our contemporary society.

In the most up-to-date survey, the English Housing Survey: HOMES 2010, out of the 22.4 million dwellings in England (21.4 million occupied), 66 per cent were owner-occupied and the rest were rented, split evenly between the private rented sector (17 per cent) and the social rented sector (17 per cent). As regards the high-rise stock numbers, 46 per cent of local authority homes were flats, 9 per cent of these in high-rise blocks (390,000 dwellings).[41]

In particular, according to a report from 2012,[42] there were still around 3,500 council housing high-rise blocks in Britain taller than ten storeys. Whether these buildings are a worthy legacy to be kept is still controversial. Tower blocks keep being demolished every year all over the country. Since 2006, 25 per cent of Glasgow's high-rise housing has been demolished, to make way for new housing developments. In London, the Heygate Estate was only demolished in 2014; in the North, two 15-storey tower blocks from Seaforth, Merseyside, and the remaining three 17-storey tower blocks of Queens Park flats in Blackpool, were only demolished in April and July of 2016 respectively. In addition to approved plans, the UK government's declarations in January 2016 elicited new debates about the demolition-refurbishment issue, when plans to either bulldoze or refurbish 100 sink estates were confirmed.

The assessment of the towers involves high levels of complexity, where numerous quantitative (measurable) and qualitative (subjective) aspects have to be taken into consideration, and the weight of these measures normally depends on whether the evaluation is undertaken from a public or private perspective. In a similar way, the different proposals to retrofit the successfully retained high-rise blocks present diverse approaches in the consideration of those variables. The framework in which these retrofits are happening and the analysis of those approaches will be the focus of the following chapters.

Notes

1 Lewis Mumford, *Technics and Civilization* (New York: Harcourt, Brace & World, 1934); Le Corbusier, *La Ville Radieuse* (Paris: Vincent, Fréal & Cie, 1933).
2 See Lionel Esher, *A Broken Wave: The Rebuilding of England 1940–1980* (London: Penguin Books, 1981), p. 70: quoting the *DIA Yearbook of 1929–30*:

> Our slums are a disgrace. Everyone has said so for 50 years . . . why then do we not demolish them and build healthy flats instead! Amsterdam, Hamburg and Vienna are not afraid of the problem. But in this country we build suburbs . . . too far from work to attract the slum-dwellers.

3 Ibid. For instance, this practice doubled the built up area of London for only an increase in population of one-fifth.

4 Simon Pepper and Peter Richmond, 'Homes unfit for heroes: the slum problem in London and Neville Chamberlain's Unhealthy Areas Committee, 1919–21', *Town Planning Review*, 80(2) (2009): 143–171.

5 Ibid., p. 27: nearly one-seventh of the remainder.

6 Miles Glendinning and Stefan Muthesius, *Tower Block: Modern Public Housing in England, Scotland, Wales and Northern Ireland* (New Haven, CT: Yale University Press, pp. 1–2: These overall totals were rather unevenly distributed across the UK. Between the wars, public housing accounted for 28 per cent of all new dwellings in England and Wales, only 15 per cent in Northern Ireland, but as much as 67 per cent in Scotland (Glasgow had 71 per cent).

7 See Florian Urban, *Tower and Slab: Histories of Global Mass Housing* (London: Routledge, 2012), pp. 10–13.

8 Congrès International d'Architecture Moderne, created in 1928 to set the principles of the Modern Movement.

9 Frank Newbery, 'Liverpool's flats 1919–1939: policy and design of central area redevelopment by the Liverpool Housing Department', B.Arch. dissertation, Liverpool School of Architecture, 1980, p. 102.

10 Ibid., pp. 89–90.

11 The term 'estate' appears for the first time in 1920: both the word and concept appear in the December 1920 issue of the official journal *Housing*, which was circulated free to local authorities when they were beginning to implement the 1919 Housing Act. See Alison Ravetz, *Council Housing and Culture: The History of a Social Experiment* (London: Routledge, 2001), p. 67.

12 Simon Pepper, 'Ossulston Street: early LCC experiments in high-rise housing, 1925–29', *The London Journal*, 7(1) (1981): 45–64.

13 Simon Pepper and Peter Richmond, 'Stepney and the politics of high-rise housing: Limehouse Fields to John Scurr House, 1925–1937', *The London Journal*, 34(1) (2009): 33–54; and Simon Pepper and Peter Richmond, 'Upward or outward? Politics, planning and council flats, 1919–1939', *The Journal of Architecture*, 13(1) (2008): 53–90.

14 Building high was not actually demonstrated to be cheaper. See Alison Ravetz, *Council Housing*, p. 105.

15 Mark Swenarton, Tom Avermaete and Dirk van den Heuvel (eds), *Architecture and the Welfare State* (London: Routledge, 2015).

16 'Flats in 6-storey blocks would get more than twice the subsidy on houses, and flats in 15-storey blocks nearly three times as much' (ibid., p. 106).

17 Simon Pepper, 'High-rise housing in London c1940–1970', in Peter Guillery and David Kroll (eds), *Mobilising Housing Histories* (London: RIBA Publishing, 2017), p. 124.

18 Ibid., p. 131.

19 Pepper, 'High-rise housing', p. 129.

20 Implemented by Aneurin Bevan in the Housing Act of 1949.

21 Ravetz, *Council Housing*, p. 96.

22 Glendinning and Muthesius, *Tower Block*, p. 2.

23 Richard Turkington, "Britain. High-rise Housing as a 'Doubtful Guest". In Richard Turkington, Ronald van Kempen, and Frank Wassenberg, (eds.)

High-Rise Housing in Europe: Current Trends and Future Prospects (Delft: DUP Science, 2004), pp. 147–164: regarding the situation at the end 1990s–early 2000s:

> The numbers of high-rise dwellings (6 storeys and above) rose from 6,000 in 1956 to 17,000 in 1961, 35,000 in 1964 and 44,000 in 1966. Within the high-rise category there was a marked trend towards increasingly tall blocks. Blocks of 10–14 storeys expanded from 0.7% of public housing in 1955 to 8.4% in 1963. Blocks of 15–19 storeys expanded from 0.1% in 1955 to 8.3% in 1964.

24 For instance, Hutchesontown Gorbals in Glasgow, by 1971, had 208 towers comprising nearly 21,000 homes. Birmingham created 458 high blocks in its suburbs. See Ravetz, *Council Housing*, p. 105. Data in relation to Greater London: 25 per cent of all new council dwellings between 1945–79, 50 per cent of all new council dwellings in 1965–68; Glasgow: 75 per cent of all new council dwellings from 1961–68. See Glendinning and Muthesius, *Tower Block*, p. 4.

25 Ibid., Table 3, p. 333.

26 Official report *Flats and Houses* (Ministry of Housing and Local Government, London: HMSO, 1958).

27 See Patrick Dunleavy, *The Politics of Mass Housing in Britain 1945–75: A Study of Corporate Power and Professional Influence in the Welfare State* (Oxford: Clarendon Press, 1981), p. 280:

> [In Greater London] seventy per cent of their applicants pre-ferred a house and a garden, although at this period only nine per cent of the authority's housing output was in this form, while sixty-five per cent was in high flats.

See Ministry of Housing and Local Government. *Families Living at High Density: A Study of Estates in Leeds, Liverpool and London* (London: HMSO, 1970). p. 151.

28 Richard Turkington, Ronald van Kempen and Frank Wassenberg (eds), *High-Rise Housing in Europe: Current Trends and Future Prospects* (Delft: DUP Science, 2004), p. 12.

29 From conversation with Sam Webb, consultant at British Research Establishment, who developed reports for the Ministry of Housing between 1968 and the end of the 1980s, for instance: 'The structure of Ronan Point and other Taylor Woodrow buildings' (1985), 'Large panel system dwellings: preliminary information on ownership and condition' (1986), and 'The structural adequacy and durability of large panel system dwellings' (1987).

30 Turkington, 'Britain. High-rise', p. 152.

31 Ibid.

32 The National Tower Block Network was created in 1987 for the active involvement of tenants in blocks issues, having their own bulletin nation-wide. Nowadays tenants are sought to engage through consultation in any refurbishment process.

33 Department for Communities and Local Government), *English Housing Survey: HOMES 2010* (London: TSO, 5 July 2012), p. 9.

34 Francis G. Castles, *et al. The Oxford Handbook of the Welfare State*. Oxford Handbooks Online (Oxford: Oxford University Press, 2010). pp. 67–80. See especially Chapters 5 and 6: 'The Emergence of the Welfare State' by Stein Kuhne and Anne Sander, and 'Post-War Welfare State Development' by Frank Nullmeier and Franz-Xaver Kaufmann.

35 See the idea of a new order for the poor, expressed by Jeremy Till in his article 'Modernity and order: architecture and the welfare state', available at: https://jeremytill.s3.amazonaws.com/uploads/post/attachment/35/2006_Modernity_and_Order.pdf, p. 19:

> There is a symbiotic relationship; both the welfare state and architectural modernism are reliant on their need for order. Within the welfare estate, the poor need to be reclassified as non-poor if progress is to be announced. They need to be reordered into another system, lifting them from poverty in an attempt to throw off the Victorian associations with dirt and immorality. Importantly, it needs to be seen that the poor have been reordered, and it is here that architectural modernism comes in as a signifier of order, cleanliness and progress. And architecture is all too willing to collaborate, not just because the welfare agenda fits so well with architecture's own agenda of ordering and cleanliness (with beauty in there as an associated given), but also because architects can feel good about it. The architecture of the welfare state provides a perfect vehicle for architectural notions of social progress being affected by architectural input.

36 Turkington, 'Britain: High-rise', p. 157.

37 Department for Communities and Local Government, *English Housing Survey*, p. 24: 'Households in poverty are defined as households whose equivalised income is less than 60% of the median value.'

38 Ibid.

39 See Chapter 2.

40 Department for Communities and Local Government, *English Housing Survey*, p. 12: In 2010 of the 22.4 million dwellings existing in England, 21.4 million were occupied; the vast majority (97 per cent) were occupied by a single household or person.

41 Ibid., p. 14.

42 Katie Bates, Laura Lane and Anne Power, 'High rise hope: the social implications of energy efficiency retrofit in large multi-storey tower blocks', LSE Housing and Communities, *CASE Report* 75 (2012): 1.

Chapter 2

Carbon emissions reduction

The need for sustainable retrofits

Environmental context

The British government, through the UK Carbon Plan,[1] published in the Climate Change Act of 2008, made a long-term commitment towards a substantial decarbonisation of Britain, establishing the world's first legally binding climate change target. According to this law, the aim is to reduce the UK's greenhouse gas emissions by at least 38 per cent by 2020, and by 80 per cent by 2050, from the 1990 baseline.

This strategy is of critical relevance to the built environment. Statistics from 2009, right after the Carbon Plan was published, show that buildings were responsible for 37 per cent of the total greenhouse emissions in the UK, being higher than any other use (i.e. transportation or industry).[2] At present, at the beginning of 2017, it is still obvious that decarbonising space and water heating is one of the biggest challenges for carbon budgets, since 17 per cent of UK emissions are still produced from heating and powering homes and buildings.[3] By 2050, all buildings will need to have an emissions footprint close to zero, which mostly means that they will need to become better insulated, use more energy-efficient products and obtain their heating from low carbon sources. Currently, the use of low-carbon heat is minor, representing less than 2 per cent of buildings' heat demands.[4] Regarding the domestic sector in particular, in 2015, it consumed 29 per cent of the total final energy (leading to 24 per cent of the total emissions), and accounted for 66 per cent of the building emissions in Britain.[5] A similar situation can be seen in Europe, where in 2014 housing rep-resented 25 per cent of all energy used in the European Union, occupying the largest amount of floor area (70–75 per cent),[6] despite the majority of the EU-28 population (41.5 per cent, four out of every ten persons) living in flats.[7]

Measures created to ensure carbon reductions are having a great impact on the design of present and future buildings, but are particularly critical as a catalyst for the regeneration of existing buildings. This is true not only because refurbishing rather than building new saves more carbon, but also because the UK's housing stock is among the most inefficient in Europe, and most impor-tantly, the renewal rate of the stock is very slow, at least 80 per cent of the homes that will be standing in 2050 have already been built.[8] According to this figure, only 20 per cent of the stock will be at least at the energy-efficiency level required by current regulations for newly built housing. Improving the energy

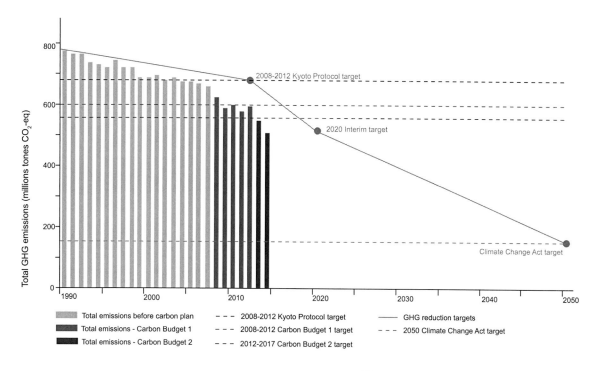

UK greenhouse gas emissions compared to targets

▲ Figure 2.1

UK GHG emissions compared to targets
Source: Department of Energy and Climate Change (31 March 2016).

efficiency of existing homes will, therefore, play a significant role in ensuring the UK's 2050 climate change targets are met (Figure 2.1).

A recent report shows that densely populated British cities have lower greenhouse emissions and energy consumption per capita than less dense cities, due to a reduced dependency on car travel.[9] The sustainable growth of cities requires compactness and diversity of use in all its areas, allowing for well-connected and car-independent communities. Sustainability also implies making the most of existing infrastructure and resources, taking advantage of the energy and capital that were invested in them. As part of this strategy, it is essential to maximise the value of the existing residential building stock.

Inspecting and appraising the existing stock are crucial to this process, not only because buildings present a variety of physical problems, but also because most of them were built at a time when energy efficiency and sustainability regulation standards were non-existent or much less demanding than today. About 70 per cent of the existing residential buildings in the UK were actually built before the oil crisis of 1973, that is, before design intentionally incorporated ecological concerns: 23 per cent were built before 1919; 17 per cent were built between 1919 and 1945, and 30 per cent were built between 1946 and 1973.[10] In the existing residential buildings, over 410,000 homes are social high-rise flats (390,000 in England, and 18,146 in Scotland;[11] there is no available surveyed data for high rise flats in Wales and Northern Ireland). Given that the oldest stock tends to consume more energy, it also offers the highest potential to improve its energy performance by resorting to retrofitting.

CHAPTER 2 Carbon emissions reduction

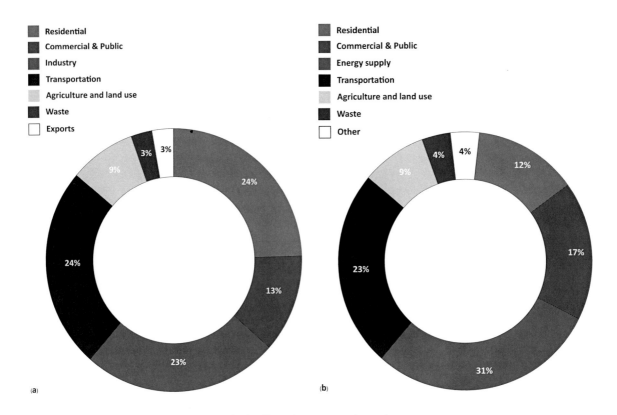

▲ Figure 2.2

(a) and (b) UK GHG emissions by sectors in 2009 and 2014
Source: Department of Energy & Climate Change (31 March 2016).

Since the 1990s, most of the British dwellings have gone through consecutive processes of modernisation and adaptation, aiming to improve their technical and energy efficiency performance (Figure 2.2). In 2013, the average energy efficiency rating (SAP09) for the English stock (80 per cent of the UK stock) was 60 (band D; 5.1 tonnes of CO_2 per dwelling per year), whereas in the social sector, the global rating was 64.6 (3.2 tonnes of CO_2 per dwelling per year), and for high-rise flats, in particular, the rating was 67.8 (top of band D; 2.9 tonnes of CO_2 per dwelling per year).[12] Only 6 per cent of homes (1.5 million) in England achieved the worst energy efficiency rating bands F and G (4 per cent of these homes were in the social sector), whereas in 1996 this proportion was 29 per cent of the total housing stock.[13] In a similar upgrading process, the SAP rating for the Scottish housing stock successively improved up to 66 (top of band D) in 2013.[14]

However, the scale of this challenge became clear in a report released by the UK government in 2013. It was estimated that an average of one home would need to be retrofitted every minute between then and 2050 if the UK was to meet its carbon reduction targets.[15] Looking at the UK residential stock, public housing represents the highest share of the housing stock developed without any energy performance considerations, and within it, high-rise concrete tower blocks offer great potential in this endeavour to lower our environmental footprint, since they already contribute to higher density and compactness, and provide economies of scale difficult to achieve in private properties. The majority of these blocks already have well-organised communities, with well-established systems to support communication among tenants. Another advantage is that there is normally one freeholder, a local authority or registered social landlord, which are easier to engage. Having just one freeholder also means that it is easier to refurbish the whole estate (in many cases over 700 dwellings) in one single comprehensive programme, where a number of practicalities can be arranged more easily too: from installing scaffoldings or acquiring building materials and labour, to granting consistency of intervention criteria for the entire block in terms of aesthetics and performance goals. An integral refurbishment permits a full treatment of the different issues of the building envelope (thermal and acoustic insulation, fabric repair, installation of renewables, etc.), rather than inefficient partial interventions detrimental to the building's performance.

The post-war residential tower blocks used experimental construction systems that were poorly insulated, and in many instances, they were not properly managed and maintained throughout their life, which have left them in even poorer technical condition: structural vulnerability to cold, draughts and damp, becoming unaffordable to heat, unattractive to view and undesirable to occupy. The ecological retrofit offers not only the instrument to update their energy and technical performance, but also to eliminate social stigmas, increase their attractiveness, and provide a positive sense of well-being and safety for tenants and landlords.

The main goals of the retrofits are:

- To deliver an ecological upgrade, leading to reductions in energy consumption, greenhouse gas emissions and energy costs. This is mainly achieved through the implementation of thermal insulation, and renewable and energy-efficient systems.
- To address the physical problems of the estate caused by poor maintenance, low construction standards and inefficient or outdated design solutions. This work implies external and internal repairs of the building fabric (cladding and structure), the definition of a new layout according to contemporary uses and types of households, implementing new and more efficient building services (lighting, heating, ventilation, electrical systems, water, waste management, passenger lifts), and cleaning (painting).
- To provide a positive environmental image for the estate and its neighbourhood. This work entails improvements to the landscape within and around the high-rise blocks, and on their communal facilities for social interaction (green areas, playgrounds, allotments, sports areas, community centres, etc.). The ultimate goal is to remove any negative social connotations and offer a safe, sustainable, pleasant and welcoming environment.

Government energy-efficiency retrofit programmes

For over twenty years, the government has launched a series of environmental schemes to incentivise the ecological upgrade of the British housing stock, by engaging dwelling owners to undertake retrofit work. Improving the current energy-inefficient housing stock offers enormous opportunities for the UK, in both

CHAPTER 2 Carbon emissions reduction

economic and environmental terms. Some studies indicate that renovating homes would not only generate investment and jobs, but could also help to avoid costly investments in additional energy infrastructure: more efficient houses present a lower energy demand, which can be minimised or even zero in those cases that incorporate power generation and resource-efficiency systems (photovoltaic cells, wind turbines, geothermal energy, water reuse, waste recycling, etc.), which can make the property completely independent from the energy networks. Apart from the obvious global carbon reductions and economic benefits already discussed, retrofitting also brings lower bills and increased well-being for residents. However, encouraging energy-efficiency improvements, despite the offered support and highly subsidised prices (often for free), turned out to be a difficult task, and take-up by households has tended to be surprisingly slow and low.[16]

Successive environmental programmes have been created to support the different stages of the decarbonisation process, in correspondence with statistical performance data supplied by regular reports commissioned by independent bodies, such as the Climate Change Committee and the British Research Establishment, who provide advice and recommendations to the UK government. A timeline in Figure 2.3 shows the different programmes chronologically ordered, and they are also explained in more detail in this section.

Energy Efficiency Standards of Performance (EESoP) and Energy Efficiency Commitment (EEF) (1994–2005)

The Energy Efficiency Standards of Performance (EESoP) and the Energy Efficiency Commitment (EEC) schemes were established with social and environmental goals. The EESoP, in its three consecutive stages, ran from 1994 to 2002; after that, the EEC ran from 2002 to 2008 in two consecutive stages. They were set to deliver energy-efficiency measures to the most vulnerable homes, mainly focused on insulation, lighting, heating and appliances, although thermal insulation was at the centre of the strategy as the most important resource to deliver comfort while saving residents money on their fuel bills.[17] These schemes were open to all types of housing, and despite their benefits and successful outcomes, they would not have as great an impact on public residential tower blocks as the Decent Homes Standard, also created at that time.

Decent Homes Standard (2000–2012)

The Decent Homes Standard[18] was a technical standard specific to public housing, introduced to improve the quality of the stock to ensure that all social housing was of a decent standard (achieves minimum quality conditions) within ten years. The target was set in 2000, using the policy as a vehicle

> [to] promote social cohesion, well-being and self-dependence, and ensure that all social housing meets set standards of decency by 2010, by reducing the number of households living in social

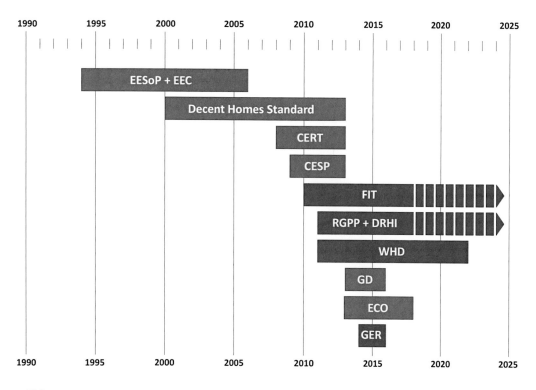

EESoP: Energy Efficiency Standards of Performance; EEC: Energy Efficiency Commitment; CERT: Carbon Emission Reduction Target; CESP Community Energy Saving Programme; FIT: Feed-in Tariffs; RGPP: Renewable Heat Premium Payment; DRHI: Domestic Renewable Heat Incentive; WHD: Warm Home Discount; GD: Green Deal Policy; ECO: Energy Company Obligation; GER: Government Electricity Rebate.

▲ Figure 2.3

UK decarbonisation incentives timeline

housing that does not meet these standards by a third between 2001 and 2004, with most of the improvement taking place in the most deprived local authority areas.[19]

This policy required all local councils to set out a programme to evaluate the entirety of their housing stock and undertake modifications and replacements when the conditions laid out in the standard were not met. Some of them found out that an extensive proportion of their stock was actually in need of an upgrade, with works that required major regeneration and long time frames. Putting in place the operational logistics to undertake the different jobs that would meet their maintenance obligations (from assessing to tackling extensive repairing, but also enabling the financial resources to fund the different interventions) was a demanding task for many local authorities, considering their inability to generate private capital. The policy was flexible enough to allow them to delegate part or the totality of their housing stock to registered social landlords, who could seek funding under the Private Finance Initiative to undertake the scheduled interventions. They could resort to three strategies: (1) private finance

CHAPTER 2 Carbon emissions reduction   27

initiative (PFI) already mentioned; (2) the arm's-length management organisations (ALMOs); and (3) stock transfer.

- ALMOs were first established in 2002 and currently, manage over 500,000 council homes in 40 local authorities.[20] They were created to ensure high-quality management, effective investment, and the increased involvement of tenants while maintaining the ownership of the housing stock in council control. They provide the opportunity for tenants to be well represented, since one-third of members on the board are council tenants, with the remaining positions occupied by serving councillors and independent members with relevant business and housing experience. Since tenants keep local authorities as their legal landlords, they also keep the same rights: rights to buy, repair and manage.
- PFI has been in effect since 1998, and its foremost aim was to enable the involvement of the private sector (private capital) in public sector projects, by creating public-private partnerships. Through PFI, the private sector handles the up-front costs, and offers an instrument for increasing efficiency to public spending, bringing a wide range of skills to the provision of public services.
- Many local councils decided to transfer some or all of their housing stock to a housing association, as another way of bringing private investment to the public sector, to better repair and maintain the stock. Housing associations can focus on management and development that can be funded by private loans, working in close collaboration with tenants, who have a greater say in the services and improvements provided. This solution permits local authorities to reduce their debts, use their funding to finance other projects and concentrate on housing strategy and planning rather than management and development.

The implementation of the Decent Homes Standard was regarded by many of the involved stakeholders as highly successful, resulting in many tower blocks being improved, with new kitchens, bathrooms, heating systems, insulation and windows.[21]

Halfway the upgrade process it became clear that the target of 100 per cent decency was unlikely to be met, but nonetheless, the 47.5 per cent non-decency homes reported in 2001 dramatically declined to 14.5 per cent in 2010.[22] Some interventions went beyond the thermal efficiency requirements, which were seen to be low, running their own Decent Homes Plus schemes with additional energy-efficiency measures. The Decent Homes Standard is actually a minimum standard, and, as in 2001 nearly half of the public housing stock was below that standard, gives stark evidence of the precarious conditions presented by a very high proportion of the stock. This fact makes the case for going beyond the standard to keep delivering improvements in living quality, which together with the critical new goals of reducing carbon dioxide emissions set in the Carbon Plan of 2008, of clear relevance in the social sector, suggested the need for new governmental incentives.

According to government reports, having massively invested in the social sector during that decade implied underinvestment in the private sector programme, and therefore the new incentives would need to be more inclusive, despite being aware of the fact that a significant backlog of works remained. For this reason, the Energy Act 2011 required the UK government to introduce regulations to improve the energy efficiency of buildings (Minimum Energy Efficiency Standards) in the private rented sector no later than 1 April 2018. From this moment, 'it will be unlawful to rent out a residential or business premises that does not reach a minimum energy performance rating of E' on their Energy Performance Certificate (EPC).[23] That is, this policy will come into force for new lets and renewals of tenancies with effect from 1 April 2018, and for all existing tenancies on 1 April 2020, requiring private landlords to update their stock, as they have access to the government's incentives, such as the Green Deal and Energy Company Obligation (described below), therefore expanding competition for these schemes.

First Carbon Plan Instruments (2008–2012): the Carbon Emission Reduction Target (CERT) and the Community Energy Saving Programme (CESP)

In the following years, two new policies supported the delivery of energy-efficiency measures to domestic premises: the Carbon Emission Reduction Target (CERT), which ran from 2008 to 2012 to assist the general decarbonisation, and the Community Energy Saving Programme (CESP), which ran from 2009 to 2012, and was specially focused on geographic areas with fuel-poor and vulnerable households.[24] Both programmes required an active contribution from energy (gas and electricity) suppliers and generators, who had to implement different carbon-saving measures. At first, carbon savings were planned to be accomplished through lighting optimisation, and nearly 304 million compact fluorescent lamps were replaced in 25 million households. Since 2010, the focus was on achieving targets related to thermal insulation, leading to more than 4 million lofts being insulated as well as 2.5 million cavity walls and almost 150,000 solid walls. Both schemes were considered successful in fulfilling their goals: energy companies were required to achieve an overall target of 19.25 Mt CO_2 saving by 31 December 2012, and they actually achieved a saving of 16.31 Mt CO_2, almost 85 per cent of the overall target.[25]

According to an independent study, by the end of these two programmes in 2012, it was estimated that 5 million lofts still remained to be properly insulated, as well as 4–5 million unfilled cavity walls and the majority of the UK's 7–8 million inefficient solid walls.[26]

The Green Deal (2013–2015)

The next programme was the Green Deal, offering the opportunity to finance the installation of a wide range of energy-efficiency measures to householders between January 2013 and July 2015. This scheme specifically worked on an individual basis, so it inherently presented barriers to individual tower block properties, given the lack of benefit in punctual thermal-control retrofit interventions (insulation and double glazing), unless the whole block agreed to the retrofit. On the other hand, tower blocks could take advantage of it for small-scale interventions, such as energy-efficient lighting and water management measures (LED lighting, and water-efficient taps).[27] To ensure the engagement of local authorities with the programme, the government additionally contributed £13 million between October 2012 and May 2013 to the creation of eight Green Deal Low Carbon Cities (Birmingham, Bristol, Leeds, Liverpool, Manchester, Newcastle, Nottingham and Sheffield).[28]

The Department of Energy and Climate Change launched this scheme, together with the Energy Company Obligation, the characteristics of which would particularly fit the high-rise housing estates needs, and therefore better benefit retrofits in these buildings, leading to a poor take-up of the Green Deal. Statistics revealed that the total number of measures installed financed by the Green Deal was 20,347 up to the end of October 2015: most of them boilers (31 per cent), followed by photovoltaics (29 per cent) and solid wall insulation (15 per cent).[29]

Recent retrofit schemes

There are several recent retrofit schemes, some of them currently in operation:

- Energy Company Obligation (ECO) (2013–2017);
- Government Electricity Rebate (Autumns 2014 and 2015);
- Warm Home Discount (current);
- Feed-in Tariffs (current);
- Renewable Heat Premium Payment and Domestic Renewable Heat Incentive (current).

The Energy Company Obligation (ECO) (2013–2017), was structured in two obligation periods, ECO1 from January 2013–March 2015, and ECO2, launched on 1 April 2015 and effective until 31 March 2017. This scheme was devised again to require energy suppliers to deliver energy-efficiency measures to domestic properties, at no up-front cost to the consumer. Improvements were focused on hard-to-treat cavity wall insulation and solid wall insulation (internal or external), with low-income geographical areas qualifying to benefit from further benefits, such as loft insulation and gas boilers. The policy also regarded additional subsidies for those with certain benefits who live in a private property, such as boiler repairs or replacements.

According to a recent study, ECO provides the best framework for funding large-scale tower block retrofits 'with the potential to support a more holistic set of retrofit measures than CERT, which was targeted at insulation', making all tower blocks stakeholders predominantly interested in this programme.[30] Apart from the obvious benefits to residents in getting more comfortable homes with lower energy bills, the opportunity to refurbish a high number of premises in one go is particularly advantageous to the energy companies, as a cost-effective way to meet their targets. ECO is conceived to increase improvements in hard-to-treat properties, and the majority of tower blocks had solid walls in need of treatment, making them eligible candidates and therefore providing a higher chance of getting the subsidy, making the retrofit substantially more afford-able for housing providers. Overall, 1,300,232 properties have benefitted from one or more ECO measures installed up to the end of September 2015. Of the 100,591 solid wall insulation measures installed, the majority (94 per cent) were external wall insulation.[31]

The government also created two key social programmes offering support in the use of domestic energy, the Government Electricity Rebate (GER), which only ran in the autumns of 2014 and 2015, and the Warm Home Discount (WHD), launched in 2011 and effective until 2021. GER helped to reduce cus-tomers' electricity bills by forcing licensed electricity suppliers to refund £12 per bill. WHD is a ten-year programme that places obligations on larger energy sup-pliers to assist fuel-poor pensioners and customers. Each year the government spends £320 million, rising with inflation, to help around 2 million low-income and vulnerable homes, through a direct rebate of £140 per household to their electricity or gas account.[32]

As part of the current strategy, the government introduced two types of renewable technology incentives, focused on clean heat and electricity gen-eration respectively: the Renewable Heat Premium Payment (RHPP)/Domestic Renewable Heat Incentive (DRHI), and Feed-in Tariffs (FIT).

RHPP was a grant scheme available to install domestic renewable heating systems, which ran from August 2011 until 31 March 2014, being the forerunner of the current Domestic Renewable Heat Incentive policy. It was envisioned as a one-off grant to help households with the cost of installing renewable heating technologies. Individual householders were eligible to bid for funds, includ-ing registered providers of social housing: local authorities, charities, private companies and partnerships. The application process requested householders to apply for a voucher to the Energy Saving Trust, which was used to request a rebate after the technology installation was completed.

DRHI, the present financial incentive, started in April 2014 and equally promotes the increased use of renewable heating systems in domestic premises both off and on the gas grid. Householders get paid quarterly for each unit of heat generated from renewable technologies (biomass boilers, solar thermal systems or heat pumps) for seven years.[33] This scheme provides a good oppor-tunity to high-rise housing to become energy self-sufficient communities, taking advantage of their scale to generate and benefit from the energy produced. In terms of carbon footprint, these interventions can achieve carbon reductions at a lower cost than the actual retrofit of the flats, and with less disruption to residents.[34] Another important factor is that by creating their own clean heating and energy generation system, estates or even each block can manage their own energy, something that in many of them is happening for the first time, and this is critical to mitigating fuel poverty. A paradigmatic example of a system promoted through this initiative is the EcoPod,[35] a green clean heating system first installed on the roof of Barton Village estate in Greater Manchester, which will be described further in Chapters 4 and 6.

CHAPTER 2 Carbon emissions reduction

FIT is a programme designed to promote the uptake of small-scale renewable and low-carbon electricity generation technologies (solar photovoltaic (PV), wind power, micro combined heat and power (CHP), and hydro and anaerobic digestion (AD)). Introduced on 1 April 2010, the scheme requires participating licensed electricity suppliers to make payments on both generation and export from eligible installations during twenty years.[36] Figure 2.4 presents the measures available through government schemes since the UK Carbon Plan.

None of the above-described policies were primarily designed for high-rise flats and therefore fail to specifically support and incentivise sustainable living for high-rise residents, acknowledging their particular problems and barriers to access some of these programmes.[37] Of course, many of the post-war residential tower blocks have benefitted from some of these programmes, but we will see in Chapter 4 that the majority of the works undertaken aimed at achieving the Decent Homes Standard as the minimum required quality improvement, and only a few have benefitted from the Green Deal or ECO to go beyond those minimum conditions and invest in higher quality living standards and innovative solutions.

Meeting the minimum decent requirements was obviously not only a great concern, but also an obligation, which therefore triggered an active response from stakeholders. In England, in particular, the proportion of dwellings failing the Decent Homes Standard declined steadily from 35 per cent in 2006 to 27 per cent in 2010, and noticeably, the local authority stock showed the largest reduction in the proportion of non-decent homes, dropping from 32 per cent in 2006 to 22 per cent in 2010.[38] Of those homes, 22 per cent of high-rise flats failed

▼ Figure 2.4

Number of measures installed through government schemes since the UK Carbon Plan
Source: Based on chart published by the National Audit Office (2016).

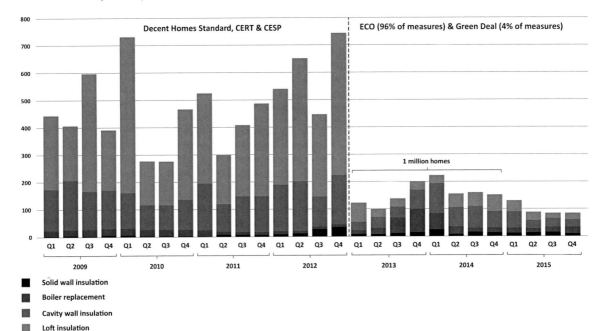

CHAPTER 2 Carbon emissions reduction

to meet the standard, due to thermal comfort and lack of modern facilities.[39] Thermal comfort remained the primary concern across the stock, thus most of the interventions aimed at improving this performance, reducing the proportion of households failing this criterion from 17 per cent to 10 per cent. The proportion of public housing failing this aspect decreased by 56 per cent in this period (dropping from 15 per cent to 6 per cent). Although in less proportion, measures were also taken to reduce the number of homes failing the Housing Health and Safety Rating System (HHSRS) and disrepairs, and nothing has been done to the proportion that failed the standard due to lack of modernisation.

According to the most recent government reports in 2015 and 2016, around 1.66 million measures were installed in around 1.35 million properties through ECO, Cashback, GD Plans and the Green Deal Home Improvement Fund up to the end of September 2015 in England and Wales. Of these, 96 per cent of the installed measures were delivered through ECO in the following distribution: 38 per cent were for cavity wall insulation, 26 per cent were for loft insulation, and 21 per cent were for boiler upgrades. With regards to solid wall insulations, over 100,000 were installed, accounting for 6 per cent of all measures.[40] However, it is estimated that about 5.5 million British homes lack cavity wall insulation, 92 per cent of solid walled homes are uninsulated, and about 65 per cent of English homes are in need of energy-efficiency improvements. In addition to this, 11 per cent of English households were classed as being fuel-poor, and 20 per cent were experiencing difficulties meeting their heating and fuel costs.[41]

These reports do not specify in which building types the different measures have been installed; therefore, we are unable to globally quantify how well public high-rise blocks are benefitting from each of the green schemes and the different measures. Independent organisations such as the UK Green Building Council and the Green Alliance seemed to have monitored part of this process, producing reports that analyse the success in take-up and the suitability of these programmes for particular typologies of the building stock, while proposing ideas for new potential incentives. Their conclusions and proposals will be fully discussed in Chapter 6.

Key UK bodies (the Department of Business, Energy and Industrial Strategy, the BRE Group, NAO and Energy Systems Catapult) are scheduled to discuss the future of energy-efficiency schemes in businesses and homes across England, as well as the next steps for energy-efficiency policy, in a forthcoming seminar entitled 'The future for energy efficiency policy in England: Issues for businesses and suppliers, and domestic priorities post-Green Deal'.[42] This will be the most up-to-date review of the current situation, coinciding with the end of ECO in March 2017. In these sessions, the focus will again be on proposals to mitigate fuel poverty, the creation of new incentive schemes and supplier obligations, establishing the standards of home efficiency measures and value for money in domestic energy efficiency, and the new trends in technology and smart systems.

At the European level, research on refurbishment has been extensively promoted through European Union-funded projects, involving different countries and a diversity of research-specific aspects. These projects not only aimed at providing a comprehensive survey of the existing stock and its needs but also at setting collaborations to work together on common challenges: renovation of housing stock; sustainable growth; helping young, disadvantaged and vulnerable groups to access the housing market; encouraging energy efficiency among homeowners; fighting poverty and social exclusion, etc. We will also discuss in Chapter 6 how the retrofit strategies and interventions undertaken in the UK sit within the European context.

Notes

1 Department of Energy and Climate Change, *Energy Efficiency Statistical Summary 2015* (London: Energy Efficiency Deployment Office, January 2015). Available at: www.gov.uk/government/policies/reducing-the-uk-s-greenhouse-gas-emissions-by-80-by-2050

2 *The Carbon Plan: Delivering Our Low Carbon Future* (2011). Presented to Parliament pursuant to Sections 12 and 14 of the Climate Change Act 2008. Amended 2nd December 2011 from the version laid before Parliament on 1st December 2011, p. 5. Available at: www.gov.uk/government/uploads/system/uploads/attachment_data/file/47613/3702-the-carbon-plan-delivering-our-low-carbon-future.pdf

3 Committee on Climate Change (2017), available at: www.theccc.org.uk/charts-data/ukemissions-by-sector/buildings/

4 Ibid.

5 Department for Business, Energy and Industrial Strategy, *Energy Consumption in the UK* (November 2015). p. 20. Available at: www.gov.uk/government/uploads/system/uploads/attachment_data/file/573269/ECUK_November_2016.pdf; also Committee on Climate Change, *Meeting Carbon Budgets I 2013: Progress Report to Parliament I*,. Chapter 3: 'Progress reducing emissions from buildings', available at: www.theccc.org.uk/wp-content/uploads/2013/06/CCC-Prog-Rep_Chap3_singles_web_1.pdf.

6 Thaleia Konstantinou, *Façade Refurbishment Toolbox: Supporting the Design of Residential Energy Upgrades* (Delft: Delft University of Technology. Faculty of Architecture and the Built Environment, 2014), p. 43.

7 See http://ec.europa.eu/eurostat/statistics-explained/index.php/Housing_statistics#Type_of_dwelling

8 UK Green Building Council 'Retrofit incentives: boosting take-up of energy efficiency measures in domestic properties' (July 2013), p. 10. Available at: www.ukgbc.org/sites/default/files/130705%2520Retrofit%2520Incentives%2520Task%2520Group%2520-%2520Report%2520FINAL_1

9 The Royal Institute of Chartered Surveyors (2011) 'Hotting up? An analysis of low carbon plans and strategies for UK cities', available at: www.rics.org/uk/knowledge/research/research-reports/hotting-up-low-carbon-analysis-of-uk-cities/

10 Laure Itard and Frit Meijer, *Towards a Sustainable Northern European Housing Stock: Figures, Facts and Future* (Delft: TU Delft/ IOS Press, 2008), vol. 22, p. 35.

11 Statistics for England, Department for Communities and Local Government (DCLG) (July 2012). *English Housing Survey: Homes 2010*, Chapter 1 annex Table 1.5. Available at: www.gov.uk/government/statistics/english-housing-survey-homes-report-2010. Statistics for Scotland in *Housing Statistics for Scotland* (2015), available at: www.gov.scot/Topics/Statistics/Browse/Housing-Regeneration/HSfS/Stock. Statistics for Northern Ireland in Department for Communities, Housing (December 2016). Northern Ireland Statistics and Research Agency, Housing Statistics. Available at: www.communities-ni.gov.uk/sites/default/files/publications/communities/ni-housing-stats-15-16-full-copy.pdf. Statistics for Wales in Stats Wales, Housing (2015). Available at: www.statswales.gov.wales/Catalogue/Housing

12 Source of data: Department for Communities and Local Government (July 2015) *English Housing Survey: Energy Efficiency of English Housing 2013: Annual Report on England's Housing Stock*, 2013 available at: www.gov.uk/government/collections/english-housing-survey; also, p. 13, and Department for Communities and Local Government (July 2014) *English Housing Survey. Energy Efficiency of English Housing 2012*: *Annual Report on England's Housing Stock 2012*, available at: www.gov.uk/government/collections/english-housing-survey, p. 14.

The average Standard Assessment Procedure (SAP) in 2001 was 46. The energy-efficiency rating is defined as follows:

> The SAP rating is based on each dwelling's energy costs per square metre and is calculated using a simplified form of the Standard Assessment Procedure (SAP). The energy costs take into account the costs of space and water heating, ventilation and lighting, less any cost savings from energy generation technologies. The rating is expressed on a scale of 1–100 where a dwelling with a rating of 1 has poor energy efficiency (high costs) and a dwelling with a rating of 100 represents a completely energy efficient dwelling (zero net energy costs per year). The energy efficiency rating is also presented in an A to G banding system for an Energy Performance Certificate, where Energy Efficiency Rating (EER) Band A represents low energy costs (i.e. the most efficient band) and EER Band G represents high energy costs (i.e. the least energy efficient band).

13 Department for Communities and Local Government (July 2014) *English Housing Survey. Energy Efficiency of English Housing 2012*, p. 11.

14 Scotland's centre of expertise connecting climate change research and policy (November 2016), *BB20 Energy Performance of Scottish Housing Stock. Indicators and Trends. Monitoring Climate Change Adaptation*, p. 3. Available at: www.climatexchange.org.uk/adapting-to-climate-change/indicators-and-trends/resilient-and-resource-use/bb20-energy-performance-scottish-housing-stock/

15 UK Green Building Council (July 2013) 'Retrofit incentives: boosting take-up of energy efficiency measures in domestic properties', Campaign for a Sustainable Built Environment. Task Group Report, p. 3. Available at:

www.ukgbc.org/sites/default/files/130705%2520Retrofit%2520Incentives%2520Task%2520Group%2520-%2520Report%2520FINAL_1.pdf

16 Ibid., p. 10.

17 Ofgem and the Energy Saving Trust (July 2003), 'A review of the Energy Efficiency Standards of Performance 1994–2002'. Available at: www.ofgem.gov.uk/ofgem-publications/58653/4211-eesopreportjuly03-pdf

18 The criteria for the standard are: 'It must meet the current statutory minimum standard for housing; it must be in a reasonable state of repair; it must have reasonably modern facilities and services; and it must provide a reasonable degree of thermal comfort.' Department for Communities and Local Government, *The Decent Homes Standard*, available at: http://webarchive.nationalarchives.gov.uk/+/http://www.communities.gov.uk/index.asp?id=1153927

19 House of Commons, Communities and Local Government Committee, UK Parliament (March 2010). *Beyond Decent Homes*. Available at: www.publications.parliament.uk/pa/cm200910/cmselect/cmcomloc/60/6005.htm

20 National Federation of ALMOs, available at: www.almos.org.uk/almos

21 House of Commons, Communities and Local Government Committee, *Beyond Decent Homes*, vol. I, p. 3. Available at: www.publications.parliament.uk/pa/cm200910/cmselect/cmcomloc/60/60i.pdf

> An estimated £40 billion has been made available for the work in the social sector alone, which has paid for, among other things, the installation of 700,000 new kitchens, 525,000 new bathrooms, over 1 million new central heating systems and the re-wiring of 740,000 homes.

22 Ibid., p. 16.

23 Department of Energy and Climate Change, *Energy Act 2011*, p. 1. Available at: www.gov.uk/government/uploads/system/uploads/attachment_data/file/48199/3211-energy-act-2011-aide-memoire.pdf

24 Office of Gas and Electricity Markets (Ofgem), which is a non-ministerial government department and an independent National Regulatory Authority. See www.ofgem.gov.uk/environmental-programmes/eco/overview-previous-schemes:

> CESP was created as part of the government's Home Energy Saving Programme. This obligation was placed on all licensed gas and electricity suppliers that had at least 50,000 domestic customers and all licensed electricity generators that had generated on average 10 TWh/yr or more in a specified three-year period. CESP was designed to promote a 'whole house' approach and to treat as many properties as possible in defined geographical areas selected using the Income Domain of the Indices of Multiple Deprivation (IMD) in England, Scotland and Wales.

25 Ibid.: the Gas and Electricity (Carbon Emissions Reduction) Order 2008 and subsequent amendments set out the levels of savings required and the way in which these were to be achieved.

26 UK Green Building Council, 'Retrofit incentives'.

27 Hannah Kyrke-Smith, *Towering Ambitions: Transforming High-Rise Housing into Sustainable Homes* (London: Green Alliance, 2012), p. 10.

28 Committee on Climate Change, *Meeting Carbon Budgets: 2013 Progress Report to Parliament* (2013), Chapter 3, p. 14. 'Progress reducing emissions from buildings'. Available at: www.theccc.org.uk/wp-content/uploads/2013/06/CCC-Prog-Rep_Chap3_singles_web_1.pdf

29 Department of Energy and Climate Change, *Domestic Green Deal and Energy Company Obligation in Great Britain*, headline report (November 2015). p. 8. Available at: www.gov.uk/government/uploads/system/uploads/attachment_data/file/477288/Headline_Release_-_GD___ECO_in_GB_19_Nov_Final.pdf

30 Kyrke-Smith, *Towering Ambitions*, p. 12.

31 Department of Energy and Climate Change, *Domestic Green Deal*, p. 11.

32 Department of Energy and Climate Change (8 April 2016), *Warm Home Discount Scheme*, 16D/029, p. 8. Available at: www.gov.uk/government/uploads/system/uploads/attachment_data/file/514324/Final_Warm_Home_Discount_consultation_for_publication.pdf

33 See www.ofgem.gov.uk/environmental-programmes/domestic-rhi/about-domestic-rhi

34 Kyrke-Smith, *Towering Ambitions*, p. 14. Information source: Bioregional, 2012, Retrofitting district heating systems: creating replicable retrofit models in Hackbridge.

35 EcoPod Energy Systems, available at: www.ecopodenergy.com/

36 Office of Gas and Electricity Markets (Ofgem), available at: www.ofgem.gov.uk/environmental-programmes/fit/about-fit-scheme

37 Kyrke-Smith, *Towering Ambitions*, p. 2.

38 DCLG, *English Housing Survey: Homes 2010*, p. 59: Definition of a decent home: be in a reasonable state of repair, have reasonably modern facilities and services, and provide a reasonable degree of thermal comfort.

39 Ibid., p. 68.

40 Department of Energy and Climate Change, *Domestic Green Deal*, p. 1.

41 Peter Bonfield, *Each Home Counts: An Independent Review of Consumer Advice, Protection, Standards and Enforcement for Energy Efficiency and Renewable Energy*. Department for Business, Energy and Industrial Strategy. Department for Communities and Local Government (December 2016). p. 11. Available at: www.gov.uk/government/uploads/system/uploads/attachment_data/file/578749/Each_Home_Counts__December_2016_.pdf

42 Westminster Energy, Environment & Transport Forum Keynote Seminar, London, 21 March 2017.

Chapter 3

Types and techniques
A retrofit manual

Original façade construction types

In the framework of this research project, 39 residential estates located in Greater London, Greater Manchester, Leeds, Liverpool and Sheffield were inspected and analysed (Figures 3.1 and 3.2). They contain a sample of 89 housing blocks in total, which share similar characteristics regarding their structure, layout, and façade construction type. Looking at the early post-war construction technology, prefabrication and standardisation dominate the *Zeitgeist*.

In the early 1950s, frames and infilling or frames and claddings formed the commonly accepted multi-storey construction principle. Even though steel is the main material for high rises, during this period, council housing was almost entirely built of reinforced concrete) because of its lower price.[1] Standardised shuttering was used for walls, slabs, beams and columns. Infills and cladding are usually made of brick or monolithic, wall-to-floor concrete walls/panels. In the late 1950s, the slab block system was gradually being replaced by the 'box frame' often described also as 'cross-wall'.[2] Entire block units, including walls and floor slabs, were now being prefabricated and assembled on site. During the 1960s the 'system building' method was introduced, where housing production as a 'whole' was entering the phase of industrialised building components as parts of a system. Large prefabricated panel factories start to make their appearance, starting to integrate one layer of polystyrene, in order to provide panels with thermal insulation.

All the housing blocks investigated during this survey were constructed as concrete load-bearing frame constructions (Figure 3.3), filled or clad either by brick masonry or prefabricated concrete panels. In some cases, such as the Great Arthur House, part of the Golden Lane Estate, the main parts of the façade were constructed as an aluminium-framed, single-glazed curtain wall system (Figure 3.4).

Windows and balcony doors in all towers were single-glazed window frame systems made out of either timber or aluminium. Thermal insulation was either completely absent or very poor, if present at all. Structural elements such as concrete columns, beams, floor slabs and balconies were exposed to weather conditions, suffering various types of physical damage and functioning as cold bridges. Central heating, powered by petrol, was commonly found and used extensively in order to replace thermal energy loss caused by non-existent insulation.

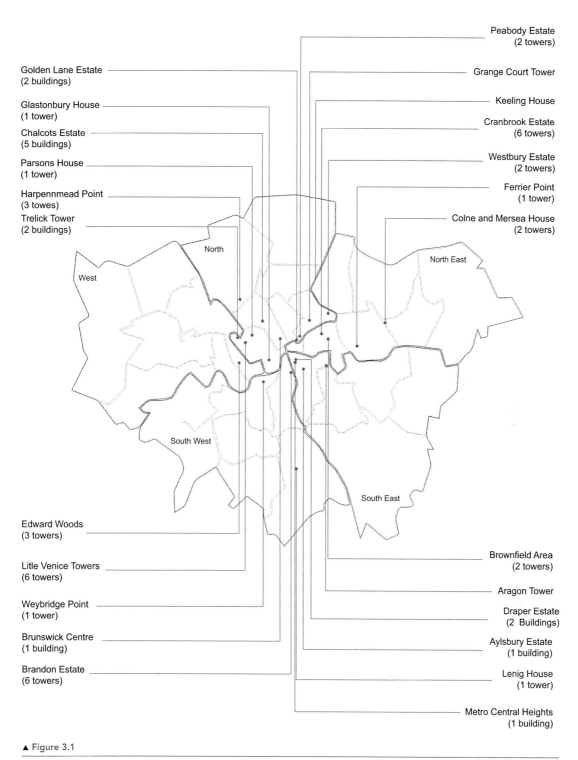

▲ Figure 3.1

Tower retrofits map, Greater London

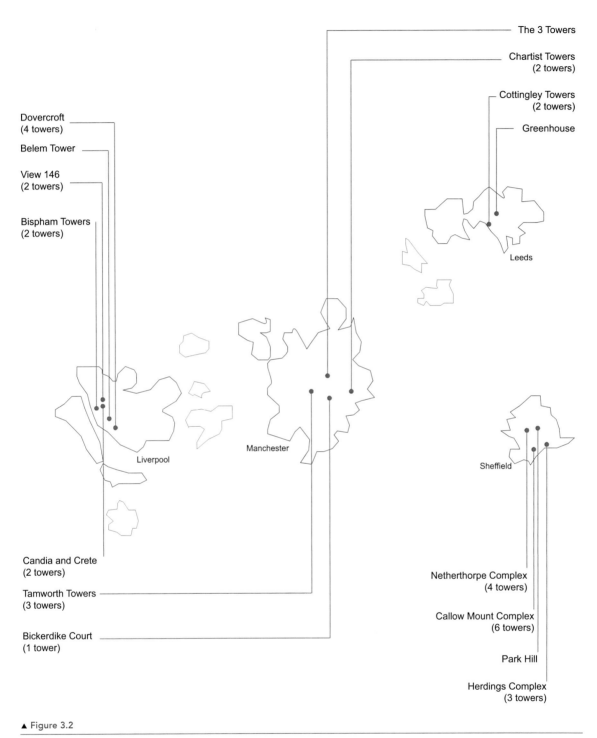

▲ Figure 3.2

Tower retrofits map, North-west England

40 CHAPTER 3 Types and techniques: a retrofit manual

▼ Figure 3.3

Typical load-bearing concrete frame construction filled by brick masonry, Park Hill, Sheffield

▼ Figure 3.4

Aluminium-framed single-glazed curtain wall façade, during the retrofit, Great Arthur House, London

The main materials used were concrete, brick, metal, wood or glass. They were applied untreated, left in their natural colour and texture. In some cases such as the Park Hill complex in Sheffield (see Figure 3.3), brickwork was laid in different shades, using brick as a design element, producing a gradient iteration from light yellow to dark red-brown.

Ever since the retrofit interventions started in the early 1990s, the addition of thermal insulation became the architects' main aim. External overcladding became the primary insulation technique applied, focusing on techniques, such as the use of composite panels or insulated render systems in addition to the replacement of single-glazed by double-glazed window frames. In many cases, central heating, electrical and mechanical systems were upgraded, while only in a few cases were renewable energies applied.

About thermal insulation

The addition of thermal insulation is the key element in all retrofit strategies investigated in this sample. It requires a material with high thermal resistance, that opposes heat transfer between elements of different temperature.[3] Contemporary material technologies offer a wide range of insulating products.[4] Depending on its ingredients and texture, insulation can be subdivided into fibre- foamed and granulate or loose fill insulation.[5] Insulation can be applied for different occasions and different purposes, either externally, within a cavity or internally. It can be classified according to its origination into inorganic/mineral (e.g. rock wool, glass wool) and organic (e.g. polystyrene).[6] Moreover, a vacuum can offer a form of immaterial insulation.

Façade retrofitting strategies: the state of the art

By looking into the current state of the art of façade retrofitting strategies, five categories can be identified: 'Replace', 'Add-in', 'Wrap-it', 'Add-on' and 'Cover-it'.[7]

CHAPTER 3 Types and techniques: a retrofit manual

- The *replace* strategy consists of replacement of old façades' elements with new ones. This could include parts of the façade or even its entirety. New components, with better thermal and physical performance, eliminate the existing problems. The shortcoming of the replace strategy is that it usually requires the building to be unoccupied. In addition, certain thermal bridging projects might not be solved with the replaced component and will require special attention.
- The *add-in* strategy is usually applied to buildings where façade changes are not permitted or are not possible. In this case, improvements take place from the inside, by adding secondary glazing and insulation between the wall cavity or on the interior walls. However, the add-in strategy cannot eliminate thermal bridging problems entirely. In addition to the disturbance it causes to the occupants, it also partly limits the actual size of the various apartment rooms affected by internal insulation.
- *Wrapping* the building around its exterior surfaces is another very common strategy. It includes external insulation, over-cladding of balconies and the addition of a second skin façade. It helps eliminate thermal bridging and has relatively small disturbance for occupants. It is a strategy which cannot be applied to listed buildings.
- Building *add-ons* (e.g. building extension, floor addition or balcony addition) are often observed during retrofit interventions. The new building part offers an exterior skin which meets the modern standards and offers a better thermal performance. It is a strategy which requires an additional retrofit strategy to meet the efficiency standards for the building parts not affected by the extension.
- The *cover-it* strategy occurs in cases where courtyards and atria are being covered by an additional roof, usually by glazed elements. It creates a thermal buffer zone between inside and outside and protects the outdated façade from weather exposure. It's a strategy which can only be applied to a particular building type.

Often some of this strategies are applied in combination, in order to match the building's complex requirements. In the sample investigated in this book, both wrap-it and replace strategies are the most commonly applied, often in combination. Wrap-it techniques include over-cladding with insulated rain screens or insulated render. Often building extensions take place as well, especially in the form of additional floors.

Common types of retrofit observed in Greater London and the North-west

As part of the wrap it strategy, over-cladding with insulated rain screen panel systems is the most common retrofit technique observed in the 39 housing estates we have investigated (Figures 3.5 and 3.6). Such systems are applied in the form of a metallic post and beam, or a vertical rail substructure fixed directly onto the existing load-bearing skeleton or wall (Figure 3.7). Following the outer

▶ Figure 3.5

Percentage of retrofit intervention types, Greater London

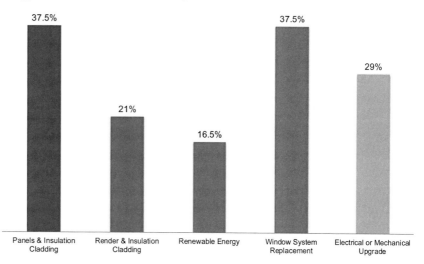

▶ Figure 3.6

Percentage of retrofit intervention types, North-west England

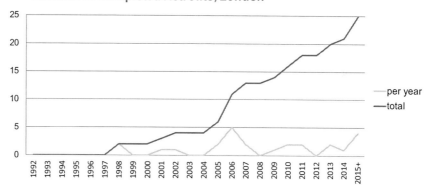

water protection layer comes an air gap (cavity) enabling back ventilation and drainage, then a thermal fibre/rock wool insulation layer concluding on a waterproof membrane placed between furring and sheathing.[8]

The materiality and texture of the outer finishing layer vary. Anodised aluminium panels are very popular, allowing a large variety in colour and coating (Figure 3.8). In other cases, terracotta rain screens (e.g. Weybridge Point, London), or sanded glass (e.g. Aragon Tower, London) have been used. Other commonly used panel materials such as fibre cement boards, high-pressure laminates or ceramic tiles have not been observed in this research sample. The case study of the 3 Towers Complex in Manchester must be mentioned as the only retrofit using structurally insulated timber panels as a self-supported curtain wall, an alteration to a post and beam substructure. Of the overall sample examined in this survey, 42 per cent of the estates had

CHAPTER 3 Types and techniques: a retrofit manual

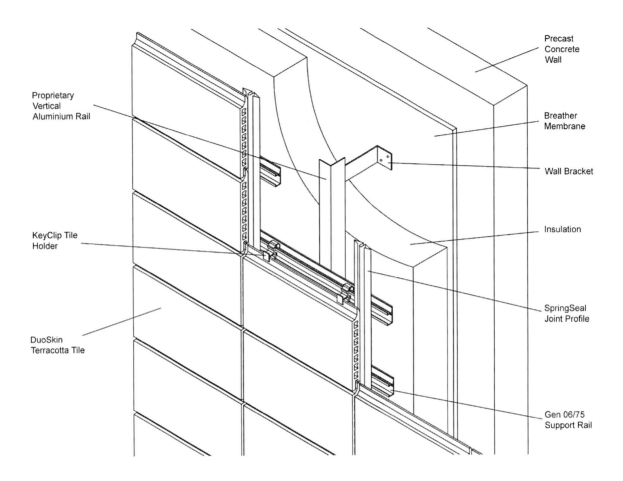

▲ Figure 3.7

Typical insulated rain-screen construction detail

applied rain screen over-cladding as the main type of retrofit intervention (Figures 3.9–3.11).

Over-cladding with insulated render is another very popular retrofit technique used (Figures 3.12, 3.13). It has been used for decades, particularly on external insulation of existing buildings of all types and size and height. Due to its wide standardisation, it has become extremely time- and cost-effective; 24 per cent of the housing blocks presented here have applied this technology. Phenolic insulation foam boards are fixed directly onto the existing external brick or blockwork wall, using mechanical or adhesive fixing methods. Once the boards have been installed, a variety of silicone, acrylic, polymer or special render finishes can be applied, in almost any possible colour. The Peabody Towers in Central London and the Greenhouse in Leeds are among the most characteristic case studies of retrofitted housing blocks using this technology. In many cases, thermal insulation has been added on the roof often alongside upgrades of waterproof insulation.

In some cases, both techniques have been combined, in order to emphasise certain building parts, such as extrusions or balconies. On the Crossways Estate in London, insulated render has been applied to the main

▶ Figure 3.8

Anodised rain-screen panels, Park Hill, Sheffield

▶ Figure 3.9

Insulated render over-cladding, Crescent Grange Sheltered Housing, Leeds

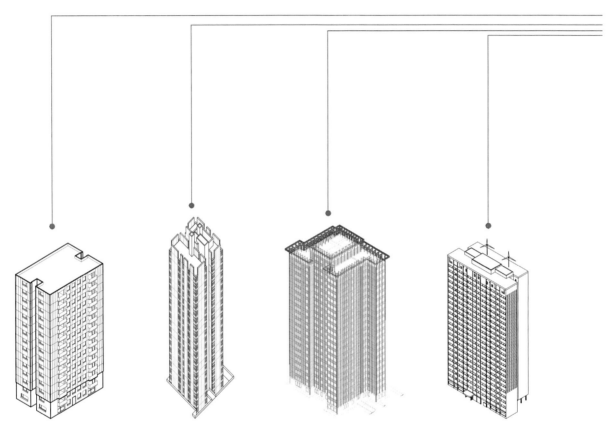

Harpenmead Point

- Over-cladding with thermally insulated aluminium screens
- Replacement of old windows and doors by aluminium-wood composite double-glazed frame systems
- Over-cladding of brick work on the ground floor area with thermally insulated render

Chalcots Estate

- Over-cladding with thermally insulated aluminium screens
- Replacement of old windows and doors by new active, double glazed self-cleaning frames

Parsons House

- Re-cladding with thermally insulated aluminium screens
- Replacement of old windows and doors by new double-glazed frame systems

Edward Woods Estate

- Over-cladding with thermally insulated aluminium screens
- Replacement of old windows and doors by new double-glazed frame systems

▲ Figure 3.10

Towers which have been over-cladded with thermally insulated panels, Greater London

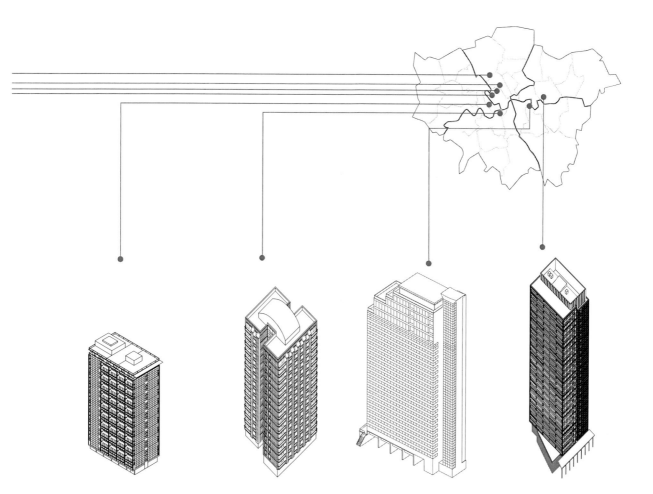

Little Venice Towers

- Over-cladding with thermally insulated aluminium screens
- Replacement of old windows and doors by new double-glazed frame systems

Weybridge Point

- Over-cladding with thermally insulated terracotta rain-screens
- Replacement of old windows and doors by new double-glazed frame systems

Aragon Tower

- Re-cladding with thermally insulated aluminium screens
- Replacement of old windows and doors by new double-glazed frame systems

Ferrier Point

- Over-cladding with thermally insulated aluminium screens
- Replacement of old windows and doors by new triple-glazed frame systems

CHAPTER 3 Types and techniques: a retrofit manual

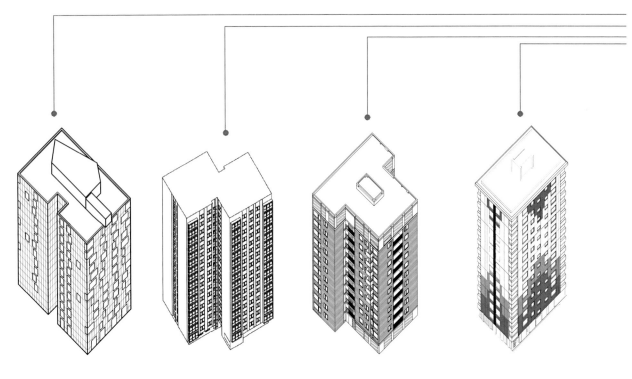

Towers

Over-cladding with thermally insulated insulated timber composite panels
Reinforcement of the balcony floor slabs
Enclosure of the balconies into the living space
Replacement of old windows and doors by new double-glazed frame systems

Bickerdike Court

- Over-cladding with thermally insulated aluminium screens
- Replacement of old windows and doors by new double-glazed frame systems
- Repairment of concrete walls

Belem Tower

- Over-cladding with thermally insulated aluminium screens
- Replacement of old windows and doors by new double-glazed frame systems

Netherthorpe Complex

Over-cladding with thermally insulated aluminium screens
- Replacement of old windows and doors by new double-glazed frame systems
- Enclosure of balconies

▲ Figure 3.11

Towers which have been over-cladded with thermally insulated panels, North-west England

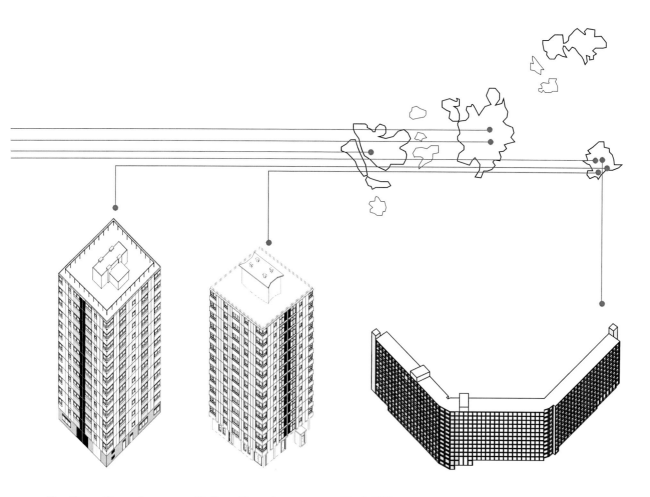

Herdings Complex

- Over-cladding with thermally insulated aluminium screens
- Replacement of old windows and doors by new double-glazed frame systems

Callow Mount

- Over-cladding with thermally insulated aluminium screens
- Replacement of old windows and doors by new double-glazed frame systems
- Enclosure of balconies

Park Hill

- Repairment of concrete structure
- Over-cladding of brickwork with anodised aluminium panels
- Replacement of old windows and doors by new double-glazed frame systems (the ratio of facade solid/void has been reversed into 2/3 glazed surface and 1/3 aluminium panels)

CHAPTER 3 Types and techniques: a retrofit manual

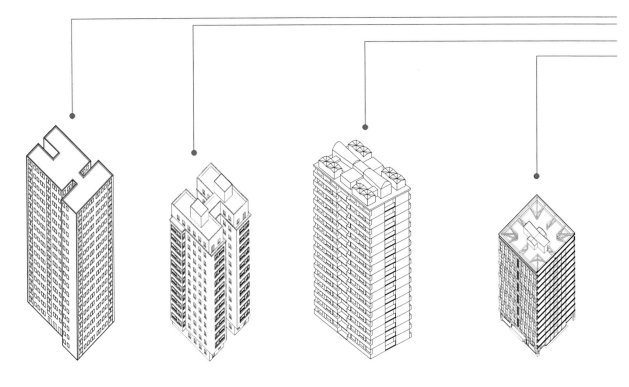

Colne & Mersea House

- Over-cladding with thermally insulated render
- Insulation of the roof
- Replacement of old windows and doors by new triple-glazed frame systems
- Installation of integral blinds on south-facing windows

Peabody Towers

- Over-cladding with thermally insulated render
- Replacement of old windows and doors by new double-glazed frame systems

Brandon Estate

- Over-cladding of concrete façade with insulated render
- Replacement of old windows and doors by new double-glazed frame systems

Cranbrook Estate

- Over-cladding with thermally insulated render
- Replacement of old windows and doors by new double-glazed frame systems

▲ Figure 3.12

Towers which have been over-cladded with thermally insulated render, Greater London

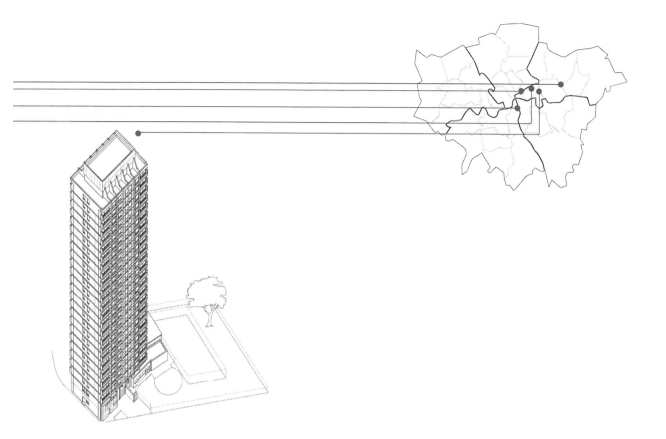

Bow Cross Estate

- Over-cladding with thermally insulated render
- Replacement of old windows and doors by new double-glazed frame systems
- Reduction of glazed surface/partial replacement by non-structural infill side panels
- Over-cladding of balcony areas and slab edges with coloured aluminium panels
- Insulation of new waterproof membrane and a ballast system
- Rooftop enclosure made with galvanised steel mesh
- Repairment of the concrete skeleton

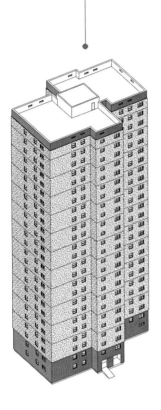 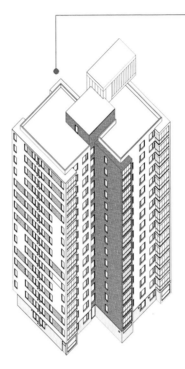 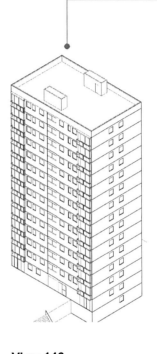

- Over-cladding of concrete façade with insulated render
- Replacement of old windows and doors by new double-glazed frame systems

Tamworth Towers

- Over-cladding of concrete façade with insulated render
- Replacement of old windows and doors by new double-glazed frame systems
- Enclosure of balconies

View 146

- Over-cladding of concrete façade with insulated render
- Replacement of old windows and doors by new double-glazed frame systems

▲ Figure 3.13

Towers which have been over-cladded with thermally insulated render, North-west England

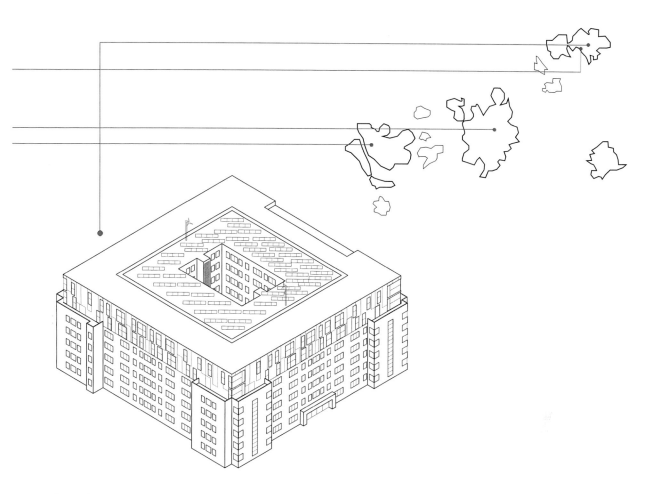

Greenhouse, Leeds

- Over-cladding of concrete façade with insulated render
- Replacement of old windows and doors by new double-glazed frame systems

CHAPTER 3 Types and techniques: a retrofit manual

exterior walls with aluminium cladding on the vertical column elements. A similar approach has been followed on the Tamworth Towers' refurbishment in Manchester, again, insulated render is the main over-cladding technique followed, but the balcony balustrades have been clad by anodised aluminium panels.

Minor skin repairs and window replacement

Replacing the outdated single-glazed windows and doors with high-performing double- or triple-glazed frame systems has been practised in all retrofits, as it is a major source of energy loss. Decaying timber and aluminium frames are usually replaced by PVC and composite systems. In quite a few cases where the refurbishment budget was limited (e.g. Westbury Estate) or where the housing blocks were listed buildings, window replacement was the only insulation improvement provided, in addition to concrete repairs and painting works (Figures 3.14, 3.15). This situation occurs mostly in London, where the highest number of listed tower blocks is located; 37.5 per cent of this survey's sample in London falls into that category. In the case of the Keeling House, the retrofit intervention was strictly restricted to minor skin repairs, painting works and spatial improvements (e.g. new entrance and penthouse addition), forcing many of the tenants/leaseholders to add interior secondary glazing on their own initiative.

◄ Figure 3.14

Windows replacement, Trellick Tower, London

Electrical and mechanical upgrades

Mechanical and electrical system upgrades have been another common sustainable retrofitting technique applied. The most common interventions include replacement of outdated central heating systems with new, efficient gas or electrical boilers, installation of smart heating meters in every home, new ventilation systems in kitchens and bathrooms, replacement of elevators, renewal of fire protection and sprinklers, electrical cabling rewiring, replacement of drainage and water system pipes, installation of LED lighting in communal areas, water saving fittings, installation of modern, energy-saving appliances in kitchens and bathrooms. Heating and water heating system replacement has been recorded in the Ferrier Point, Edward Woods Estate, Chalcots Estate, Balfron Tower, Golden Lane Estate, Westbury Estate, Crossways Estate, Colne & Mersea House, Peabody Towers, Cranbrook Estate, Bickerdike Court, Belem Tower, Callow Mount, Greenhouse and Chartist House. Greenhouse in Leeds and Glastonbury House in London are the most advanced precedents observed, having applied all possible electrical and mechanical upgrades, adopting innovative technologies for intelligent home control systems that manage heat and water control efficiently.

Building extensions, functional conversion, floor plan and landscape improvements

In many cases, the retrofit intervention included floor plan improvements, the addition of extra stories on the rooftop, and communal and outdoor space improvements. The Crossways Estate, in London, for instance, underwent major floor plan changes, connecting kitchens and living areas and providing more variety in available flat types with one, two or three bedrooms. The Greenhouse in Leeds underwent a massive extension, with two extra penthouse stories on the rooftop, as well as an addition of an entire wing of flats around its interior courtyard. Both Aragon Tower (Figure 3.16) and Keeling House received additional penthouse flats. An embodiment of balconies into the building envelope often takes place to enlarge the living area, as well as reducing energy losses or cold bridges. The Callow Mount in Sheffield and the 3 Towers in Manchester are typical cases of such an intervention. In other cases, balconies have been glazed and transformed into winter gardens (e.g. Glastonbury House).

Entrance lobbies are often expanded or refurbished, equipped with CCTV, aiming to improve the building's safety situation (e.g. Peabody Towers and Keeling House). Outdoor spaces and landscape interventions are applied in many cases (e.g. Park Hill and Crossways Estate) improving microclimate and building accessibility.

In some of the housing blocks, additional functions have been added, thus former apartments, rooftops, and outdoor areas have been converted into working, communal or amenity spaces. In Park Hill in Sheffield, for instance, ground floor and first-floor apartments have been converted into working

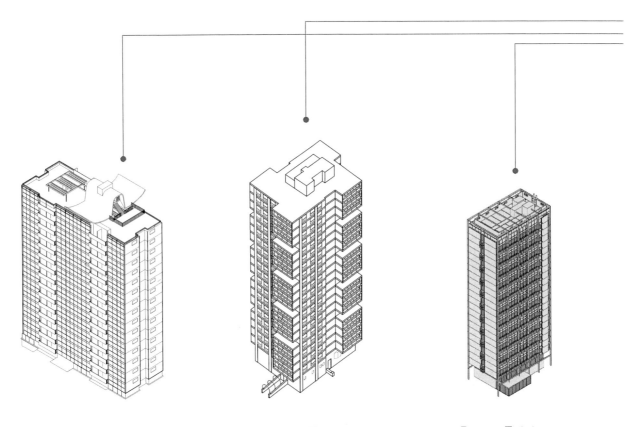

Golden Lane Estate

- Replacement of old windows and doors by new double-glazed frame systems
- Repainting of exposed concrete structure

Westbury Estate

- Re-cladding with new-double glazed anodised aluminium frame curtain wall system
- Replacement of old windows and doors by new double-glazed frame systems
- Repairment of the balconies and concrete structure

Draper Estate

- Replacement of old windows and doors by new double-glazed frame systems
- Recovering and insulating the roof
- Repeating of concrete panelling
- Repairment of balconies and staircase repair

▲ Figure 3.15

Towers which have undergone minor skin repairs and window replacement, Greater London

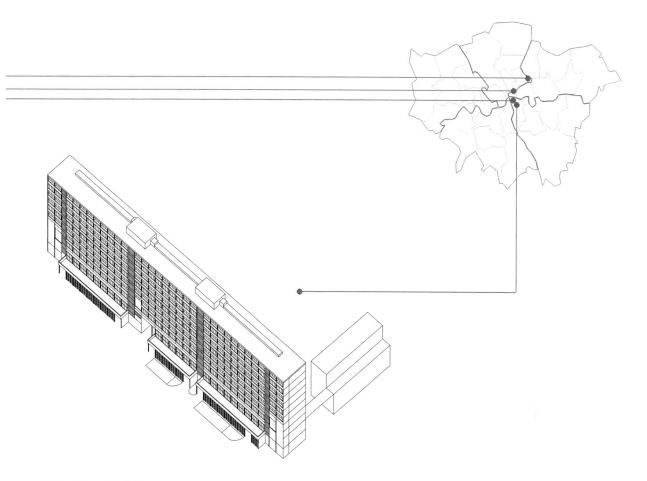

Aylesbury Estate

- Replacement of old windows and doors by new double-glazed frame systems
- Recovering and insulating the roof

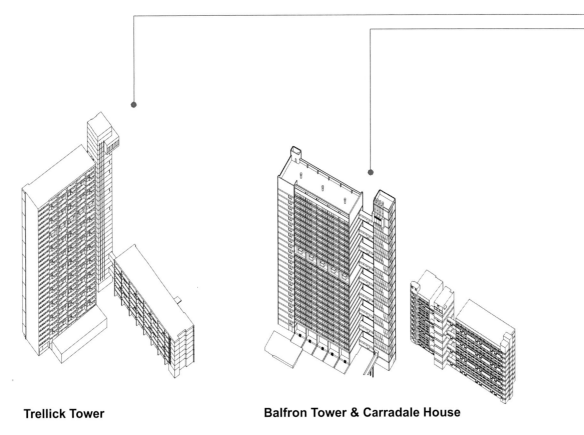

Trellick Tower

- Replacement of old windows and doors by new double-glazed frame systems
- Repairment of concrete facade
- Reduction of glazing surface reduced

Balfron Tower & Carradale House

- Replacement of old windows and doors by new double-glazed frame systems
- Repainting/repairment of concrete walls

▲ Figure 3.15 (Continued)

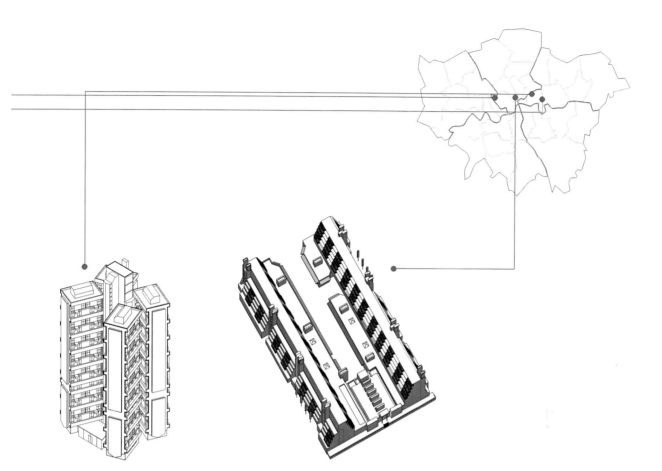

Keeling House

- Repainting/repairment of concrete walls
- Addition of internal second layer of glazing
- Addition of penthouses storey

Brunswick Centre

- Repainting/repairment of concrete walls
- Replacement of old windows and doors by new double-glazed frame systems
- Redesign of glazed winter garden roofs to increase their thermal performance

◀ Figure 3.16

Six-storey extension, Aragon Tower, London

spaces for creative businesses, while the Greenhouse in Leeds created working spaces, a gym, bike rental facilities, and café on the ground floor level.

Change of function is strongly related to the ownership change. All blocks underwent an ownership and/or management change, moving from public ownership to mixed models of private and public or private, shared and public ownerships. In Park Hill in Sheffield, the ratio between public, shared and private ownership is about 1/3 each, while Keeling House in London has been completely privatised. Such changes have had an acute impact on the buildings' social structure, changing their entire anthropogeography. In some cases, where the blocks were abandoned before the retrofit (e.g. Greenhouse), the property was sold to a private investor who took charge of the entire refurbishment process.

Application of renewable energies

Renewable energy technologies are only applied in a minority of projects. Installation of photovoltaic panels is the most common renewable energy source recorded, having been applied in the Bickerdike Court, Belem Tower, Greenhouse, Ferrier Point (Figure 3.17), Glastonbury, Colne and Mersey House, Peabody Towers and Edward Woods Estate. In most cases the panels are placed on the tower's roof but sometimes, as in the case of Edward Woods Estate and Ferrier Point, they are placed on the south-facing façade, becoming an essential design element. Thermosolar panels have been installed on the Chartist House in Liverpool, while Edward Woods and the Greenhouse use wind energy turbines on their rooftops. The Greenhouse in Leeds uses also geothermic energy to pre-heat water as well as technologies which collect rainwater and recycle grey water to use it for the building's draining system. Figures 3.18 and 3.19 show the towers where renewable energy technologies have been applied in our case studies.

▶ Figure 3.17

Photovoltaic façade, Ferrier Point, London

CHAPTER 3 Types and techniques: a retrofit manual

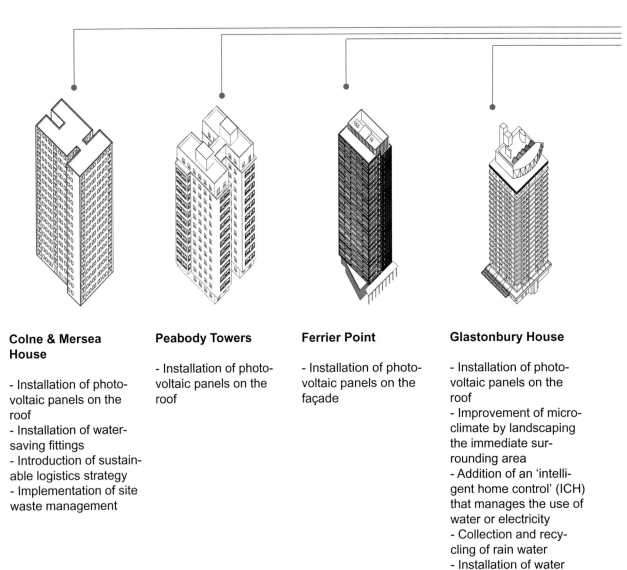

Colne & Mersea House

- Installation of photo-voltaic panels on the roof
- Installation of water-saving fittings
- Introduction of sustainable logistics strategy
- Implementation of site waste management

Peabody Towers

- Installation of photo-voltaic panels on the roof

Ferrier Point

- Installation of photo-voltaic panels on the façade

Glastonbury House

- Installation of photo-voltaic panels on the roof
- Improvement of microclimate by landscaping the immediate surrounding area
- Addition of an 'intelligent home control' (ICH) that manages the use of water or electricity
- Collection and recycling of rain water
- Installation of water saving toilet flushes

▲ Figure 3.18

Towers where renewable energy technologies have been applied, Greater London

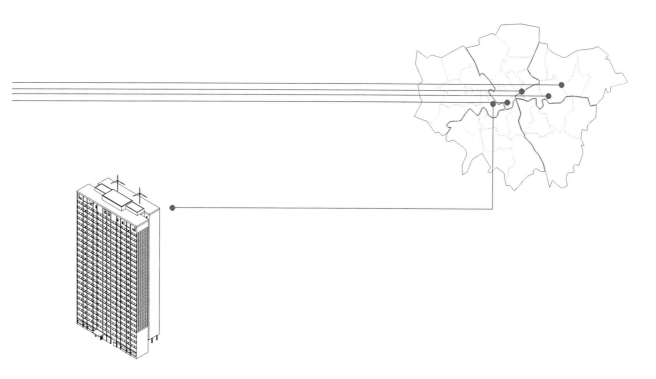

Edward Woods Estate

- Installation of photo-voltaic panels on the facade
- Installation of wind turbines on the roof

CHAPTER 3 Types and techniques: a retrofit manual   63

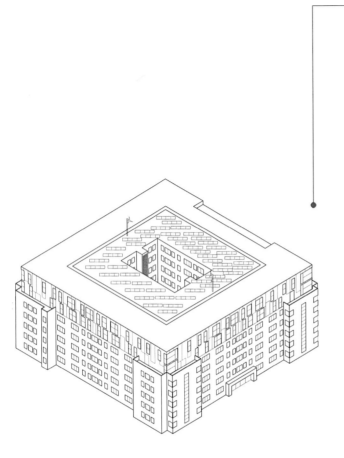

Greenhouse, Leeds

- Installation of photovoltaic panels on the roof
- Installation of two medium sized wind turbines on the roof
- Application of geothermic energy for heating purposes
- Recycling of grey water from sinks and showers
- Collection of rainwater
- New ventilation system (central fans in each apartment)
- Installation of energy saving light fittings and appliances

Bickerdike Court

- Installation of photo-voltaic panels on the roof

▲ Figure 3.19

Towers where renewable energy technologies have been applied, North-west England

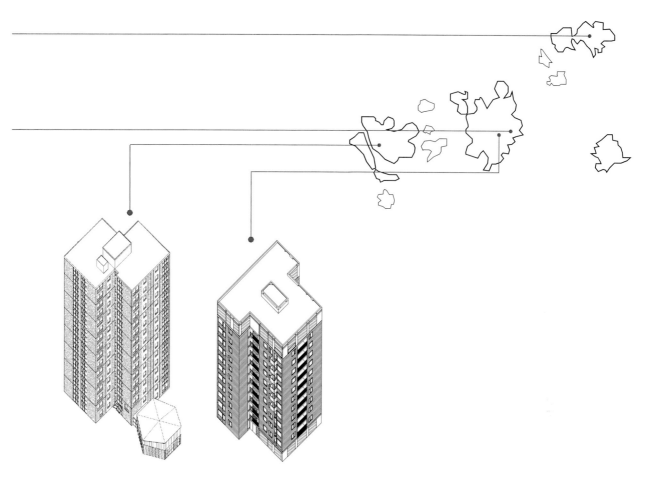

Chartist House

- Installation of thermo-solar panels on the roof
- Installation LED light in communal areas

Belem Tower

- Installation of thermo-solar panels on the roof

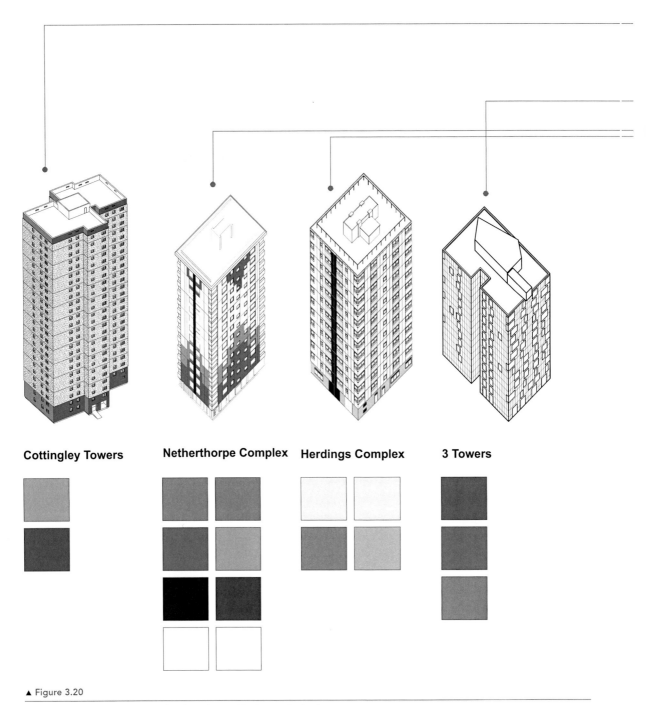

▲ Figure 3.20

Towers that have undergone trough colour change, North-west England

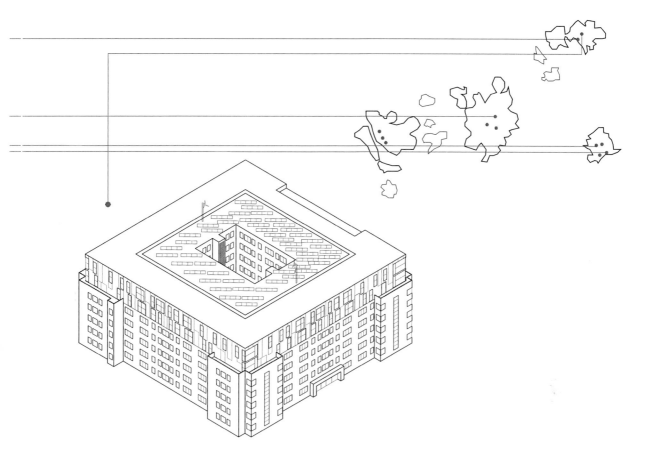

Greenhouse

Change of materiality and colour is the predominant retrofit trend observed. Concrete and brick colour and texture are being replaced with light or shiny colours. In many cases, especially in North-west England (e.g. Park Hill and Callow Mount in Sheffield), the colour pallets used are very intense (Figure 3.20), while for others, mostly in London, light grey and pale tones are preferred (e.g. Little Venice Towers, Aragon Tower) (Figure 3.21). Overall, 69 per cent of the estates included in this survey have undergone a change in their colour and materiality. The remaining 31 per cent are mostly listed housing blocks in the greater London area (Figures 3.22 and 3.23). In particular, London's grade II housing blocks Keeling and Carradale Houses, Balfron and Trellick Towers, Golden Lane Estate, Brunswick Centre and Metro Central Heights have all maintained their original colour, materiality, and appearance, while Park Hill, another grade II building in Leeds has partly changed its materiality, by over-cladding its brickwork walls with shiny, anodised aluminium panels.

CHAPTER 3 Types and techniques: a retrofit manual   **67**

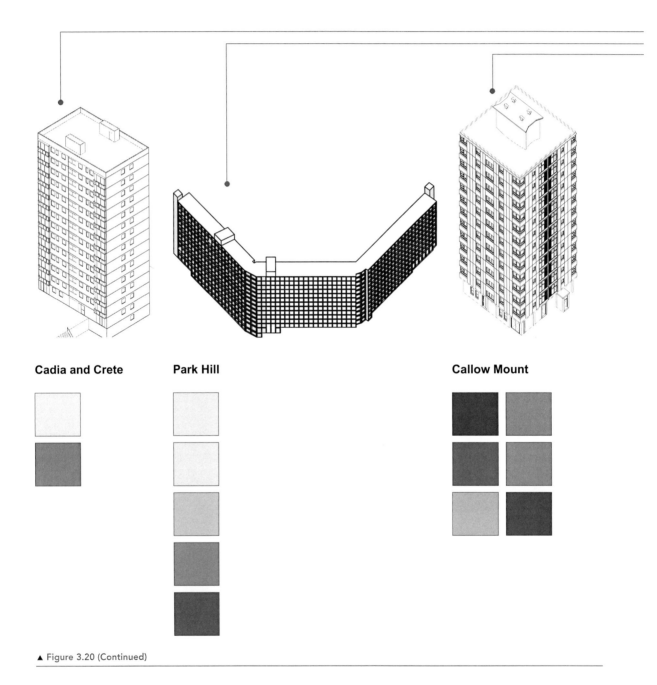

▲ Figure 3.20 (Continued)

68　　　CHAPTER 3 Types and techniques: a retrofit manual

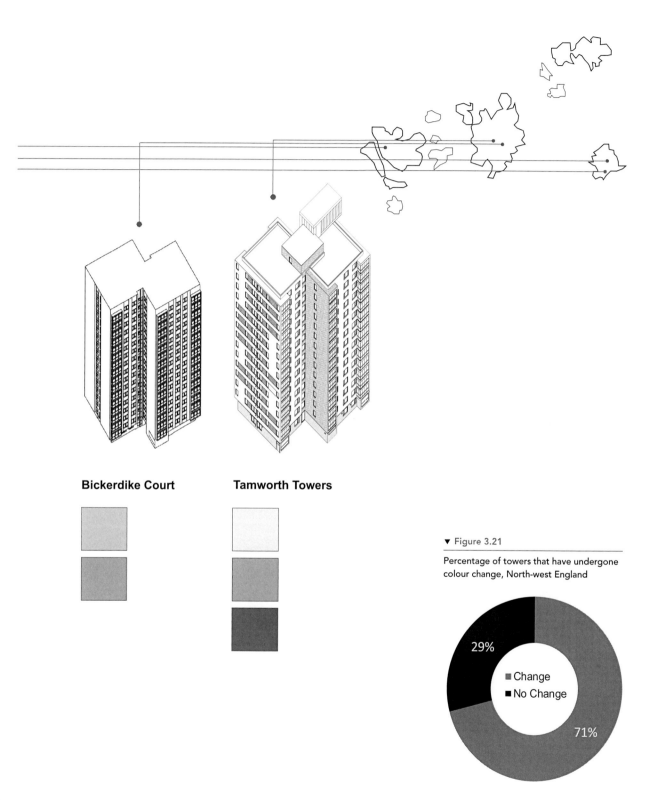

▼ Figure 3.21

Percentage of towers that have undergone colour change, North-west England

CHAPTER 3 Types and techniques: a retrofit manual

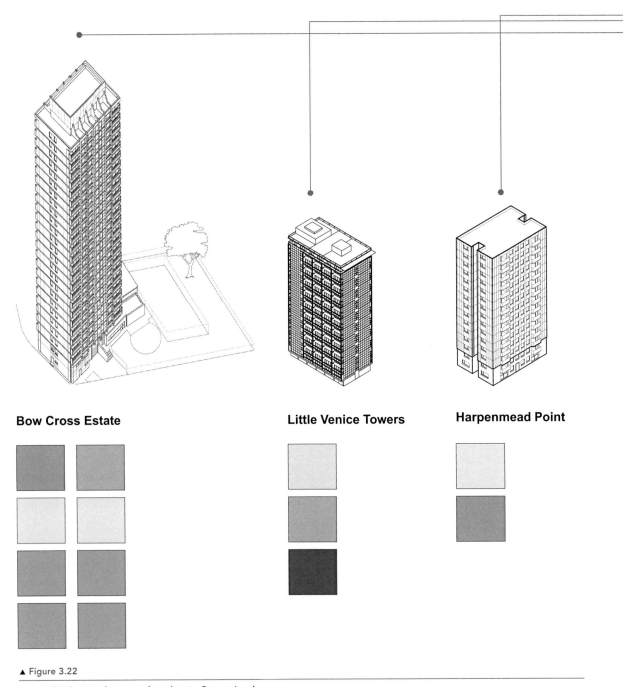

▲ Figure 3.22

Towers that have undergone colour change, Greater London

70　　　　　CHAPTER 3 Types and techniques: a retrofit manual

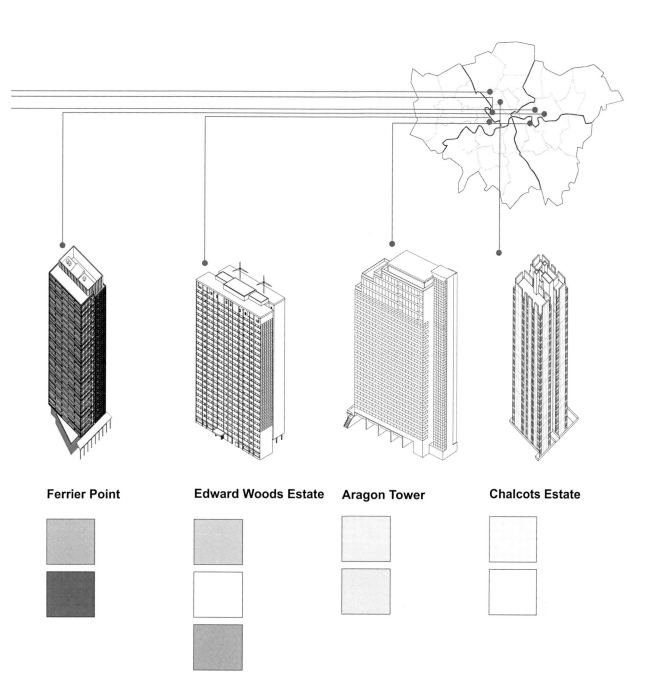

Ferrier Point   **Edward Woods Estate**   **Aragon Tower**   **Chalcots Estate**

CHAPTER 3 Types and techniques: a retrofit manual

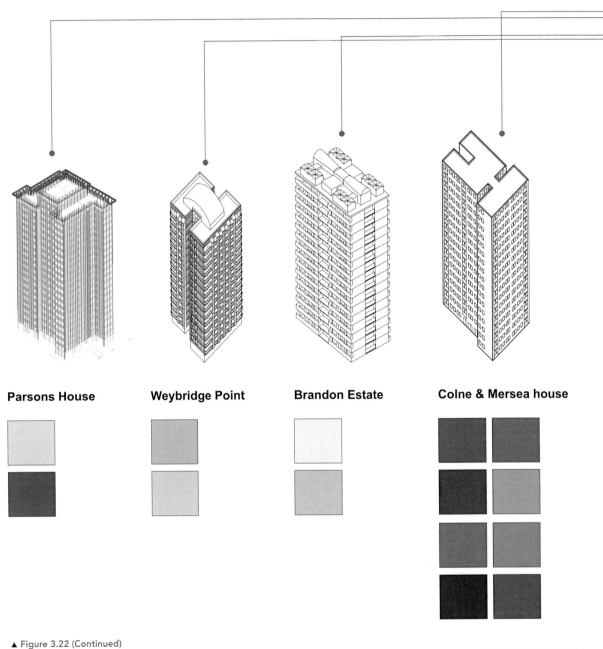

▲ Figure 3.22 (Continued)

72 CHAPTER 3 Types and techniques: a retrofit manual

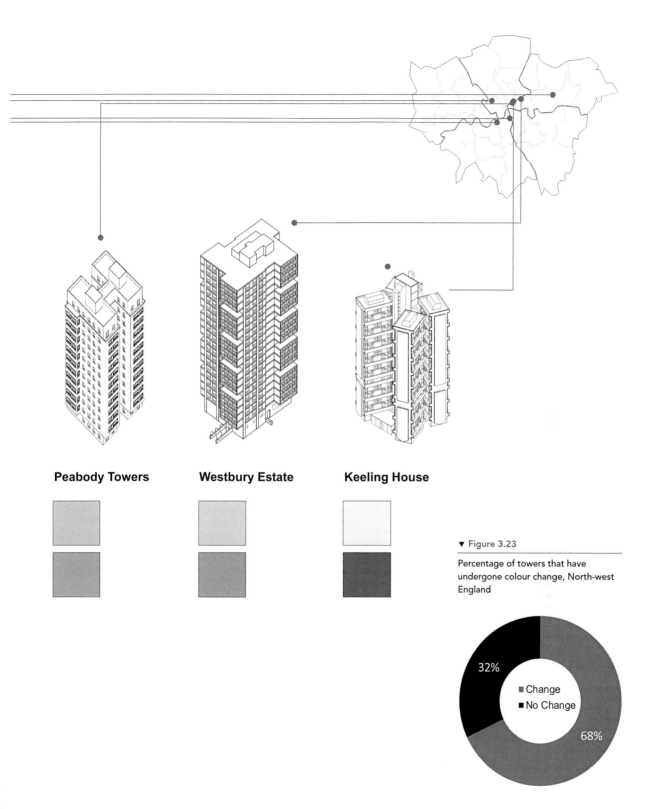

▼ Figure 3.23

Percentage of towers that have undergone colour change, North-west England

CHAPTER 3 Types and techniques: a retrofit manual

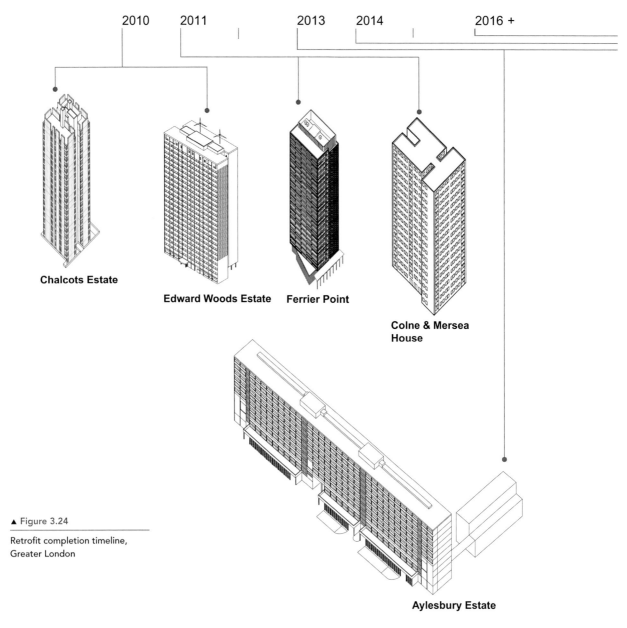

▲ Figure 3.24

Retrofit completion timeline, Greater London

Looking at the retrofit completion timelines, we can draw some interesting observations (Figures 3.24–3.26). The retrofit activity starts to take off in the mid-to-late 1990s. The activities were boosted around the beginning of the twenty-first century (2000–2002) with additional highlights around 2006–2007 and 2011–2012. Many projects are retrofitted after 2015. Retrofit picks in London match the picks in North-west England (Figure 3.27).

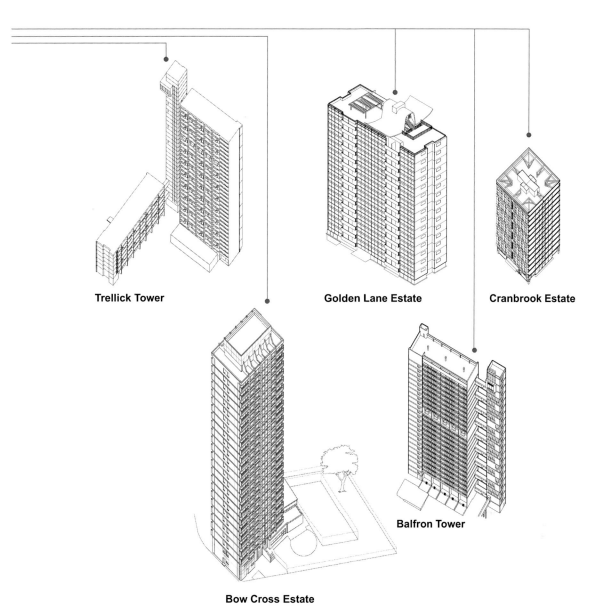

▼ Figure 3.24 (Continued)

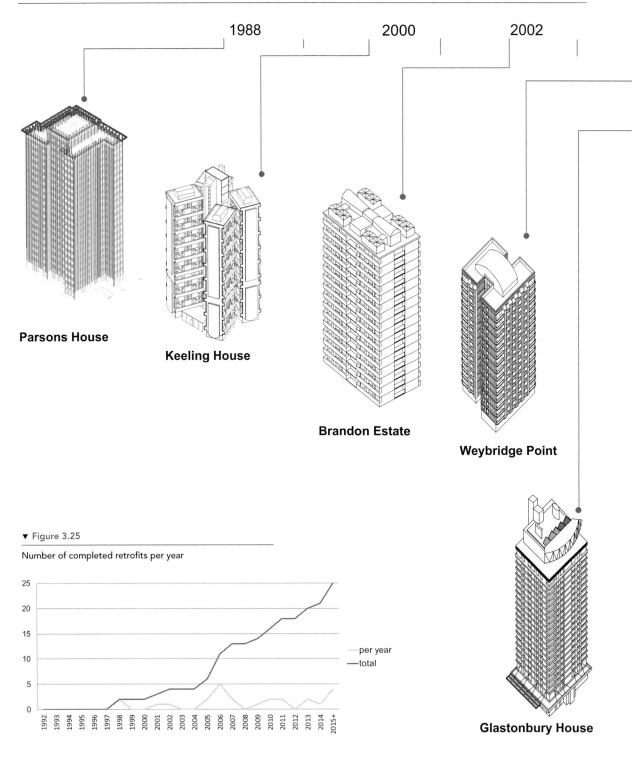

▼ Figure 3.25

Number of completed retrofits per year

CHAPTER 3 Types and techniques: a retrofit manual

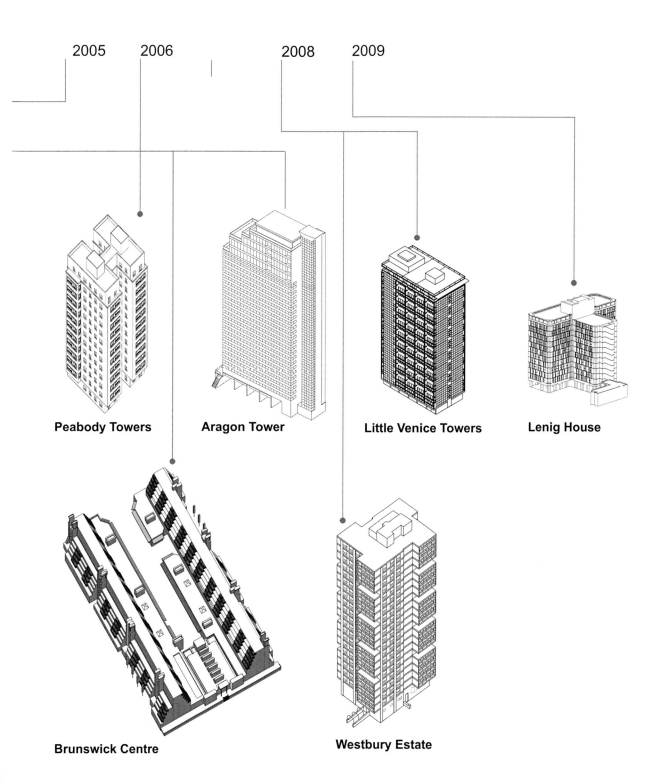

CHAPTER 3 Types and techniques: a retrofit manual

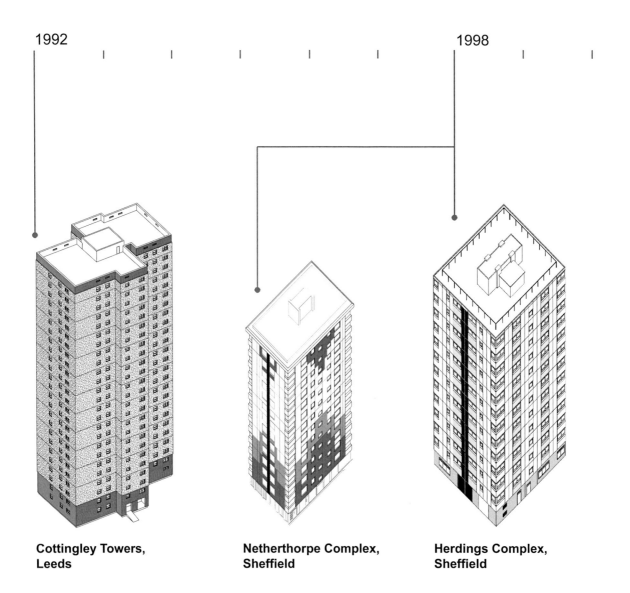

▲ Figure 3.26

Retrofit completion timeline, North-west England

78　CHAPTER 3 Types and techniques: a retrofit manual

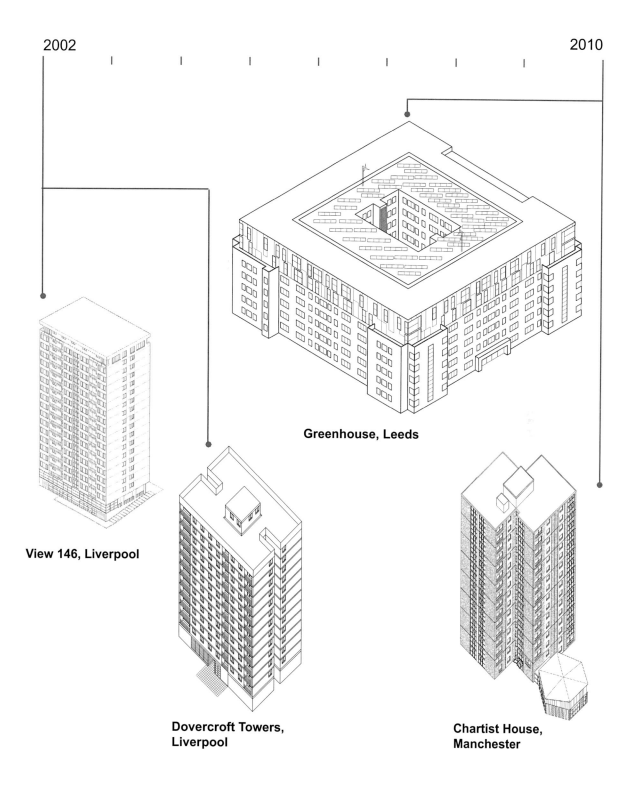

CHAPTER 3 Types and techniques: a retrofit manual

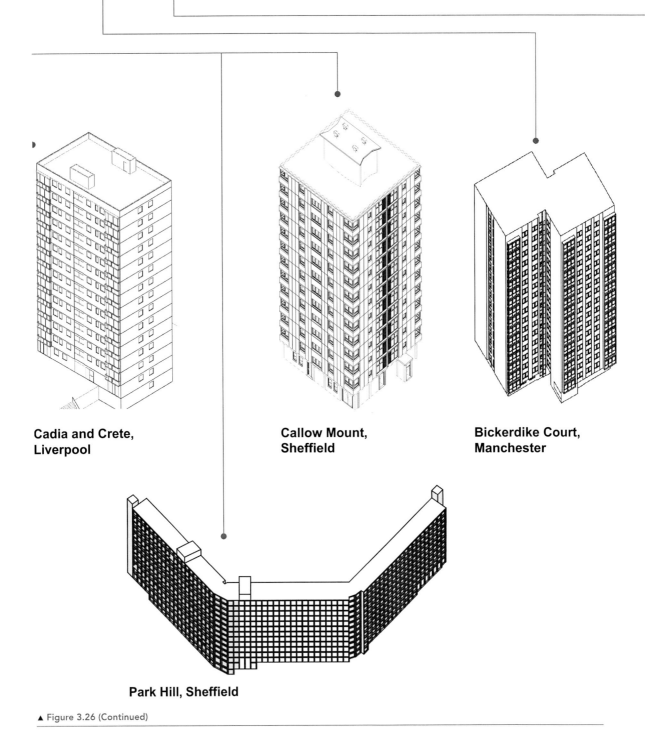

▲ Figure 3.26 (Continued)

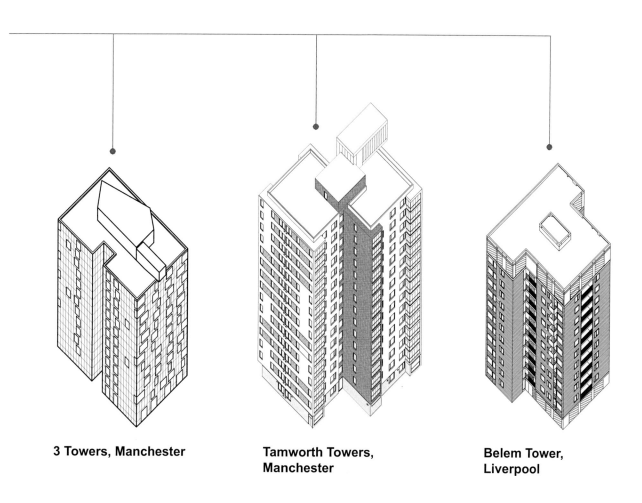

3 Towers, Manchester

Tamworth Towers, Manchester

Belem Tower, Liverpool

▼ Figure 3.27

Number of completed retrofits per year, North-west England

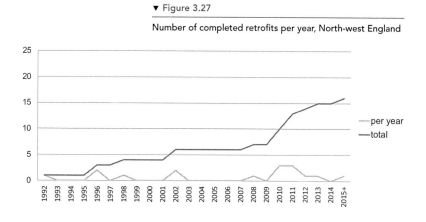

CHAPTER 3 Types and techniques: a retrofit manual

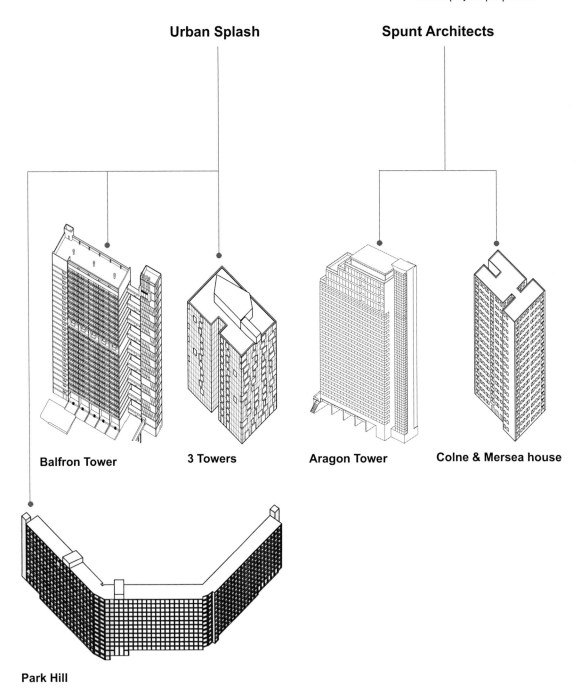

▼ Figure 3.28

Retrofit projects per practice

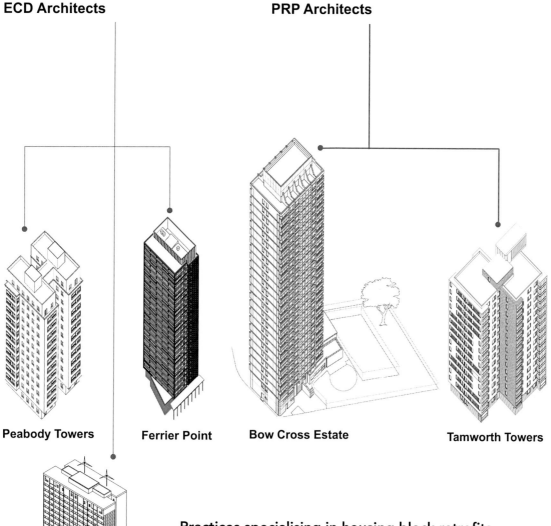

Practices specialising in housing block retrofits

Some architectural practices have specialised on tower block retrofits and are getting repeatedly involved in related projects (Figure 3.28). PRP Architects have completed sustainable retrofits of Crossway Estate (London) and Tamworth Towers (Manchester), ECD Architects completed Peabody Towers, Edward Woods Estate and Ferrier Point (London), Sprunt Architects retrofitted Aragon Tower and Colne and Mersea House (London) while Urban Splash completed the 3 Towers (Manchester) and Phase 1 in Park Hill (Sheffield) and are currently working on Park Hill Phase 2 as well as on Balfron Tower and Carradale House (London).

CHAPTER 3 Types and techniques: a retrofit manual

Full list of estates that have undergone retrofit interventions, research sample, Greater London

▼ Figure 3.29

(a)–(d) Full list of estates that have undergone retrofit interventions, research sample, Greater London

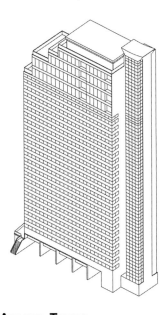 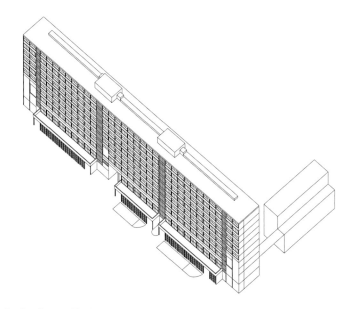

Aragon Tower **Aylesbury Estate**

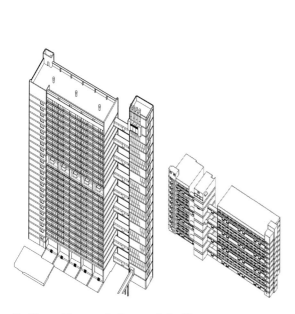

Balfron Tower & Carradale House

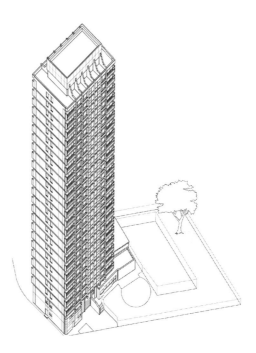

Bow Cross Estate

CHAPTER 3 Types and techniques: a retrofit manual

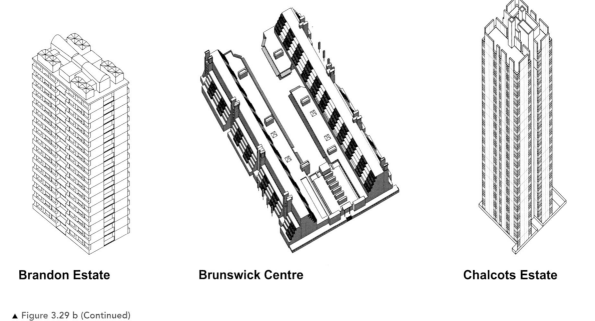

▲ Figure 3.29 b (Continued)

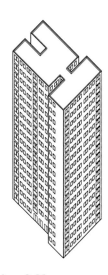 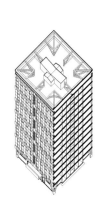 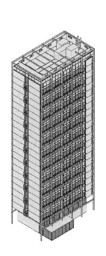 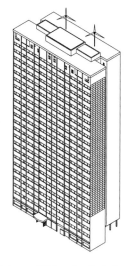

Colne & Mersea House   **Cranbrook Estate**   **Draper Estate**   **Edward Woods Estate**

CHAPTER 3 Types and techniques: a retrofit manual

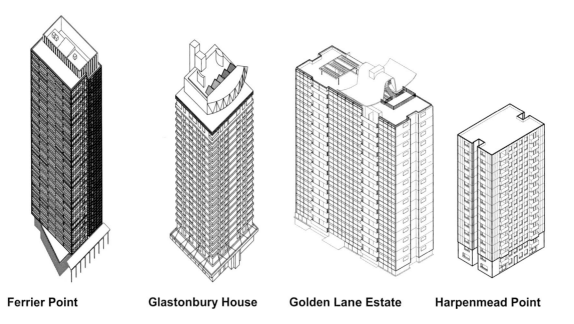

▲ Figure 3.29 c (Continued)

88　　　　　　　　　　　CHAPTER 3 Types and techniques: a retrofit manual

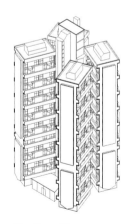 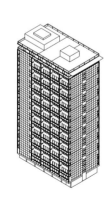 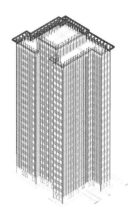 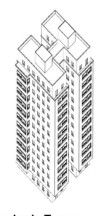

Keeling House **Little Venice Towers** **Parsons House** **Peabody Towers**

CHAPTER 3 Types and techniques: a retrofit manual

89

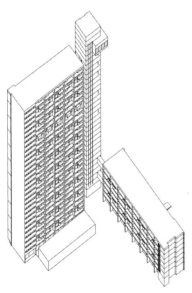
Trellick Tower

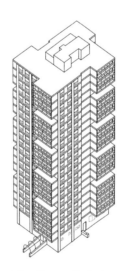
Westbury Estate

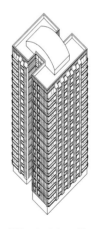
Weybridge Point

▲ Figure 3.29 d (Continued)

Aragon Tower

- Re-cladding with thermally insulated aluminium screens
- Replacement of old windows and doors by new double-glazed frame systems
- Addition of five floors on the rooftop
- Replacement of the old fires

Aylesbury Estate

- Replacement of old windows and doors by new double-glazed frame systems
- Recovering and insulating the roof
- Rearrangement of the floor plans (the main corridor moved at north, the old corridor space at south turned into a living space)

Balfron Tower and Carradale House

- Replacement of old windows and doors by new double-glazed frame systems
- Repainting/repair of concrete walls
- Installation of new heating system and boilers
- Installation of new ventilation system

Bow Cross Estate

- Over-cladding with thermally insulated render
- Replacement of old windows and doors by new double-glazed frame systems
- Reduction of glazed surface/partial replacement by non-structural infill side panels
- Over-cladding of balcony areas and slab edges with coloured aluminium panels
- Insulation of new waterproof membrane and a ballast system
- Rooftop enclosure made with galvanised steel mesh
- Repair of the concrete skeleton
- Installation of new heating system
- Installation of new ventilation system

Brandon Estate

- Over-cladding of concrete façade with insulated render
- Replacement of old windows and doors by new double-glazed frame systems

Brunswick Centre

- Repainting/repair of concrete walls
- Replacement of old windows and doors by new double-glazed frame systems
- Redesign of glazed winter garden roofs to increase their thermal performance
- Replacement of old pipework
- Revitalisation of the plaza and the communal areas

Chalcots Estate

- Over-cladding with thermally insulated aluminium screens
- Replacement of old windows and doors by new active, double-glazed self-cleaning frames
- Installation of new heating system

Colne and Mersea House

- Over-cladding with thermally insulated render
- Insulation of the roof
- Replacement of old windows and doors by new triple-glazed frame systems
- Installation of integral blinds on south-facing windows
- Installation of photovoltaic panels on the roof
- Installation of water-saving fittings
- Introduction of a sustainable logistics strategy
- Implementation of site waste management

Cranbrook Estate

- Over-cladding with thermally insulated render
- Replacement of old windows and doors by new double-glazed frame systems
- Installation of photovoltaic panels on the roof
- Installation of new heating system

Draper Estate

- Replacement of old windows and doors by new double-glazed frame systems
- Recovering and insulating the roof
- Replacing of concrete panelling
- Repair of balconies and staircase repair

Ferrier Point

- Over-cladding with thermally insulated aluminium screens
- Replacement of old windows and doors by new triple-glazed frame systems
- Installation of photovoltaic panels on the façade
- Installation of new, gas-powered heating system
- Installation of new boilers

Glastonbury House

- Installation of photovoltaic panels on the roof
- Improvement of micro-climate by landscaping the immediate surrounding area
- Addition of an 'Intelligent Home Control' (ICH) that manages the use of water or electricity
- Collection and recycling of rainwater
- Installation of water-saving toilet flushes

Golden Lane Estate

- Re-cladding with new double-glazed anodised aluminium frame curtain wall system
- Replacement of old windows and doors by new double-glazed frame systems
- Repair of the balconies and concrete structure
- Installation of new heating and ventilation systems

Harpenmead Point

- Over-cladding with thermally insulated aluminium screens
- Replacement of old windows and doors by aluminium-wood composite double-glazed frame systems
- Over-cladding of brickwork on the ground floor area with thermally insulated render
- Improvement of waterproof insulation on the roof

Keeling House

- Repainting/repair of concrete walls
- Addition of internal second layer of glazing
- Addition of penthouses storey on the roof
- Addition of entrance foyer

CHAPTER 3 Types and techniques: a retrofit manual

Little Venice Towers

- Over-cladding with thermally insulated aluminium screens
- Replacement of old windows and doors by new double-glazed frame systems

Parsons House

- Re-cladding with thermally insulated aluminium screens
- Replacement of old windows and doors by new double-glazed frame systems

Peabody Towers

- Over-cladding with thermally insulated render
- Replacement of old windows and doors by new double-glazed frame systems
- Installation of photovoltaic panels on the roof
- Installation of new heating system and boilers

Trellick Tower

- Replacement of old windows and doors by new double-glazed frame systems
- Repair of concrete façade
- Reduction of glazed surface

Westbury Estate

- Replacement of old windows and doors by new double-glazed frame systems
- Repainting of exposed concrete structure
- Installation of new heating system
- Installation of low energy lighting

Weybridge Point

- Over-cladding with thermally insulated terracotta rain-screens
- Replacement of old windows and doors by new double-glazed frame systems.

Full list of estates that have undergone retrofit interventions, research sample, North-west England

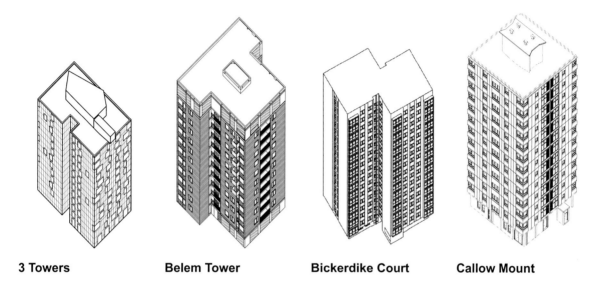

3 Towers **Belem Tower** **Bickerdike Court** **Callow Mount**

▲ Figure 3.30

(a) -(c) Full list of estates that have undergone retrofit interventions, research sample, North-west England

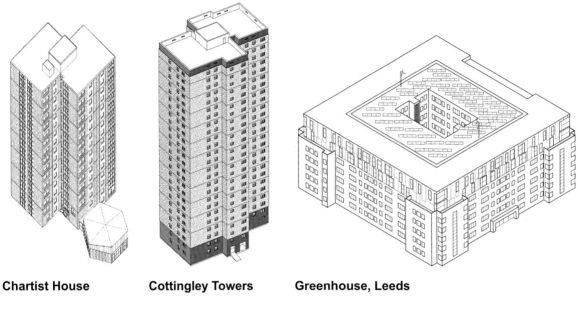

Chartist House   **Cottingley Towers**   **Greenhouse, Leeds**

▲ Figure 3.30 b (Continued)

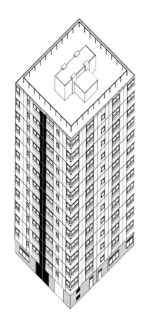

Herdings Complex

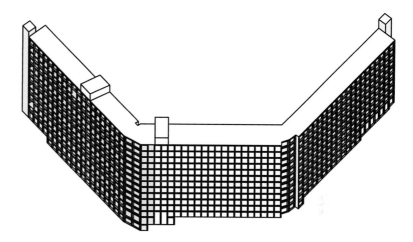

Park Hill

3 Towers

- Over-cladding with thermally insulated timber composite panels
- The balcony floor slabs have been reinforced
- The balconies have been enclosed for more living space
- Replacement of old windows and doors by new double-glazed frame systems

Belem Tower

- Over-cladding with thermally insulated aluminium screens
- Replacement of old windows and doors by new double-glazed frame systems
- Installation of thermosolar panels on the roof

 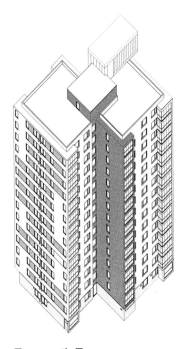 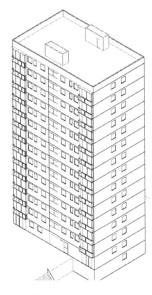

Netherthorpe Complex **Tamworth Towers** **Candia and Crete**

▲ Figure 3.30 c (Continued)

Bickerdike Court

- Over-cladding with thermally insulated aluminium screens
- Replacement of old windows and doors by new double-glazed frame systems
- Repair of concrete walls
- Installation of photovoltaic panels on the roof
- Improvements of electrical and mechanical fittings

Callow Mount

- Over-cladding with thermally insulated aluminium screens
- Replacement of old windows and doors by new double-glazed frame systems

- Enclosure of balconies
- Installation of new boilers

Candia and Crete

- Over-cladding of concrete façade with insulated render
- Replacement of old windows and doors by new double-glazed frame systems

Chartist House

- Installation of thermosolar panels on the roof
- Installation LED light in communal areas
- Replacement of heating system and radiators

Cottingley Towers

- Over-cladding of concrete façade with insulated render
- Replacement of old windows and doors by new double-glazed frame systems
- Installation of new heating system

Greenhouse, Leeds

- Over-cladding of concrete façade with insulated render
- Replacement of old windows and doors by new double-glazed frame systems
- Installation of photovoltaic panels on the roof
- Installation of two medium-sized wind turbines on the roof
- Application of geothermic energy for heating purposes
- Recycling of grey water from sinks and showers
- Collection of rainwater
- New ventilation system (central fans in each apartment)
- Installation of energy-saving light fittings and appliances
- Addition of two storeys on the roof
- Modification of the floor plan and the courtyard
- Installation of smart technologies and utility meters

Herdings Complex

- Over-cladding with thermally insulated aluminium screens
- Replacement of old windows and doors by new double-glazed frame systems

CHAPTER 3 Types and techniques: a retrofit manual

Netherthorpe Complex

- Over-cladding with thermally insulated aluminium screens
- Replacement of old windows and doors by new double-glazed frame systems
- Enclosure of balconies

Park Hill

- Repair of concrete structure
- Over-cladding of brickwork with anodised aluminium panels
- Replacement of old windows and doors by new double-glazed frame systems (the ratio of façade solid/void has been reversed into 2/3 glazed surface and 1/3 aluminium panels)

Tamworth Towers

- Over-cladding of concrete façade with insulated render
- Replacement of old windows and doors by new double-glazed frame systems
- Enclosure of balconies

Notes

1 Miles Glendinning and Stefan Muthesius, *Tower Block: Modern Public Housing in England, Scotland, Wales and Northern Ireland* (New Haven, CT: Yale University Press, 1994).
2 Ibid.
3 R. McMullan, *Environmental Science in Building* (Basingstoke: Palgrave Macmillan, 2012).
4 G. Giebeler, *Refurbishment Manual: Maintenance, Conversions, Extensions* (Basel: Birkhäuser, 2009).
5 G. Hausladen, *ClimateSkin* (Basel: Birkhäuser, 2008).
6 Greenspec (2013) *Lighting Specification and Part L: 2013*. Available at: www.greenspec.co.uk/building-design/lighting-part-l-2013/
7 Thaleia Konstantinou, *Façade Refurbishment Toolbox: Supporting the Design of Residential Energy Upgrades* (Delft: Delft University of Technology. Faculty of Architecture and the Built Environment, 2014).
8 U. Knaack, T. Klein, M. Bilow, and T. Auer, *Façades: Principles of Construction* (Boston: Birkhäuser, 2014).

Chapter 4

Tower block retrofits

The 3 Towers

Original information

Location: Manchester
Address: Dalton Street
Postcode: M40 7GX
Date of construction: 1960s
No. storeys: 13
No. flats: 187
Architect: Manchester City Council
Owner: Manchester County Council

▼ Figure 4.2

The 3 Towers, axonometric drawing

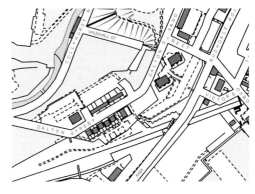

▲ Figure 4.1

The 3 Towers site plan

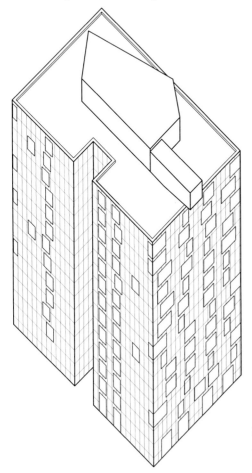

The 3 Towers formed part of a set of six towers located in Collyhurst and Miles Platting, in the Central Manchester Area, just 2.5 km north-east of the city centre. The towers were owned by Manchester City Council, originally built in the 1960s as part of the council's slum clearance and rehousing programme. In 2003, the towers were sold to the developer Urban Splash Ltd. for £900,000 with the intention of recycling those receipts back into the project. In the early 1990s, the estate was energetically outdated and fell into material and social decay. At the time of sale, the towers were vacant, had suffered a decade of dereliction within a generally neglected area, and were threatened by demolition. The estate is bordered by the River Irk, in an area lined by birch trees (originally a wooded hill), with the potential to provide a high-quality landscape that could be the starting point for the regeneration project.

▶ Figure 4.3

The 3 Towers balconies enclosed within the living spaces after the retrofit

▼ Figure 4.4

The 3 Towers post-retrofit, west view

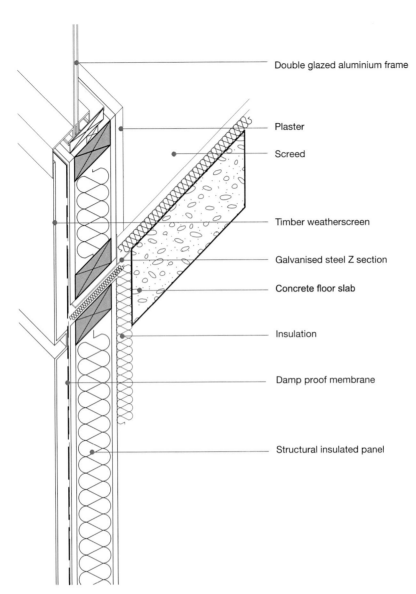

▶ Figure 4.5

Over-cladding with timber SIPs, retrofit axonometric detail

(Labels: Double glazed aluminium frame; Plaster; Screed; Timber weatherscreen; Galvanised steel Z section; Concrete floor slab; Insulation; Damp proof membrane; Structural insulated panel)

Retrofit information

Date of retrofit intervention: 2008–2013
No. storeys: 14
No. flats: 187
Architect: Union North Architects
Property owner/client: Urban Splash, partly privately owned
Contractor/developer: Urban Splash
Institutions involved: N/A
Governmental programmes: English Partnership's First Time Buyers Initiative
Cost: £12 million

▼ Figure 4.6

The 3 Towers, generic south view

Despite being subjected to a period of underinvestment, the buildings were in good structural condition and needed very little repair. The existing concrete slab was fully encased with timber SIPs (structurally insulated panels), which act as a self-supporting curtain wall. Timber SIPs are extremely thermally efficient, achieving a U-value of up to 0.10W/m^{2}k. The timber veneer used on the panels' outer faces is certified by the Forest Stewardship Council.

The old single-glazed windows have been replaced by partly floor-to-ceiling high, double-glazed aluminium frame systems. Balcony floor-slabs have been reinforced and the living area extended. The old heating system has been replaced.

In addition to the environmental upgrade, the estate's perception was radically changed through a new vision based on the transformation of the towers' materiality and landscape. Concrete was replaced by timber to connect the towers to the vertical silver lines of the existing birch trees. The new composition of the façades was designed to break the stumpy regular image of the towers, making them look taller and more elegant. The reconfiguration of openings, including corner windows, together with the emphasis on vertical joints by using narrow upright panels, transformed the previous horizontality predominant in the original elevations into verticality. This move helped to merge the towers into the surrounding, softer landscape.

▼ Figure 4.7

The 3 Towers, east view

▼ Figure 4.8

Over-cladding with timber SIPs façade close-up

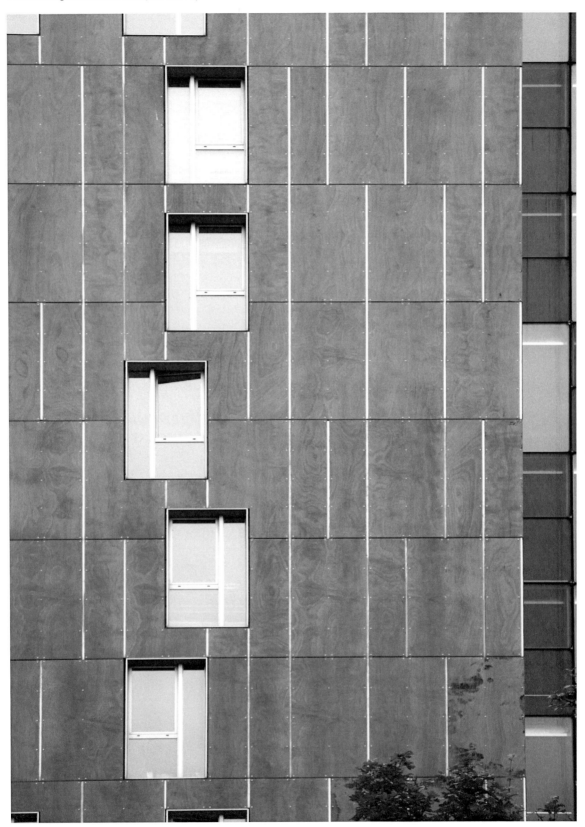

The social change towards privatisation is reflected in the characteristics of the interventions. Rather than trying to meet minimum standards and vandal-proof detailing, the design approach aims to provide attention to detail, high-quality finishes and generally high standards of specification in the three towers, independently of the type of tenancy allocated to each of them.

Sources

– *Architect's Journal Magazine* (2008) '3 Towers',10 April
– http://manchesterhistory.net/manchester/outside/3towers.html
– http://skyscraperpage.com/cities/?buildingID=26799
– www.lancerouth.com
– www.northerndesignawards.com/entry/2010/urban-splash-3-towers-manchester
– www.urbansplash.co.uk/documents/brochure/3tow_digi.pdf
– www.urbansplash.co.uk/documents/FS_CHRISTABEL.pdf
– www.e-architect.co.uk/manchester/three-towers
– www.manchesterhistory.net

▶ Figure 4.9

Over-cladding with timber SIPs corner close-up

Aragon Tower

Original information

Location: South London
Address: George Beard Road
Postcode: SE8 3AJ
Date of construction: 1962
No. storeys: 24
No. flats: 144
Architect: Ted Hollamby
Owner/client: London County Council
Institutions involved: London County Council

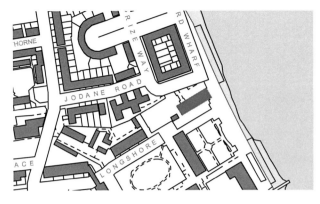

▲ Figure 4.10

Aragon Tower site plan

▼ Figure 4.11

Aragon Tower post-retrofit axonometric drawing

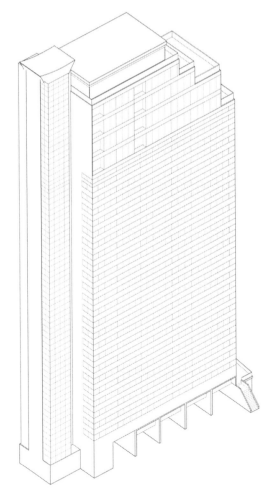

◀ Figure 4.12

Aragon Tower pre-retrofit

The Aragon Tower is located on the Pepys Estate in Deptford, south-east London, along the banks of the River Thames. It was originally built in 1962 as part of a trio of towers combined with maisonette flats on the estate. The original building comprised 24 storeys containing 144 flats, and at the time it was the tallest residential property in London, standing at 78 metres high. Pedestrian and vehicular traffics were separated, resorting to a series of elevated walkways that connected the different buildings. The estate provided for different social and convenient amenities: car park, shopping centre, maternity and child welfare centre, green areas, and youth and old folks clubs.

Aragon Tower was a social housing tower block under the ownership of the local authority until 2003. Lewisham Council sold the property to developers Berkeley Homes for approximately £11.5 million, with the proceeds going into funding for the regeneration of alternative areas of the Pepys Estate.

▼ Figure 4.13

Aragon Tower, rooftop extension, south view

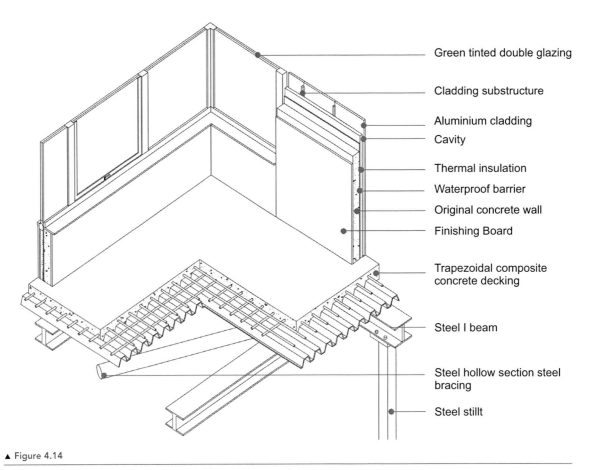

▲ Figure 4.14

Axonometric detail of the façade retrofit: over-cladding with insulated aluminium rain-screens

Retrofit information

Date of retrofit intervention: 2006
No. storeys: 29
No. flats: 158
Architect: Sprunt
Property owner/client: Berkeley Homes and some now privately owned
Contractor/developer: Berkeley Homes/Apex Construction
Cost: £20 million

The tower block structure is formed of pre-cast reinforced concrete. The original cladding was made out of pre-cast concrete panels, decorated with pebble dash, without any cavity and insulation. All glass surfaces were single-glazed windows.

The tower was suffering from thermal bridging and lack of insulation and moisture, noise and heat control. The image of the local area had greatly degenerated due to crime and poverty, as well as general disrepair caused by the absence of maintenance.

Aragon Tower has been over-clad with aluminium rain-screens, receiving a substantial layer of insulation. Double-glazed aluminium framed windows have replaced the single-glazed windows. The new insulated envelope improved the building environmental performance drastically. The building U-value dropped from 1.5 to 0.33W/m²K, lowering maintenance cost and energy consumption by 25 per cent.

All traces of the concrete tower were erased and replaced by light grey-greenish panels and glass. The rooftop, accessed by a prefabricated staircase next to the tower, has been extended by six additional stepped floors. These additional storeys have changed the building's proportions. The reception level has been raised from the ground level to the first floor. All flats have been refurbished, receiving new kitchens and toilets. However, the building's social sustainability has undergone a radical change: since the tower was sold all apartments have been privatised, and rents have increased significantly.

▶ Figure 4.15

Aragon Tower, aluminium rain-screen façade

Sources

- Lewisham Council (2003) 'Aragon Tower, Longshore, Pepys Estate, SE8', Lewisham/Deptford Planning Committee Reports.
- Potts, G. (2008) *Regeneration in Deptford*, London. British Urban Regeneration Association (BURA).
- Taylor, N. (1967) 'The failure of housing'. *Architectural Review*, 849: 341–359.
- http://singleaspect.org.uk/sustower/index.htm
- www.sprunt.net/aragon-tower.html
- www.steel-renovation.org/WP5/WP%205.3.11%20Renovation%20of%20residential%20building%20in%20East%20London.pdf
- www.telegraph.co.uk/finance/property/3336718/Tears-of-the-clown-as-his-tower-gets-a-fancy-facelift.html

◄ Figure 4.16

Aragon Tower, aluminium rain-screen, north-west façade

Balfron Tower and Carradale House

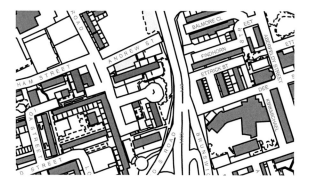

▲ Figure 4.17

Brownfield Estate's site plan

Original information

Location: East London
Address: St Leonards Road
Postcode: E14 0QT
Date of construction: 1967
No. storeys: 27
No. flats: 147
Architect: Ernő Goldfinger
Owner/client: Greater London Council

Retrofit information

Date of retrofit intervention: 2016+
No. storeys: 27
No. flats: 146
Architect: PRP Architects
Property owner/client: Poplar HARCA
Contractor/developer: Urban Splash
Institutions involved: English Heritage, Twentieth Century Society
Cost: £10 million (estimate)

◄ Figure 4.18

Balfron Tower, west view

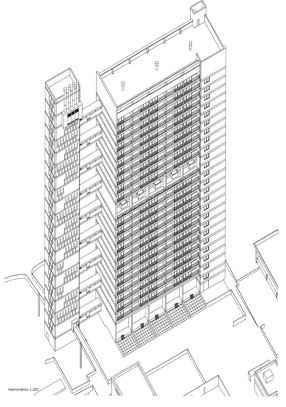

▲ Figure 4.19

Balfron Tower, axonometric drawing

Balfron Tower and Carradale House are both parts of the Brownfield estate, built as part of a wider urban housing scheme, commissioned by the London County Council in 1963, later renamed as Greater London Council. Located in East London, they are a precursor to the distinguished Trellick Tower. This fine example of Goldfinger's Brutalist style, named after a Scottish village, boasts characteristic horizontal sky bridges which are accessed on every third floor and vivid concrete towers, with signature arrowslit windows. Due to the robust nature of the detailing of this building, which has helped it to weather well, and the vital part it has played in providing a strong community for the local area, Balfron Tower and Carradale House have been listed as Grade II buildings since 1996. Their iconic design made them become suitable scenery for many film settings and video clips.

Ownership of the entire estate was transferred from the Greater London Council to the Tower Hamlets Borough Council in 1980 and to Poplar HARCA in 2007. Poplar HARCA has initiated its refurbishment, expected to take place in 2017.

PRP Architects started the Balfron Tower and Carradale House refurbishment in 2007, however, the project was taken over by Urban Splash recently. The retrofit is scheduled to start in early 2017 and will include window replacement by double-glazed, high-performing window frames, concrete envelope repairs, waste management upgrade, communal areas refurbishment and heating system replacement.

The retrofit has not been complete at this stage, but it appears to be happening with respect to the character of the building. However, there are many complaints by residents concerning the affordable housing targets of Poplar HARCA. It appears that the property is moving towards full privatisation, ignoring social sustainability.

▼ Figure 4.20

Balfron Tower, circulation core and bridges

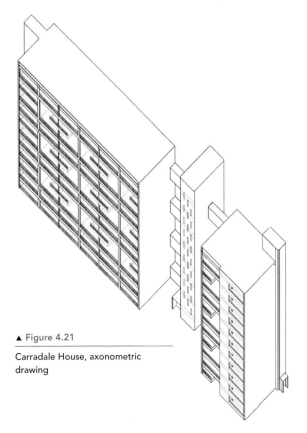

▲ Figure 4.21

Carradale House, axonometric drawing

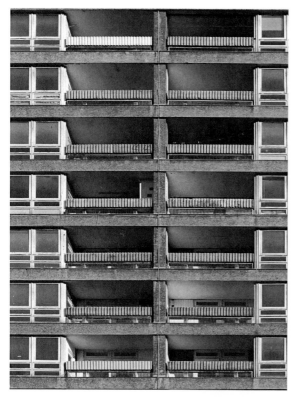

▲ Figure 4.22

Balfron Tower pre-retrofitted façade close-up

Sources

- www.archdaily.com/160672/ad-classics-balfron-tower-erno-goldfinger
- www.balfrontower.org/
- www.dezeen.com/2014/09/24/brutalist-buildings-balfron-tower-london-erno-goldfinger/
- www.eastendreview.co.uk/2015/03/24/balfron-tower-poplar-harca/
- www.theguardian.com/artanddesign/gallery/2014/sep/26/flat-130-in-the-balfron-tower-in-pictures

▶ Figure 4.23

Balfron Tower, south view

Bow Cross

Original information

Location: East London
Address: Rainhill Way, Tower Hamlets
Postcode: E3 3EY
Date of construction: 1970
No. storeys: 25
No. flats: 92 (per tower)
Owner/client: Bow City Council

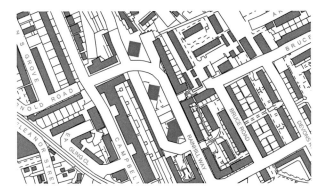

▲ Figure 4.24

Bow Cross site plan

▲ Figure 4.25

Bow Cross before the retrofit

▲ Figure 4.26

Bow Cross after the retrofit

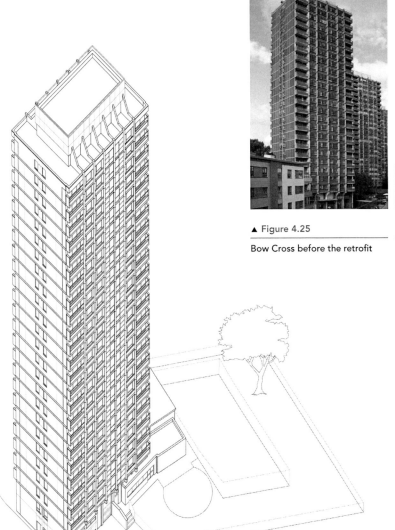

◀ Figure 4.27

Bow Cross post-retrofit, axonometric view

▶ Figure 4.28

Bow Cross post-retrofit, south view

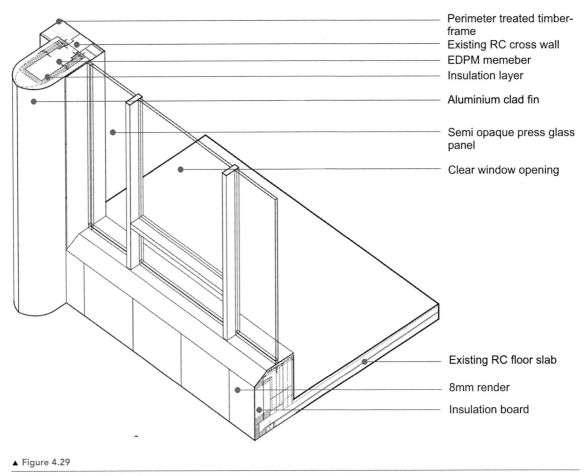

▲ Figure 4.29

Crossways Estate retrofit detail

Built in the early 1970s, Bow Cross is among the most iconic council estates in the East of London, locally known as the 'Pride of Bow'. Commissioned by the London County Council for affordable housing purposes, it includes a total of three, 25-storey-high towers located next to the DLR railway tracks. By 2003, the estate was in significant decline; the elevated walkways proved detrimental to personal safety and had also created blighted space at ground level, with graffiti and fly-tipping commonplace. The estate repairs backlog was ever increasing; high crime levels including arson had created no-go areas. Finally, the estate was sold to Swan Housing Association, which initiated its retrofit.

Retrofit information

Date of retrofit intervention: 2013–2014
No. storeys: 25
No. flats: 93 per tower
Architect: PRP Architects
Property owner/client: Swan Housing Association
Contractor/developer: Retrofit YK Ltd
Institutions involved: Countryside Properties, London Borough of Tower Hamlets

The key retrofit interventions include over-cladding in low-maintenance insulated silicone-based render, installation of new high-performance aluminium/timber composite windows, controlled ventilation systems to kitchens and bathrooms, a new heating plant serving all towers with individual heat, a new smoke ventilation system, as well as new lifts that serve all floors.

▼ Figure 4.30

Insulated render façade in combination with aluminium cladded fins

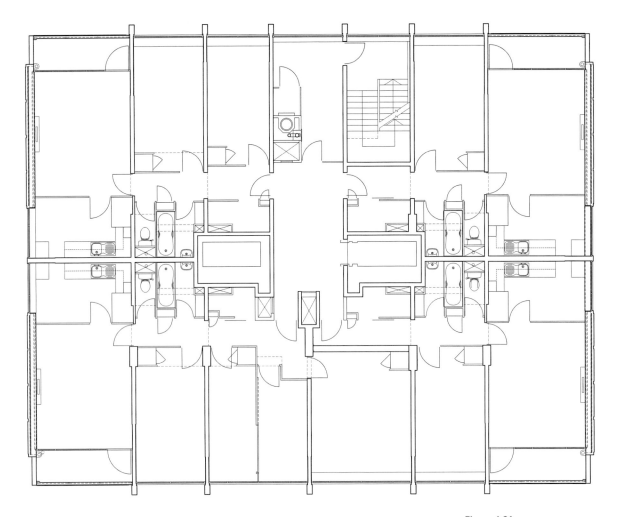

In particular, the existing walls were insulated and covered by a white rendering, with coloured detail panels on the balcony areas, and at the slab edge zones. To highlight the base of the tower and its vertical circulation, rain-screen cladding was applied. To maintain the articulation of the vertical structure, fin over-cladding was used, made of prefabricated anodised aluminium. External windows and doors were replaced with double-glazed frames. The roof was covered by a new, insulated, waterproof membrane.

The old bridges and walkways on the ground level were removed and new entrance areas were added to each tower, making them accessible on the ground floor level.

The Bow's retrofit interventions improved the environmental performance of all towers, as well as living standards as indicated by a resident feedback survey carried out in 2009: 90 per cent were satisfied with their new homes, and 100 per cent were satisfied with the improved neighbourhood. The new envelope dramatically reduced heating costs and energy consumption.

▲ Figure 4.31

Bow Cross pre-retrofit typical floor plan

▼ Figure 4.32

Aerial picture of Bow Cross during the retrofit intervention

Sources

– http://ukhousing.wikia.com/wiki/Crossways_estate
– www.countryside-properties.com/about-us/partnerships/case-studies/
– bow-cross-London/
– www.crosswayestates.com/
– www.dailystar.co.uk/showbiz/playlist/154069/Roll-Deep-plan-to-pay-homage-to-Crossways-Estate
– www.kaybridge.com/page2583/crossways-estate.aspx
– www.openhouselondon.org.uk/towerhamlets/
– www.prp-co.uk/projects/detail/bow-cross-priestman-point.html
– www.swan.org.uk/home/news/bow-cross-wins-top-planningaward.
– aspx
– www.theguardian.com/music/2014/apr/26/site-and-sound-when-cities-spawn-music-london-grime-trip-hop-bristol
– www.towerhamlets.gov.uk/

▼ Figure 4.33

Bow Cross during the retrofit intervention; original and post-retrofit façades

Brunswick Centre

Original information

Location: Central London
Address: Between Marchmont Street, Bernard Street and Brunswick Square
Postcode: WC1N 1BS
Date of construction: 1968–1972
No. storeys: 9 above ground
No. flats: 560
Architect: David Bernstein Architects and Patrick Hodgkinson as contributor.
Owner/client: Marchmont Properties Ltd

▲ Figure 4.34

Brunswick Centre, site plan

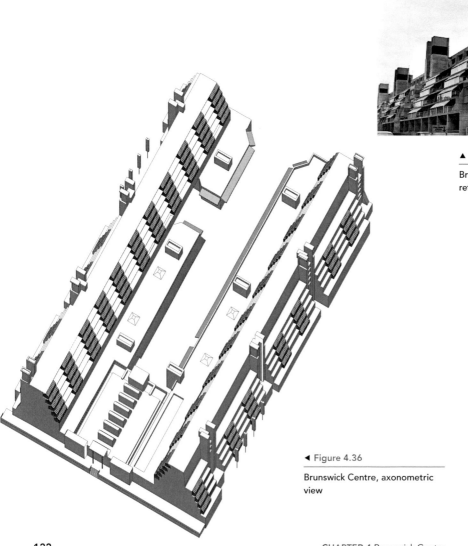

▲ Figure 4.35

Brunswick Centre before the retrofit

◄ Figure 4.36

Brunswick Centre, axonometric view

122   CHAPTER 4 Brunswick Centre

Located in central London, the Brunswick Centre was built between 1967–72 as a mixed-use private development. Its designer Patrick Hodgkinson attempted to develop a modern, holistic community with high density, open space for each apartment incorporating residential and commercial uses without social segregation and in harmony with its context.

The residential units are split into to two volumes, constructed by in situ concrete, supported by large concrete frames. Stepped in plan, these two *'Terrassenhäuser'* are looking towards each other, sitting on top of a raised stone piazza. The flat units step back to pave way for private balconies in front of partly glazed living spaces looking onto the piazza. The material pallet is a combination of concrete and glass. Although Hodgkinson wanted the concrete painted cream for it to merge with the contextual Georgian terraced housing, the Centre is stripped of any kind of ornamentation. Failing to attract private buyers, the residential section was leased by the London Borough of Camden for use as a council housing. Despite being widely disliked by many, it achieved Grade II status in 2000. By this time, the building had suffered social and physical decline and the shop premises were unoccupied.

▼ Figure 4.37

Brunswick Centre post-retrofit, west view

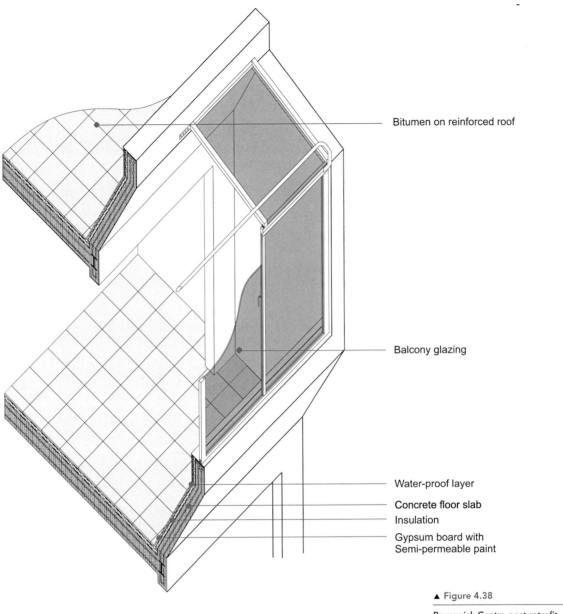

▲ Figure 4.38

Brunswick Centre post-retrofit, façade detail

Retrofit information

Date of Retrofit intervention: 2003–2006
No. storeys: 9 above ground, 2 underground
No. flats: 560
Architect: David Bernstein Architects and Patrick Hodgkinson as a contributor.
Property Owner/Client: London Borough of Camden
Contractor/Developer: Allied London
Institutions involved: Camden City Council, English Heritage, Twentieth Century Society
Cost: £30 million

Completed in 2006, the £22 million retrofit included the renewal of the winter gardens and windows glazing systems. New, double-glazed windows were installed, using self-cleaning glass. In addition, a new integrated central heating system and boiler were also installed. Metal drainage pipes were replaced with PVC, paving of balconies renewed, walls repainted, concrete damages were repaired internally and externally. The central piazza was narrowed down, repaved with a concrete finish and provided with new benches and retail stores covered with canopies. As the users of the space enter the stone piazza, they encounter a series of glazed shop façades sheltered with canopies of profiled metal decking. Finally, 75 per cent of the waste produced during the refurbishment process was recycled.

▼ Figure 4.39

Brunswick Centre post-retrofit, east courtyard façade

 Figure 4.40
Brunswick Centre post-retrofit, view of the balconies

 Figure 4.41
Brunswick Centre post-retrofit, view of the winter gardens

The refurbishment turns Brunswick Centre from an outdated building to a flourishing commercial and residential centre. New glazing systems contributed in reducing heating costs and energy consumption. Post retrofit the U value for wall insulation decreased from 1.7 W/m²k to 0.5 W/m²K. The U value for glazing dropped from 5.7 W/m²K to 2.7 W/m²K. These statistics validate that investing in the works of the building fabric was highly cost effective. Insulating cylinders and pipelines increased their efficiency by 5 per cent with an energy saving of 30.30 per cent. Recycling the waste produced during the refurbishment is another sustainable feature, which could be applied in other similar projects.

However, in the second wave of Thatcher's 'right to buy' privatisation scheme, the post-retrofit building's social structure changed entirely. Many of the flats were privatised, becoming available for higher incomes only.

Sources

– Hodgkinson, P. (2002) 'Brunswick Centre, Bloomsbury: a good bit of City?' *Twentieth Century Architecture*, no. 6, 2002, pp. 82–90.
– www.bdonline.co.uk/news/patrick-hodgkinson-(1930-2016)/5080277.article
– www.building.co.uk/brunswick-centre-refurbishment-by-patrick-hodgkinson/3074798
– www.bdonline.co.uk/richard-rogers-warns-of-threat-to-brunswick-centre/5069992.article
– www.levittbernstein.co.uk/project-stories/brunswick-centre/
– www.repository.cam.ac.uk/bitstream/handle/1810/246280/HBen
– %20%26%20KSteemers,2014.pdf?sequence=1
– www.theguardian.com/artanddesign/2006/oct/23/architecture.communities
– http://susannaheron.com/landscape/

Callow Mount Complex

Original information

Location: Sheffield
Address: Gleadless Valley, Callow Road
Postcode: S14 1LQ
Date of construction: 1963
No. storeys: 12/14
No. flats: 296
Architect: J. L. Womersley
Owner/client: Sheffield City Council

▲ Figure 4.42

Callow Mount site plan

▲ Figure 4.43

Callow Mount pre-retrofit view

◀ Figure 4.44

Callow Mount post-retrofit, axonometric view

CHAPTER 4 Callow Mount Complex

The Callow Mount Complex project was part of the high-density housing development in Sheffield's Gleadless Valley, which took place during the 1950s and 1960s. It aimed to accommodate approximately 17,000 people who had lost their homes during the Second World War. The City Council of Sheffield included high-rise social housing blocks and industrialised construction methods in its strategy for quick and inexpensive residential development.

J. L. Womersley, the council's leading architect at the time was responsible for the complex's design and planning. Hundreds of families moved from the crumbling city centre slums out to the greenfield site, attracted by affordable rents, natural landscape and excellent views. The complex contains six, 12–24-storey-high towers, accommodating 296 flats.

However, the complex's generally poor construction and problems due to lack of insulation quickly came to light. Due to poor maintenance, the complex started to deteriorate. Callow Mount got a reputation for being an undesirable, high-crime, low-cost housing complex. Its flats remained continuously occupied, however, mainly because of their low rents.

▼ Figure 4.45

Callow Mount post-retrofit, south view

Retrofit information

Date of retrofit intervention: 2010–2011
No. storeys: 12/14
No. flats: 296
Architect: Rolfe Judd
Property Owner/client: Sheffield City Council (buildings managed by Sheffield Homes)
Contractor/developer: Lovell Partnership (main contractor), Alumet Systems Ltd. & Alumet Renewable Technologies Ltd. (subcontractor), Axis Architecture, panel cladding and windows (subcontractor)
Institutions involved: Sheffield City Council, Sheffield Homes, Leverton Gardens TARA (Tenants and Residents Association)
Cost: £5 million

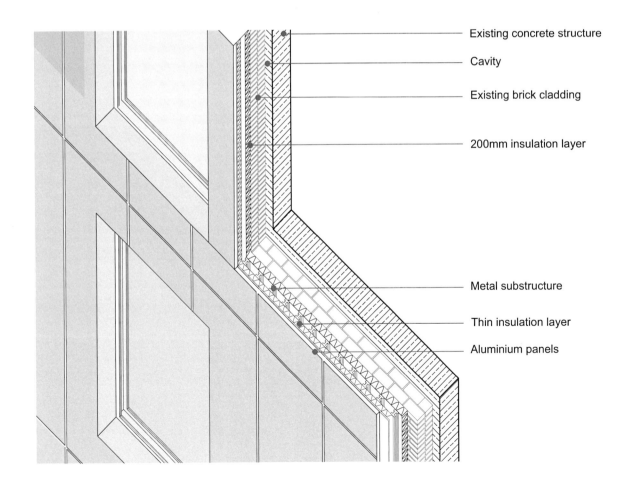

▼ Figure 4.46

Callow Mount insulated aluminium rain-screen façade, axonometric details

▲ Figure 4.47

Callow Mount insulated aluminium rain-screen façade close-up

The complex was finally retrofitted between 2010 and 2011. The retrofit interventions include over-cladding of existing brickwork with insulated aluminium cassette rain-screen panels and the replacement of the old windows by new double-glazed, high-performance frame systems. In addition, all balconies have been incorporated into the living areas, and the old electric floor heating and coal boiler have been replaced by a new biomass boiler, two gas boilers and one combined heat and power unit. Finally, new kitchens, bathrooms and sprinkler systems have been installed in all apartments.

▲ Figure 4.48

Callow Mount post-retrofit elevations

◀ Figure 4.49

Callow Mount post-retrofit colour pattern

The new building envelope improved the building's thermal performance drastically, achieving a total U-value of 0.34 w/m^{2}k put the buildings to the level of modern standards and made it possible for the project to comply with the UK's carbon plan to reduce greenhouse gas emissions. The newly added thermal insulation, in combination with the new heating system installed, helped decrease energy bills. Former problems of damp and mould were eliminated, improving living conditions for the residents.

The retrofit's aesthetic approach is trying to harmonise the towers with their natural environment through the use of colour. Concrete and brick textures have been replaced by an anodised shiny panel pattern in various green intonations, aiming to fit in with its tree-covered hillside environment. The elevations' horizontal lines have been replaced with vertical tiling.

Sources

– http://ukhousing.wikia.com/wiki/Tower_block
– https://en.wikipedia.org/wiki/List_of_brutalist_apartment_blocks_in_Sheffield
– http://sheffieldflats.blogspot.co.uk/2010/03/callow-mount.html
– https://steelcitystatic.wordpress.com/page/40/
– www.alumetregenerate.co.uk/case_study_callow_mount_sheffield.php

Chalcots Estate

Original information

Location: Camden London Borough
Address: Adelaide Road, Chalcots, Camden, London
Postcode: NW3 3RX
Date of construction: 1965–1976
No. storeys: 20 (19 above ground)
No. flats: 72 per tower (717 in total)
Architect: Dennis Lennon & Partners
Owner/client: Camden Council
Institutions involved: Dennis Lennon & Partners, S.A.G and London Borough of Camden

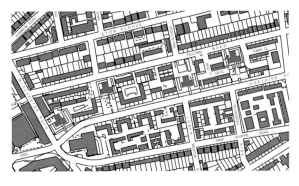

▲ Figure 4.50

Chalcots Estate site plan

The Chalcots Estate is located in Adelaide Road, Camden, in the north-west of London. It was constructed by Camden City Council between 1965 and 1968 and contains five 20-storey tower blocks named after the nearby villages of Dorney, Barry, Burnham, Taplow and Blashford. They are aligned in a parallel row and surrounded by large outdoor facilities. The estate's increasing physical and social deterioration during the late 1980s and 1990s made a retrofit intervention necessary. Its realisation finally started under the new ownership by United House London and took place from 2006–2010.

◀ Figure 4.51

Chalcots Estate before the retrofit

▶ Figure 4.52

Chalcots Estate axonometric drawing

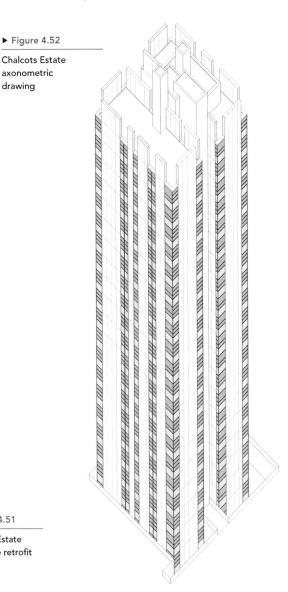

134

▼ Figure 4.53

Chalcots Estate before the retrofit

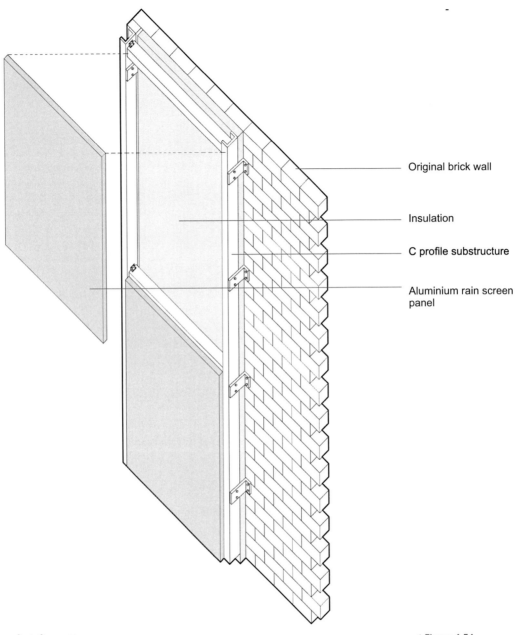

◀ Figure 4.54

Insulated aluminium screen, axonometric detail

Retrofit information

Date of retrofit intervention: 2006–2010
No. storeys: 20 (19 above ground)
No. flats: 711 (597 social; 114 leaseholds)
Architect: Hunt Thomson Architects
Property owner/client: United House; London Brought Camden
Contractor/developer: Rydon Construction Limited
Cost: £66 million
Governmental programmes: Decent Homes

The £66 million retrofit included the replacement of the old windows with aluminium, double-glazed, self-cleaning window frames, the over-cladding of the existing concrete façade by insulated aluminium rain-screens as well as the addition of insulation on the roofs. Internal refurbishment works comprised the renewal of kitchens, bathrooms, the entrance lobby and the communal areas, the installation of new lifts, central heating and electric fittings, thus achieving the 'Decent Homes Plus' standard.

▼ Figure 4.55

Aluminium screen façade close-up

The estate's carbon footprint was reduced by 30 per cent. Its exterior appearance was renewed, becoming attractive to new buyers and tenants. According to a BBC video report about the Chalcots Estate retrofit, the residents are satisfied with the retrofit results, especially the new kitchens and bathrooms. Regarding the sustainable strategies, the aluminium rain-screen system and heating/hot water systems seem to work well, contributing to reducing the building's energy consumption.

Sources

– Elrington, C. R., T. F. T. Baker, D. K. Bolton and P. E. C. Croot (1989) 'Hampstead: Chalcots', in *A History of the County of Middlesex*, vol. 9, Hampstead, Paddington (1989), pp. 63–66.
– http://projects.pilkington.com/DisplayProject.aspx?id=3843&search_id=47928000
– www.20thcenturylondon.org.uk/mol-82-622-8
– www.building.co.uk/chalcot-estate-altered-towers/3113501.article
– www.harleyfaçades.co.uk/page/chalcot-estate
– www.hta.co.uk/projects/chalcots
– www.londonmagnet.com/ce/ce1.HTM
– www.unitedhouse.net/projects/id/1275498417

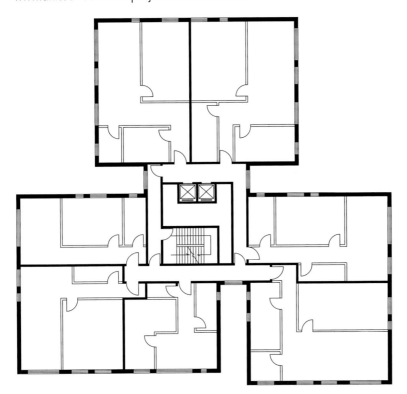

◀ Figure 4.56

Chalcots Estate post-retrofit typical floor plan

Edward Woods Estate

Original information

Location: West London
Address: Queensland Crescent, Edward Woods Estate
Postcode: W11 4TE
Date of construction: 1967
No. storeys: 24
No. flats: 176 per tower
Architect: NA
Owner/Client: Hammersmith and Fulham London Borough

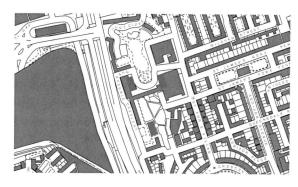

▲ Figure 4.57

Edward Woods Estate site plan

▲ Figure 4.58

Edward Woods Estate after the retrofit

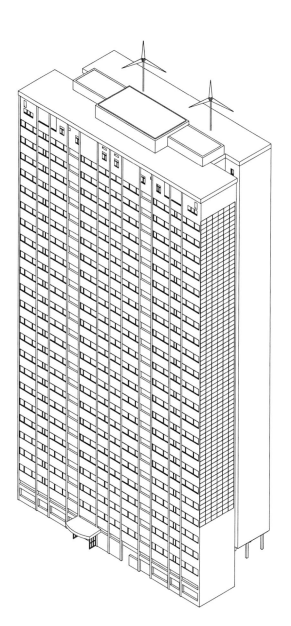

◀ Figure 4.59

Edward Woods Estate post-retrofit, axonometric view

Commissioned by the Hammersmith and Fulham London Borough, the Edward Woods Estate, built in 1966, was originally designed, aiming to provide affordable, high-quality accommodation. Located in the West of London, it consists of three identical 24-storey towers, containing 176 apartments in total. It is a reinforced concrete frame structure with concrete and brickwork panel infills.

During the late 1980s and the 1990s, the estate suffered from physical and social decline, including criminality, vandalism and outdated heating and ventilation systems, and lacked insulation. The estate had been facing potential demolition but Hammersmith and Fulham Council, in collaboration with Rockwool, ECD Architects, Breyer and British Gas, decided to undertake a refurbishment of the towers instead.

▼ Figure 4.60

Edward Woods Estate post-retrofit, south view

Retrofit information

Date of retrofit intervention: 2010
No. storeys: 23
No. flats: 176
Architect: Energy Conscious Design Architects
Property owner/client: Hammersmith and Fulham London Borough
Contractor/developer: Breyer Group
Institutions involved: London School of Economics (LSE), Hammersmith and Fulham Council, British Gas, Nu-Heat company, London Development Agency
Cost: £13.5 million

The retrofit interventions on Edwards Woods Estate include improvements of thermal insulation, a heating/electrical system upgrade and the addition of renewable energy sources. The building face was over-cladded with insulated aluminium panels and the old windows replaced by double-glazed window frames. Two wind turbines were installed on the top of each tower, generating 10,070 kilowatts per year each. The south-facing façades were covered by 318 panels, capable of producing up to 82,000 kilowatts per year.

In addition, a penthouse storey has been added, a new heating, the boiler and ventilation systems have been renewed, while all lighting in communal areas has been replaced by LED technology. The under-utilised ground level storage areas have been converted into office space for rent to local charitable organisations.

▼ Figure 4.61

Aluminium screen façade close-up

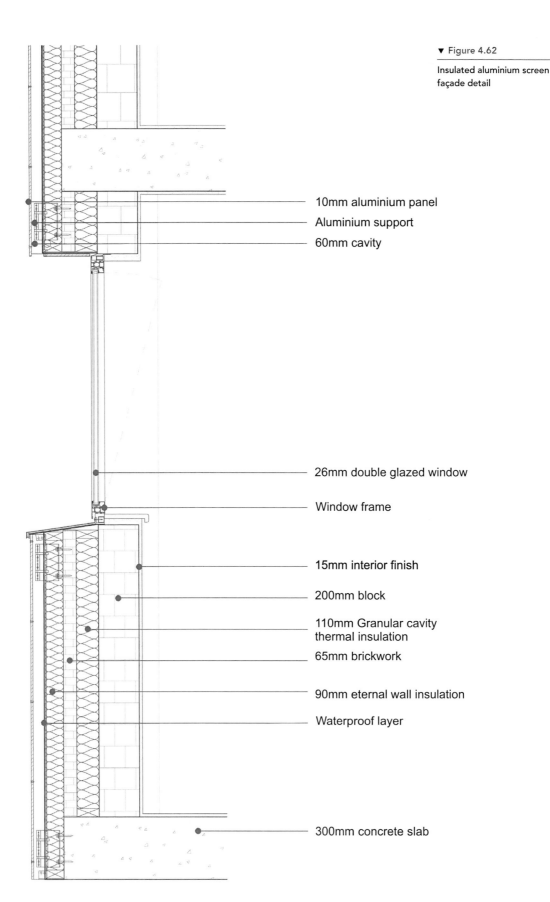

▼ Figure 4.62

Insulated aluminium screen façade detail

▼ Figure 4.63
Edward Woods Estate, south-facing photovoltaic façade

Edward Woods is among the few refurbished estates that incorporated renewable technologies, helping to reduce the building's carbon footprint. However, the estimated payoff period for the wind turbines is 14 years and even longer for the photovoltaic panels, estimated to about 25 years.

The new retrofit improved the buildings carbon footprint and reduced its energy consumption. The building's appearance changed drastically. Its concrete texture disappeared, being replaced by bright, white-greyish colours. Wind turbines and photovoltaic panels become part of the building's new appearance, symbolising the estate's eco-friendly new era.

While the building's living and safety conditions improved, its social profile decreased drastically, thus many of the flats were privatised.

Sources

– https://ecda.co.uk/portfolio/edward-woods/
– Bates, K., Lane, L. and Power, A. (2012) 'High rise hope: The social implications of energy efficiency retrofit in large multi-storey tower blocks', LSE Housing and Communities. CASE Report 75, p. 6. Available at: http://sticerd.lse.ac.uk/dps/case/cr/CASEreport75.pdf
– Kyrke-Smith, H. (2012) *Towering Ambitions. Transforming High-Rise Housing into Sustainable Homes*. London: Green Alliance, p. 13. Available at: www.green-alliance.org.uk/page_43.php.
– http://greenallianceblog.org.uk/2012/11/29/high-rise-hope-can-tower-blocks-become-models-of-energy-efficiency/
– www.insidehousing.co.uk/living-the-high-life/6506223.article
– www.london.gov.uk/sites/default/files/living-roofs.pdf

Ferrier Point

Original information

Location: Newham, London
Address: Forty Acre Lane
Postcode: E16 1QN
Date of construction: 1968
No. storeys: 23
No. flats: 115
Architect: Samuel King
Owner/client: London Borough of Newham

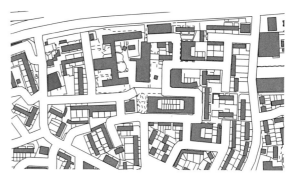

▲ Figure 4.64

Ferrier Point site plan

▶ Figure 4.65

Ferrier Point after the retrofit

Located in the heart of Canning Town, the Ferrier Point tower was built in 1968 by architect Samul King. It was built on a plot of land which was bombed during the Second World War. Post-war reconstruction was based on the master plan developed by the local authorities in 1944. The 66.5m high, 23-storey tower was part of the affordable housing scheme launched by the Borough of Newham. The Council proceeded with the tower's £9.8 million refurbishment in 2011, aiming to stop the property's increasing physical and social deterioration.

◀ Figure 4.66

Ferrier Point post-retrofit, axonometric view

CHAPTER 4 Ferrier Point

▼ Figure 4.67

Ferrier Point post-retrofit, south view

Retrofit information

Date of retrofit intervention: 2011
No. storeys: 23
No. flats: 115
Architect: Energy Conscious Design Architects
Property owner/client: London Borough of Newham
Contractor/developer: Rydon Construction Ltd
Institutions involved: London Borough of Newham
Cost: £9.7 million

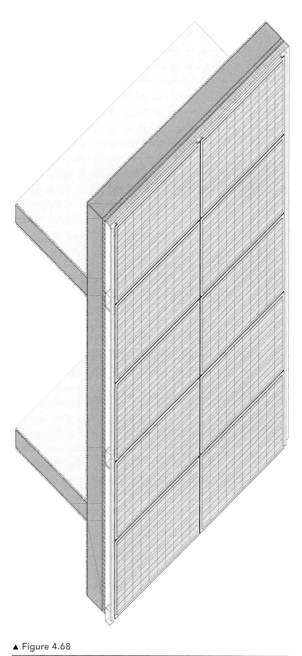

▲ Figure 4.68

Photovoltaic wall axonometric detail

The ECD Architects team aimed for a contemporary fresh image, using modern materials and innovative over-cladding technologies. The tower's concrete texture was over-cladded by insulated grey and blue anodised aluminium panels, creating a new façade pattern, which echoes the original façade's horizontal lines.

▼ Figure 4.69

Aluminium screen façade close-up

Other upgrades included the replacement of the old windows with new triple-glazed frame systems, the internalisation of the balconies as well as the replacement of kitchens, bathrooms, the entrance lobby and the central heating system.

In addition, 50 per cent of the south façade has been covered by 375m² of photovoltaic panels, which produce 40,000 kWh/year. They cover up to 10 per cent of the buildings' demands in electricity, used in the towers' electricity needs in communal areas. Any excess power produced is being sold to repay the £100,000 government grant which funded the photovoltaic panels.

Finally, the tower block's carbon emissions were reduced up to 60 per cent using extra insulation and Passivhaus windows. It is one of the few towers incorporating renewable technologies, being capable of saving 6,490 kg of CO_2 annually. All interventions contributed to the improvement of living standards, however, the buildings' social structure changed entirely, since many apartments have been privatised.

Sources

– http://blog.ibstock.com/fastwall/ferrier-point-real-brick-wall-cladding/
– www.harleycurtainwall.com/page/ferrier-point
– www.insidehousing.co.uk/tall-order/6513584.article
– www.metaltechnology.com/index.php/projects/view/ferrier-point
– www.prp.gb.com/residentialpdf/ferrierpoint.pdf
– www.rydon.co.uk/projects/case-studies/refurbishment/ferrier-point

Golden Lane Estate

Original information

Location: Central London
Address: Fann Street, Golden Lane Estate
Postcode: EC1Y 0RD
Date of construction: 1957
No. storeys: 17
No. flats: 559
Architect: Chamberlain, Powell & Bon
Owner/client: City of London
Institutions involved: N/A

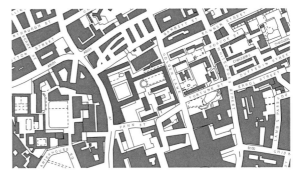

▲ Figure 4.70

Golden Lane site plan

▲ Figure 4.71

Great Arthur House before the retrofit

▲ Figure 4.72

Great Arthur House during the retrofit

▼ Figure 4.73

Great Arthur House post-retrofit, axonometric view

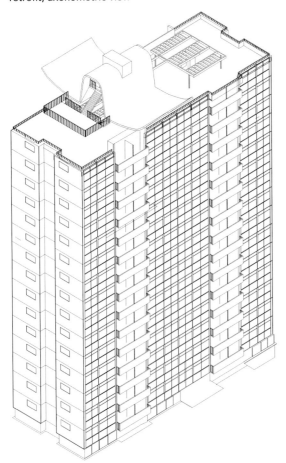

Built in 1957, the Golden Lane estate aimed to provide council housing for general needs, being part of the recovery from the Second World War rebuilding strategy of the City of London. When Geoffry Powell won the competition to build the Golden Lane estate, he formed a partnership with Christoph Bon and Peter Chamberlin. This project became their first piece of work after the partnership was formed. Today, located in central London, the estate is home to approximately 1,500 people living in 559 one-, two- or three-bedroom units. There are 385 flats and 174 maisonettes, a swimming pool as well as outdoor facilities. By 2015, 51 per cent of the flats had been sold on long leases under the 'Right to buy' scheme provisions brought in by the Thatcher government and when subsequently sold into the commercial market, leases have proved attractive to design-conscious buyers and they command good prices. The rental flats continue as council housing let at affordable rents. Great Arthur House is the tallest and most iconic buildings on the estate, which is a Grade II listed building.

Retrofit information

Date of retrofit intervention: 2014–present
No. storeys: 17
No. flats: 559 (120 for Great Arthur House)
Architect: John Robertson Architects (for Great Arthur house only)
Property owner/client: City of London
Institutions involved: English Heritage, Twentieth Century Society
Cost: £5,525,000 (estimate)

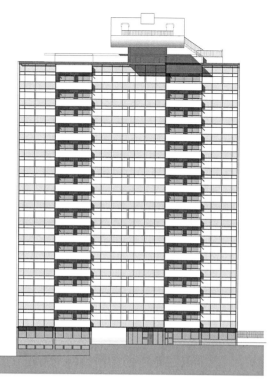

▲ Figure 4.75

Great Arthur House, west elevation

▼ Figure 4.74

Golden Lane Estate low-rise, post-retrofit view

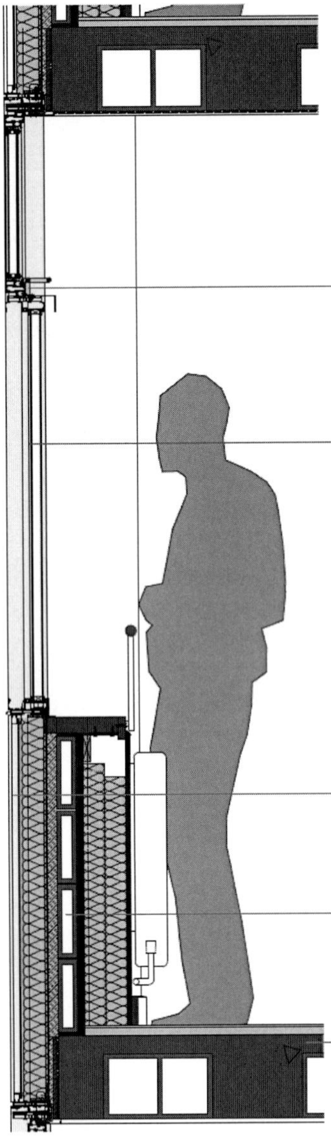

◀ Figure 4.76

Great Arthur House, retrofit façade detail

- Slender thermaly broken aluminum window frame
- Double glazed sliding windows
- Yellow opaque glazing spandrel cladding
- Existing hollow pot upstand wall retained
- Existing reinforced concrete and hollow pot floor

▼ Figure 4.77

Great Arthur House, installation of new façade

The Muro-glass single-glazed curtain wall system was replaced with a new double-glazed anodised aluminium frame curtain wall that stays true to the original design but should vastly improve the thermal performance of the building with an added curtain wall depth of 50 mm. Any junctions between the new curtain wall and the original building will be filled with insulation. Individual windows were replaced with double-glazed ones and the timber balcony doors will also be improved. This should reduce heat loss by 39 per cent, thus reducing heating bills for residents and should secure the warranty liability and whole life cost advantage.

▼ Figure 4.78

Great Arthur House, pre- and post-retrofit intervention

◀ Figure 4.79

Golden Lane estate during the retrofit intervention

◀ Figure 4.80

Great Arthur House during the retrofit intervention

The new curtain wall system is heavier, thus additional reinforcement had to be added. English Heritage and Twentieth Century Society were both very supportive of the proposed curtain wall system. Without this additional support the system could not be put in place and the improved thermal efficiency could not be achieved.

The retrofit intervention of Golden Lane Estate is indeed a very sensitive approach, practised with respect to the original design and intentions. Obviously, the aesthetic demands of a Grade II listed building did not allow complete elimination of thermal bridging, however, heating bills are expected to decrease by 31 per cent.

Sources

– www.bdonline.co.uk/greg-penoyres-inspiration-the-golden-lane-estate-london/5035997.article
– www.bdonline.co.uk/refurbishment-is-the-height-of-fashion/5050333.article
– www.bdonline.co.uk/fresh-façade-for-golden-lane-estates-great-arthur-house/5066839.article
– www.cartwrightpickard.com/news/2012/120604_golden-lane-completion.aspx
– www.jra.co.uk/projects/historic-buildings/great-arthur-house-golden-lane-estate-london-ec1.html
– www.martindelguayo.com/projects/rethinking-golden-lane-estate

Greenhouse

Original information

Location: Leeds
Address: Greenhouse, Beeston Road, Hunslet
Postcode: LS11 6AD
Date of construction: 1938
No. storeys: 5 +basement
No. flats: 115
Architect: George C. Robb, senior architectural assistant to Livett
Owner/client: Leeds City Council

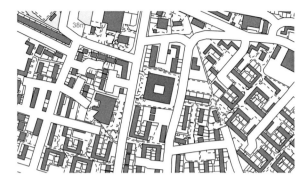

▲ Figure 4.81

Greenhouse site plan

▲ Figure 4.82

Greenhouse before the retrofit

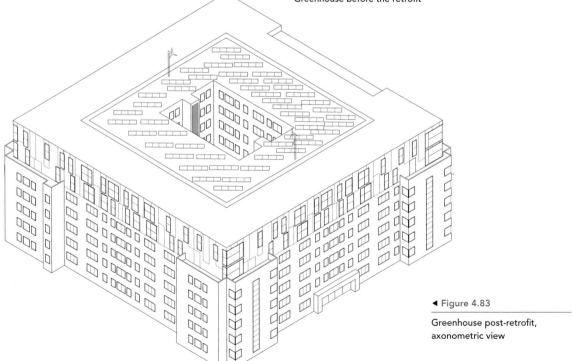

◀ Figure 4.83

Greenhouse post-retrofit, axonometric view

Built during the Modernist era, in an Art Deco style, the Greenhouse was formerly known as Shaftesbury House. Functioning as a lodging house for 500 local workers, and a hostel for homeless men and women, its construction by Leeds City Council significantly improved the standard of living for thousands of people during its functional lifetime. The original design of the building included a central cruciform structure, which created four internal courtyards. The construction methods applied, were considered revolutionary for its time. The building suffered from material and social deterioration during the 1980s, thus it was totally abandoned in the 1990s. In 2000, the Leeds City Council halted existing demolition plans and sold the property to CITU, initiating its complete refurbishment.

Retrofit information

Date of retrofit intervention: 2010
No. storeys: 7+basement
No. flats: 166 apartments, 6 offices, gym, café
Architect: West & Machell Architects
Property owner/client: CITU
Contractor/developer: Clegg
Institutions involved: Sheffield City Council, Woods Environmental
Cost: £12.5 million

▼ Figure 4.84

Greenhouse post-retrofit, south view

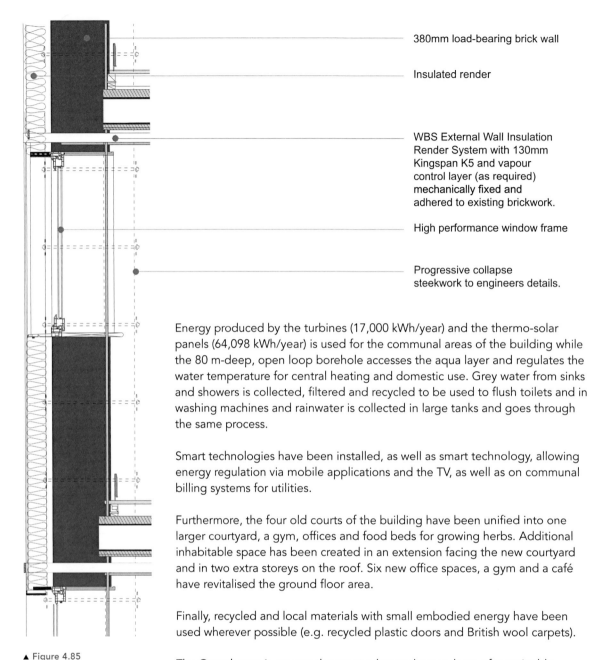

- 380mm load-bearing brick wall
- Insulated render
- WBS External Wall Insulation Render System with 130mm Kingspan K5 and vapour control layer (as required) mechanically fixed and adhered to existing brickwork.
- High performance window frame
- Progressive collapse steekwork to engineers details.

Energy produced by the turbines (17,000 kWh/year) and the thermo-solar panels (64,098 kWh/year) is used for the communal areas of the building while the 80 m-deep, open loop borehole accesses the aqua layer and regulates the water temperature for central heating and domestic use. Grey water from sinks and showers is collected, filtered and recycled to be used to flush toilets and in washing machines and rainwater is collected in large tanks and goes through the same process.

Smart technologies have been installed, as well as smart technology, allowing energy regulation via mobile applications and the TV, as well as on communal billing systems for utilities.

Furthermore, the four old courts of the building have been unified into one larger courtyard, a gym, offices and food beds for growing herbs. Additional inhabitable space has been created in an extension facing the new courtyard and in two extra storeys on the roof. Six new office spaces, a gym and a café have revitalised the ground floor area.

Finally, recycled and local materials with small embodied energy have been used wherever possible (e.g. recycled plastic doors and British wool carpets).

The Greenhouse is among the most advanced precedents of sustainable retrofitting. The project currently produces only 0.5 tonnes of CO_2 and uses 50 kWh/m^2 per year per flat, reaching high-performance standards on the code for sustainable homes. Its insulated walls have achieved a U-value of 0.150 W/m^{2}K, the windows 1.32W/m^{2}K and the roof 0.1W/m^{2}K. The combination of renewable technologies and insulation have reduced utility bills by 60 per cent.

▲ Figure 4.85

Insulated aluminium panel over-cladding detail

▼ Figure 4.86

Greenhouse retrofit façade, roof extension and wind turbine

The building's appearance has been changed drastically. Brick colour and texture have been replaced by white render and green colour tones on the roof extension. The newly added wind turbines have become part of the Greenhouse's new image.

Its social structure has changed entirely. Once a hub of crime and decay, the Greenhouse has generated a new eco-friendly community, acting as a catalyst for the entire neighbourhood.

Due to its outstanding innovation achievements, the Greenhouse has won many awards from prestigious institutions.

▶ Figure 4.87

View through the courtyard

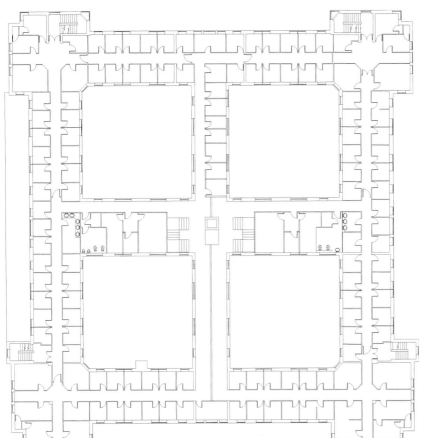

◀ Figure 4.88

Pre-retrofit typical floorplan

▲ Figure 4.89

Photovoltaic roof and wind turbine

Sources

- https://theculturevulture.co.uk/blog/reviews/greenhouse-leeds-eco-development-regeneration-scheme-or-gated-community/
- www.ajbuildingslibrary.co.uk/projects/display/id/3424
- www.greenhouseleeds.co.uk/
- www.greenhouseleeds.net/press/sustainability_awards.pdf
- www.greenhouseleeds.net/press/hb_dec10_dotm.pdf
- www.yorkshiretimes.co.uk/article/LEEDS-DEVELOPMENT-LEADS-AS-UKS-COMMUNITY-BLUEPRINT-Microgeneration-Project-Held-up-as-Exemplary-Mode

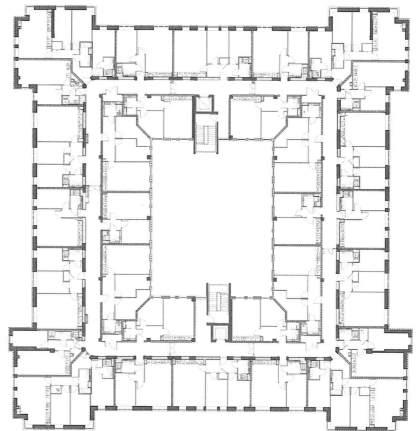

▶ Figure 4.90

Post-retrofit typical floor plan

Keeling House

Original information

Location: East London
Address: Claredale Street
Postcode: E2 6PG
Date of construction: 1952–1957
No. storeys: 15
No. flats: 56
Architect: Denys Lasdun
Owner/client: Tower Hamlets City Council
Institutions involved: Peabody Trust

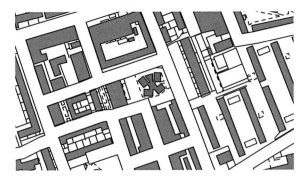

▲ Figure 4.91

Keeling House site plan

▲ Figure 4.92

Keeling House before the retrofit

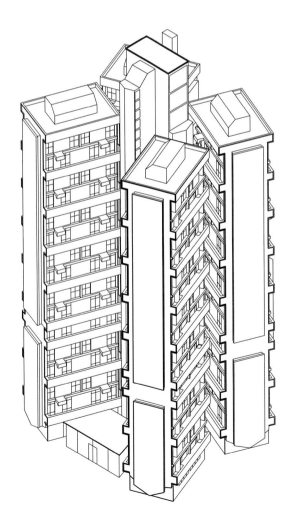

◀ Figure 4.93

Heeling House post-retrofit, axonometric view

▼ Figure 4.94

Keeling House post-retrofit, south-west view

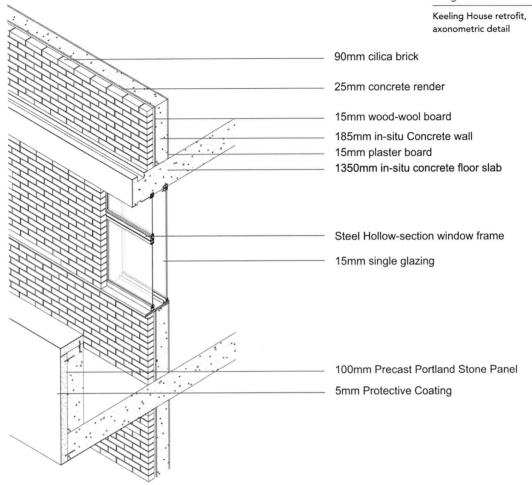

▼ Figure 4.95

Keeling House retrofit, axonometric detail

- 90mm cilica brick
- 25mm concrete render
- 15mm wood-wool board
- 185mm in-situ Concrete wall
- 15mm plaster board
- 1350mm in-situ concrete floor slab
- Steel Hollow-section window frame
- 15mm single glazing
- 100mm Precast Portland Stone Panel
- 5mm Protective Coating

Sir Denys Lasdun was commissioned in 1954 to design the Keeling House (c.1957) in Bethnal Green, London, a social housing complex which would house council tenants. In an era of reigning Modernism, Lasdun's attempt was to break away from the norms and cultivate a design which fostered sociability and at the same time gave importance to the privacy of the residents. He conceptualised the solution of a cluster block, with the design of four blocks of concrete with maisonettes stacked upon one another placed around a central service core, which encouraged interaction between neighbours as the wings looked onto one another. At the same time, the design offered privacy with each balcony facing outwards, capturing the view of the city. It received Grade II listed status in 1993. The building was sold to Lincoln Holdings, who initiated its renovation by Munkenbeck + Marshall, completed in 2001.

Retrofit information

Date of retrofit intervention: 1999–2000
No. storeys: 16
No. flats: 64
Architect: Munkenbeck & Marshall
Property owner/client: Lincoln Holdings
Contractor/developer: Lincoln Holdings
Institutions involved: Tower Hamlets Council, English Heritage, Twentieth Century Society

▶ Figure 4.96

Keeling House retrofit façade close-up

◀ Figure 4.97

Keeling House post-retrofit, south-west view

CHAPTER 4 Keeling House

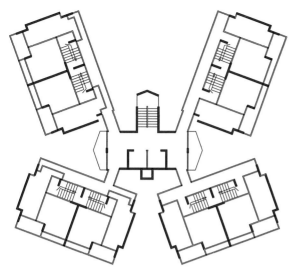

▲ Figure 4.98

Keeling House typical post-renovation floor plan

The retrofit interventions focused mainly on repairing damages in the concrete structure of the tower, which was additionally covered by a protective coating. A new penthouse floor was added, including roof insulation and double-glazing for the new apartments. A new double-glazed entrance area was added and flats were internally modernised, including the water supply and electrical systems. Secondary glazing was installed only partially by individual residents. No insulation was added on the external walls.

The retrofit interventions have brought some improvement to the building's carbon footprint, but there is still room for much more, such as the installation of secondary glazing and internal insulation. The refurbishment changed the social character of the building, the entire building was privatised in 1999. However, the building's design character has remained unchanged. The renovation scheme by Munkenbeck and Marshall is considered to be among the best of its kind, receiving a RIBA award in 2002.

Sources

– Budd, A., Leedham, A., Rodrigues, R. and Vitali, M. 'Building study.'
– http://en.wikipedia.org/wiki/Keeling_House
– www.britishlistedbuildings.co.uk/en-441463-keeling-house-bethnal-green-greater-lond
– www.educate-sustainability.eu/kb/content/keeling-house-bethnal-green-london-0
– www.emporis.com/building/keelinghouse-london-unitedkingdom
– www.keelinghouse.co.uk/
– www.mandp.uk.com/projects/communities/keeling_house.html
– www.themodernhouse.com/past-sales/keeling-house-2
– REPORT KHWT(2010) Disused Water Tank, Keeling House Available from http://planreg.towerhamlets.gov.uk/WAM/doc/Other-601909.pdf?extension=.pdf&id=601909&appid=&location=VOLUME5&contentType=application/pdf&pageCount=1

Little Venice Towers

Original information

Location: West London
Address: Bourne Terrace
Postcode: W2 5TQ
Date of construction: 1960–1970
No. storeys: 22
No. flats: 750
Owner/client: City of Westminster
Contractor/developer: Wates Living Space Limited
Cost: £32 million

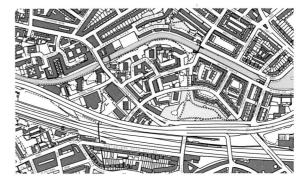

▲ Figure 4.99

Little Venice Towers site plan

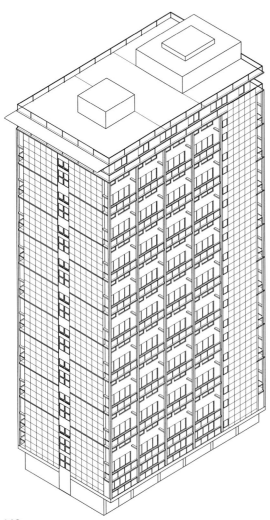

◄ Figure 4.100

Little Venice Towers post-retrofit, axonometric view

▼ Figure 4.101
Little Venice Towers West façade

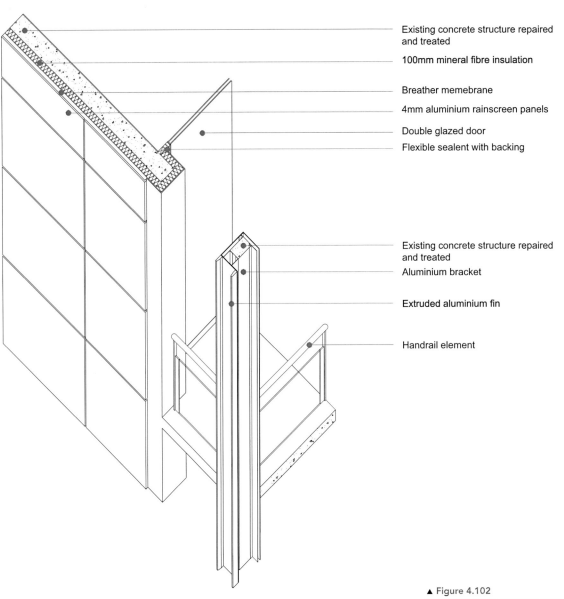

▲ Figure 4.102

Little Venice Towers, axonometric detail

The Little Venice Towers complex was commissioned by Westminster City Council and was constructed between 1960 and 1970. It consists of six 22-storey residential towers and is located in West London, next to a series of canals. Their location between the canals inspired the name 'Little Venice'. They were constructed as typical for the time: exposed concrete structure, infilled by brick walls. They accommodate 750 two-storey dwellings, which are clearly expressed on the towers' façades. Once considered modern and desirable, the complex fell into social and physical decay, making them highly unpopular. City West Homes, the company set up by Westminster City Council, initiated their retrofit in 2008 as part of the UK government's 'Decent Homes' programme.

▲ Figure 4.103

Little Venice Towers post-retrofit, west elevation close-up

Retrofit information

Date of retrofit intervention: 2008
No. storeys: 22
No. flats: 750
Architect: Kemp Muir Wealleands (KMW)
Property owner/client: Westminster Homes
Contractor/developer: Wates Living Space
Institutions involved: Westminster City Council, Westminster Homes
Governmental programmes: Decent Homes
Cost: £32 million

KMW's £32 million retrofit includes the repair of the existing concrete structure, the towers' over-cladding with mineral fibre-insulated aluminium rain-screen panels, the addition of double-glazed window frames, as well as the insulation of roof and balconies. The use of dual frame reversible windows allows internal cleaning, without the opening light intruding into the interior space, fouling curtains or blinds, as all of the rotation takes place outside the building line. In addition, internal refurbishment took place.

◀ Figure 4.104

Little Venice Towers, south-west view

The over-cladding design intentions aimed to emphasise the building's vertical solid elements and the varied appearance of the two-storey dwellings. The natural dark grey concrete texture was covered by light grey aluminium shades. Residents were included in decision-making of the refurbishment process.

In conclusion, the sustainable retrofit intervention of Little Venice Tower reduced the estate's carbon footprint and the residents' energy bills. Its materiality changed entirely, however, all the design elements of the original scheme were kept. The complex's ownership status changed completely as the complex was transferred to Westminster Homes, prior to its 2008 renovation.

Sources

– http://farm9.staticflickr.com/8107/8551271640_c2744b5705.jpg
– www.architecture.com/FindAnArchitect/ArchitectPractices/KempMuirWealleans/Projects/LITTLEVENICETOWERS-98860.aspx
– www.harleycurtainwall.com/page/little-venice
– www.kmw.co.uk/little-venice-towers/
– www.sapagroup.com/companies/Sapa%20Building%20System%20BE/documenten/SBS-housing.pdf

Netherthorpe Complex

Original information

Location: Sheffield, South Yorkshire
Address: Netherthorpe Road
Postcode: S3 7NG
Date of construction: 1962
No. storeys: 15
No. flats: 208
Owner/client: Sheffield City Council

▲ Figure 4.105

Netherthorpe Complex site plan

▲ Figure 4.106

Netherthorpe Complex before the retrofit

◀ Figure 4.107

Netherthorpe Complex post-retrofit, axonometric view

▼ Figure 4.108

Netherthorpe Complex, west view

The Netherthorpe complex is located in the Netherthorpe inner-city district of Sheffield. The area of Netherthorpe was first built during the second half of the nineteenth century, consisting of Victorian terraced housing. Their demolition began in 1956 to be replaced between 1959 and 1972 by modern housing tower blocks and three-to-four-storey maisonettes. The four currently existing towers, completed in 1962, were planned by the Sheffield City Council. After social and physical deterioration during the 1980s, the council initiated their retrofit in 1998. They are also known as Brook Hill complex.

▲ Figure 4.109

Aluminium screen façade close-up

Retrofit information

Date of retrofit intervention: 1998
No. storeys: 15
No. flats: 208
Property owner/client: Sheffield City Council
Architect: Henry Boot
Contractor/developer: Henry Boot
Institutions involved: Sheffield City Council

The retrofit includes enclosure of the balconies, installation of double-glazed windows, and over-cladding with insulated aluminium rain-screen panels. The brown brick texture colour was replaced by a pastel colour scheme. It is one of the first retrofits observed and it carries a very characteristic symmetric pattern. The towers remained inhabited during the refurbishment process.

In summary, the retrofit of Netherthorpe generally achieved the goals set at the time. The insulated rain-screen cladding solved the problem of thermal insulation and protected the building from dampness as well. Enclosed balcony and double glazing were both common and utility changes on residential buildings. However, several drawbacks were observed strongly related to the quality of the materials used. As it was one of first of the complexes which were retrofitted, it does not meet current standards and has partly aged worse than expected.

Sources

– http://jimbo1312.tumblr.com/post/141063922709/shefeld-netherthorpe-tower-blocks-sheffield
– http://ukhousing.wikia.com/wiki/Cornhill
– https://en.wikipedia.org/wiki/Netherthorpe,_Sheffield
– Punter, J. (2010) 'The city of dreams: Sheffield and the modern movement', in *Urban Design and the British Urban Renaissance*, London: Routledge.
– www.flickr.com/photos/jrjamesarchive/9562656456/
– www.emporis.com/complex/106249/brook-hill-sheffield-united-kingdom
– www.geograph.org.uk/photo/3776765
– www.towerblock.eca.ed.ac.uk/development/netherthorpe-redevelopment-area-brook-hill

▶ Figure 4.110

Netherthorpe Complex, south view

Park Hill

Original information

Location: Sheffield
Address: Park Hill, Sheffield
Postcode: S2 5PN
Date of construction: 1957–1961
No. storeys: 4–13 storeys high
No. flats: 995
Architect: Jack Lynn and Ivor Smith
Owner/client: Sheffield City Council
Institutions involved: Sheffield City Council

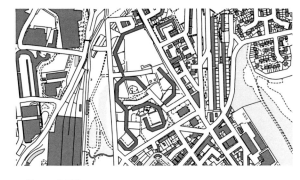

▲ Figure 4.111

Park Hill site plan

Park Hill, constructed between 1957 and 1961, is a council housing estate East of the Sheffield city centre, by Ivor Smith and Jack Lynn. At that time, Park Hill was considered one of the most ambitious inner-city housing projects. The 'streets in the sky' concept aimed to recreate the traditional neighbourhood streets within a high rise. Unfortunately, owing to the collapse of the steel industry, the radical ideals of Park Hill came to an end. It was constructed as an exposed reinforced concrete structure with brick wall infills. The brick walls come in different intonations forming a gradient pattern from top to bottom. The complex entered the phase of gradual social and physical decay. However, the future of the complex changed in 1997 when Park Hill was granted a Grade II listing by English Heritage and turned into the largest listed building in Europe. After that, property developer Urban Splash, Hawkins\Brown partner and urban designers Studio Egret West were commissioned to renovate this housing estate. Its first phase was completed in 2011 and has received numerous awards, including the prestigious RIBA Stirling Prize 2013. Sold for £77 million to Places for People in the same year, its second and third phases are in full progress.

▲ Figure 4.112

Park Hill before the retrofit

▲ Figure 4.113

Park Hill after the retrofit

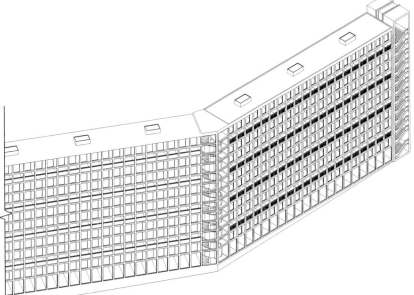

◀ Figure 4.114

Park Hill post-retrofit, axonometric view

▼ Figure 4.115

Bridge between retrofitted and non-retrofitted parts of Park Hill

Retrofit information

Date of retrofit intervention: First stage development completed 2011
No. storeys: 4–13 stories high
No. flats: 75
Architect: Hawkins Brown with Studio Egret West. Grant Associates Landscape Architects.
Property Owner/client: Places for People
Contractor/developer: Urban Splash Build Ltd (North)
Institutions involved: Homes and Communities Agency, The Housing Corporation, Transform South Yorkshire, English Heritage, Sheffield City Council
Cost: Estimated £146 million for entire scheme

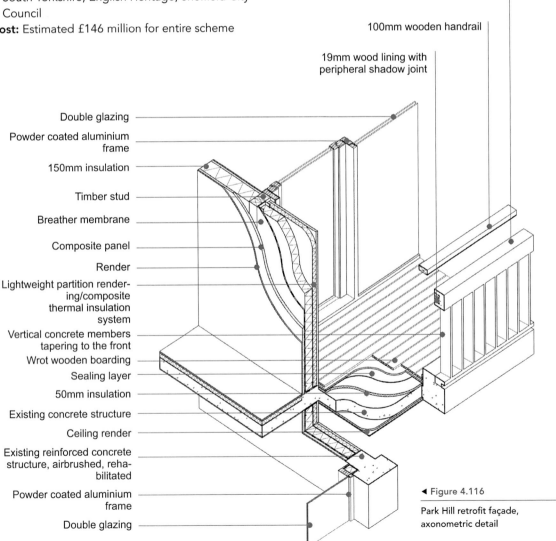

◀ Figure 4.116

Park Hill retrofit façade, axonometric detail

▲ Figure 4.117

Park Hill, retrofit façade close up

During the retrofit, Park Hill's exposed concrete structure was retained and repaired. These approximately 5,500 individual repairs, using anti-carbonation mortar, have been left visible as an aesthetic symbol of restoration.

The coloured exterior brickwork façade has been over-cladded with anodised aluminium panels in bright colour gradience (yellow-orange-red), following the concept of the original colour scheme. In addition, window frames were converted in double glazing, and the balconies, new entrances, outdoor and communal areas were refurbished. The concrete rails of the so-called 'streets in the sky' exterior hallways were replaced. Furthermore, some of the apartments on the ground and first floors were converted into commercial use, targeting innovative businesses.

▼ Figure 4.118

Park Hill west elevation and colour scheme of retrofitted wing

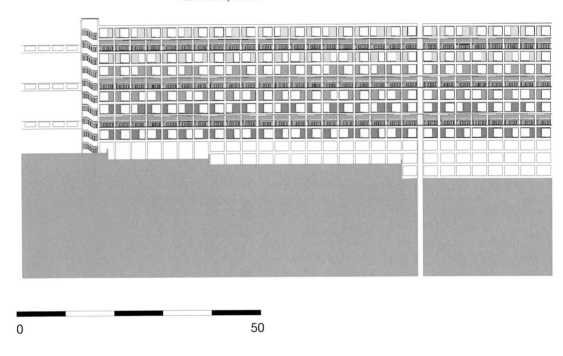

▼ Figure 4.119

Park Hill west elevation panorama of retrofitted wing

Flank B Courtyard Side

Flank C Courtyard Side

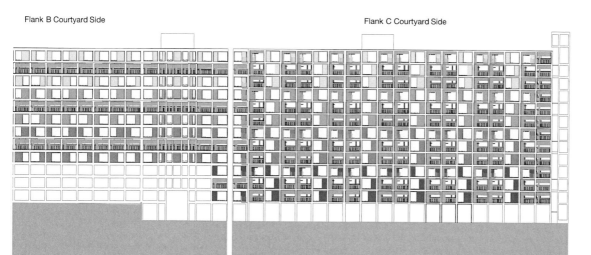

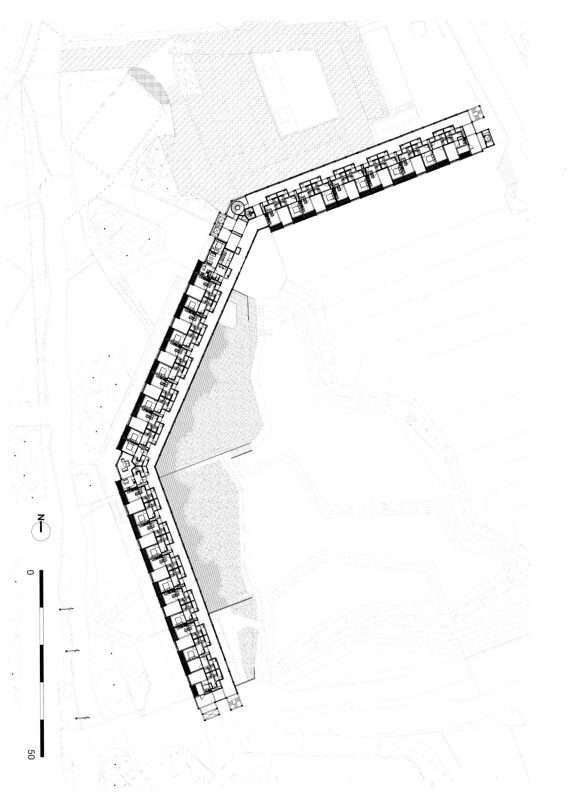

▲ Figure 4.120

Park Hill plan

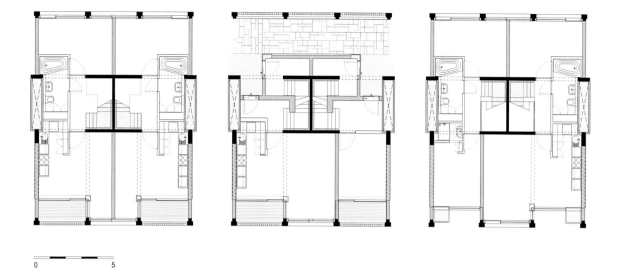

▲ Figure 4.121

Typical floor plans of retrofitted apartment units

The retrofit intervention aimed to respect the original design idea and managed to improve all the critical issues which had occurred through the years. The old brickwork colours of the exterior façade have been replaced by strong, vivid colours of the same range, renewing its image. Even though the building's thermal performance improved, thermal bridges linked to the exposed concrete structure still remain. The design team had to compromise in thermal insulation, in order to respect the building's design ethos.

The former social housing block is now partly fully privatised or in a shared ownership status, while only one-third of the apartments remain in the affordable housing status. Criminality and social problems have been eliminated, while the newly introduced commercial uses have attracted various types of users, revitalising the ground floor area.

Park Hill is considered to be among the most successful retrofits, gaining high publicity and being awarded numerous prestigious prizes.

Sources

– *Architects Journal* (2013) 'Sheffield Council urged to cut financial ties with Park Hill', 1 October 2013. ww.architectsjournal.co.uk/news/sheffield-council-urged-to-cut-financial-ties-with-park-hill/8653813.article
– http://egretwest.com/projects/homes/park-hill-2/#more-390
– www.archdaily.com/174968/
– www.hawkinsbrown.com/projects/park-hill-sheffield
– www.grant-associates.uk.com/projects/74-housing/2908-park-hill.aspx
– www.urbansplash.co.uk/residential/park-hill

Parsons House

Original information

Location: City of Westminster, London
Address: Edgware Road
Postcode: W2 1NF
Date of construction: 1969
No. storeys: 21
No. flats: 120
Owner/client: City of Westminster
Institutions involved: Westminster City Planning and Development Planning Department

Located on Edgware Road in Central London, Parsons House was planned as a social housing tower in the low rise area of Paddington Green. It was completed in 1969 by architect T.P. Bennett. The 21-storey building contains 120 flats and an underground car park for 100 cars. It is a reinforced concrete structure with a brickwork infill and had

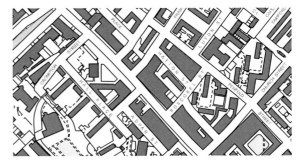

▲ Figure 4.122

Parsons House site plan

◀ Figure 4.123

Parsons House post-retrofit, axonometric view

▼ Figure 4.124

Parsons House post-retrofit, south-east view

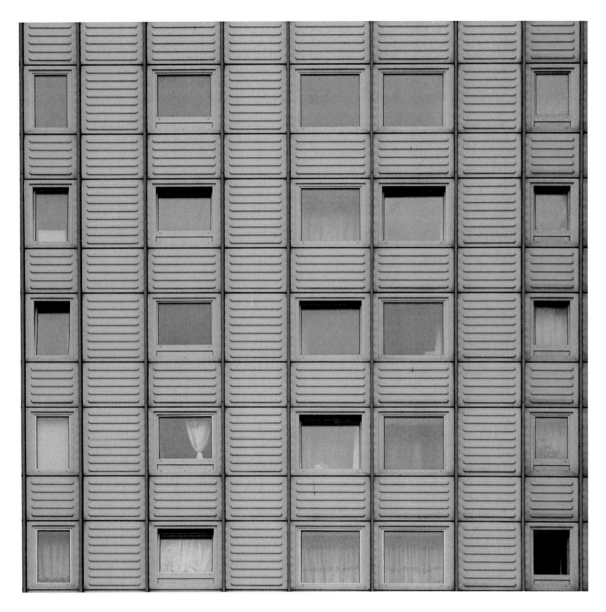

wooden framed windows originally. Being retrofitted in 1988, it was the first renovated tower in London.

▲ Figure 4.125

Parsons House post-retrofit aluminium screen cladded façade

Retrofit information

Date of retrofit intervention: 1988
No. storeys: 21
No. flats: 120
Property owner/client: City of Westminster
Contractor/developer: Henry Boot
Institutions involved: Westminster City Council
Cost: £14 million

During the retrofit, all the old, decayed timber framed windows were replaced by double-glazed aluminium window frames. In addition, the building envelope has been over-cladded by Peter Bell's composite aluminium panels, providing efficient thermal insulation. Brick and concrete texture colours were replaced by pale grey and strong red colours, giving the building a slight high-tech appearance. The building was given a top, by adding a maintenance cradle rail, and a bottom by adding vandal-proof tiling.

The retrofit project achieved its goals in reducing energy consumption and carbon emissions. Its appearance was changed drastically from a brown brick-cladded building to a light grey metal box, with colourful red vertical elements, a base and a crown top. However, a substantial amount of the flats have been privatised since Thatcher's 'right to buy' scheme, gradually changing the tower's social structure.

Sources

– http://transact.westminster.gov.uk/docstores/publications_store/Parsons_Hse_Summary_Brief_Jan12.pdf
– www.peterbellarchitects.co.uk/parsons.htmlh
– www.skyscrapernews.com/buildings.php?id=2077

▼ Figure 4.126

Parsons House post retrofit façade detail

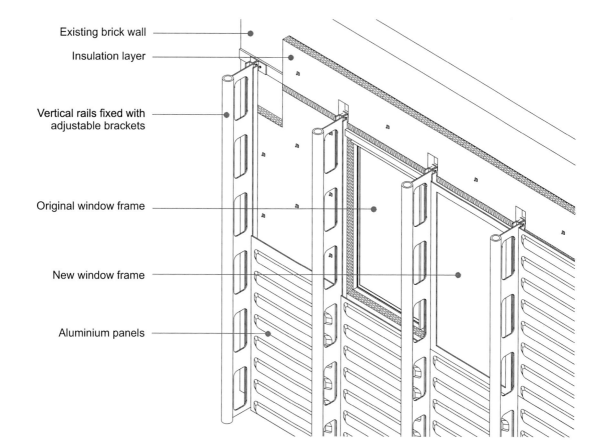

Peabody Estate

Original information

Location: Islington, London
Address: 1 Golden Lane, Peabody Estate
Postcode: EC1Y
Date of construction: 1959
No. storeys: 13
No. flats: 107
Owner/client: The Peabody Trust
Architect: John Gray & Partner
Institutions involved: Islington City Council

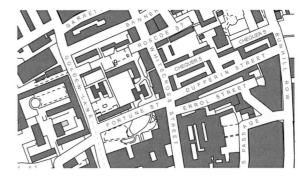

▲ Figure 4.127

Peabody Estate site plan

◀ Figure 4.128

Peabody Estate post-retrofit, axonometric view

▼ Figure 4.129

Peabody Estate after the retrofit

▲ Figure 4.130

Insulated render façade close-up

The Peabody Donation Fund built two estates on both sides of Whitecross Street in 1883. Through the years, both estates merged into one known as 'Peabody town'. 'Peabody town' was severely damaged during the Second World War, but began to get its current form during its reconstruction, completed in 1957 by John Gray and Partners. Located in Islington, next to the Barbican, the estate consists of two 13-storey towers, constructed as a reinforced concrete frame structure with brick and concrete panel infills. ECD Architects took over the estate's retrofit, which was completed in 2006.

Retrofit information

Date of retrofit intervention: 2006
No. storeys: 13
No. flats: 107
Property owner/client: The Peabody Trust
Architect: ECD Architects
Institutions involved: Islington City Council
Cost: £3.5 million

The refurbishment focused on insulating walls and the roof as well as the layout and structural optimisation. New double-glazed, timber/aluminium frames were installed, concrete and brickworks were repaired. The building was over-cladded with an insulated acrylic render in a light grey-white colour finish. The entrance area was redesigned and enlarged, and photovoltaic panels installed on the roof.

Due to the renovation, the Peabody Estate's carbon emissions were reduced by 60 per cent. Energy bills were drastically reduced. Double glazing helped to reduce the noise rising from the neighbouring streets. The original concrete texture colour was covered by bright, pale grey acrylic render.

Sources

– Arestis, A., *et al.* (2010). *Whitecross Street Estate*. 1st ed. London: Publica.
– www.peabody.org.uk/our-neighbourhoods/islington/roscoe-street/facilities-developments
– www.skyscrapernews.com/buildings.php?id=3161
– www.superhomes.org.uk/superhomes/london-islington-roscoe-towers-peabody-trust/

▼ Figure 4.131

Insulated render façade axonometric detail

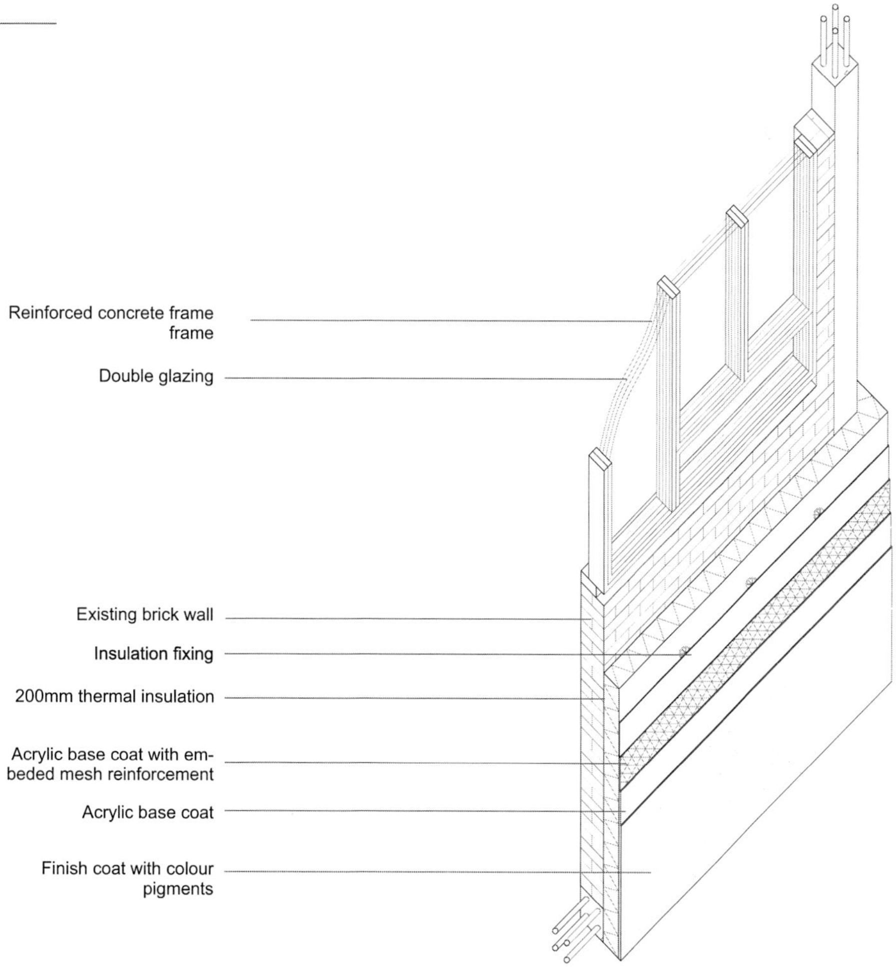

Reinforced concrete frame frame

Double glazing

Existing brick wall

Insulation fixing

200mm thermal insulation

Acrylic base coat with embeded mesh reinforcement

Acrylic base coat

Finish coat with colour pigments

Tamworth Towers

Original information

Location: Manchester, Old Trafford
Address: Bold Street
Postcode: M15 5QH
Date of construction: Late 1960s
No. storeys: 15
No. flats: 90
Architect: Trafford City Council
Owner: Trafford City Council

▲ Figure 4.132

Tamworth Towers site plan

▲ Figure 4.133

Tamworth Towers before the retrofit

◀ Figure 4.134

Tamworth Towers post-retrofit, axonometric view

CHAPTER 4 Tamworth Towers

The borough of Old Trafford was a typical working-class area. Between 1960 and 1970, many uninhabitable Victorian houses were demolished and replaced by seven tower blocks, built by the Old Trafford City Council as an exposed reinforced concrete structure with a brickwork infill: three 'balcony blocks' and four 'bird blocks'. After many years of social and physical decay, the newly introduced regeneration master plan proposed the demolition of the four 'bird blocks' and the retrofitting of the three remaining towers. Trafford Housing Trust gained ownership of the towers from Trafford Council in 2005 and commissioned PRP architects to do the £8.5 million retrofit. The project won the Architects' Journal Retrofit 2013 Award for Housing, immediately after completion.

▼ Figure 4.135

Tamworth Towers after the retrofit intervention

CHAPTER 4 Tamworth Towers

195

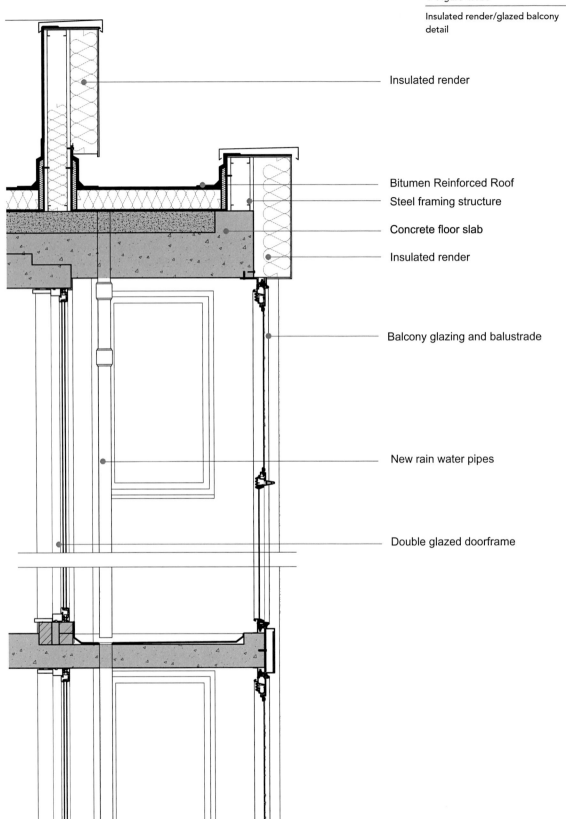

▼ Figure 4.136

Insulated render/glazed balcony detail

Retrofit information

Date of retrofit intervention: 2013
No. storeys: 15
No. flats: 87
Architect: PRP Architects
Property owner/client: Trafford Housing Trust
Contractor/developer: Seddon Construction
Institutions involved: Trouffard City Council
Cost: £7.5 million
Governmental programmes: Community Energy Saving Programme (CESP), Action for Sustainable Living

The retrofit adopts the strategy of wrapping insulation and rendering around the existing façade and roof structure. The walls have been covered by an additional external layer of 200 mm thermally insulated cement boards, while balcony balustrades have been cladded with insulated aluminium panels. Existing single-glazed windows have been replaced by double-glazed aluminium frames and the balconies fully were glazed.

▶ Figure 4.137

South façade

The roof was insulated with an additional layer of water insulation, a 200 mm layer of thermal insulation and a new parapet, eliminating existing thermal bridges at that part of the building. Bitumen sheets were used to cover all layers of the roof as well as the existing and the new parapets. Furthermore, heating and ventilation systems have been replaced, the entrance area was refurbished, and CCTV installed.

The towers' appearance was entirely transformed as the brickwork's natural colour was replaced by a white/greyish render. Coloured aluminium panels differentiate each tower's identity from its neighbouring ones. The towers received a distinguishable bottom and top zone, breaking their previously existing symmetrical order. The project is among the boldest design approaches observed within this book.

The retrofit interventions drastically improved the buildings' environmental performance, lowering power consumption, maintenance costs and the

▼ Figure 4.138

Insulated render façade close-up

▶ Figure 4.139

Tamworth Towers typical floor plan

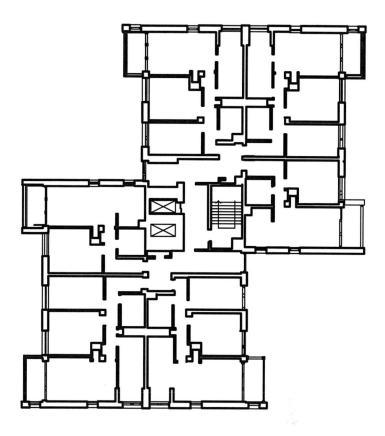

residents' energy bills. However, the Trafford Housing Trust proceeded with its common privatisation and shared ownership policy changing the pre-retrofit social structure.

Sources

– Finch, P., Slavid, R., Sedgwick, A, Chikaher, G., House, D., Mayfield, M., and Lam, F. (2012) 'Retrofit Awards 2012', *Architects' Journal*, 236: 22–24.
– Soros, M. S. (2009) *The Oxford Companion to Global Change*, Oxford: Oxford University Press.
– http://apollocradles.co.uk/tamworth.html
– www.mancunianmatters.co.uk/content/180456965-trafford-set-%C2%A385million-housing-transformation-brutalist-tower-blocks-demolished
– www.messengernewspapers.co.uk/news/9081055.Multi_million_pound_facelift_for_tower_blocks/
– www.prparchitects.co.uk/news/news-releases/2013/tamworth-towers-refurbishment-wins-key-retrofit-award.html
– www.traffordhousingtrust.co.uk/your-community/old-trafford-masterplan/project-1-tamworth-neighbourhood
– www.urbed.coop/projects/old-trafford-masterplan-0

Trellick Tower

Original information

Location: North Kensington, West London
Address: 7 Golborne Road
Postcode: W10 5NY
Date of construction: 1967–1972
No. storeys: 31
No. flats: 217
Architect: Ernő Goldfinger
Owner/client: Greater London Council

▲ Figure 4.140

The Cheltenham estate's site plan

Retrofit information

Date of retrofit intervention: 2013
No. storeys: 31
No. flats: 217
Architect: John McAslan & Partners
Property owner/client: Royal Borough of Kensington & Chelsea/K&C Tenant Management Organisation
Contractor/developer: Bieber
Institutions involved: Greater London Council, English Heritage, Twentieth Century Society
Cost: £4 million

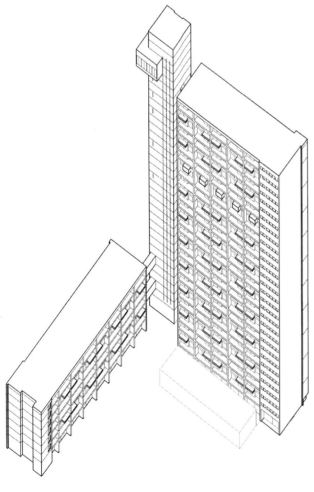

▲ Figure 4.141

Trellick Tower, axonometric drawing

▲ Figure 4.142

Trellick Tower post-retrofit, west view

The Trellick Tower is part of the Cheltenham estate which also contains two six-storey blocks of flats and five terraces of three-storey houses. It is located in North Kensington in West London. In 1966, the Greater London Council (GLC) commissioned architect Ernő Goldfinger to design the entire Cheltenham estate. It was finally completed in 1972, becoming the tallest public apartment building in Great Britain. The unique 'bush-hammered in-situ reinforced concrete' with pre-cast pebble-finished panels and high-quality brickwork defines the external appearance of both the tower and the whole estate.

It was listed as a Grade II building in 1988. Its iconic design made the Trellick Tower a symbol and landmark for many Londoners. However, like many other council housing blocks, the building suffered from material and social decay, during the 1980s and 1990s.

▼ Figure 4.143

Trellick Tower, retrofit detail

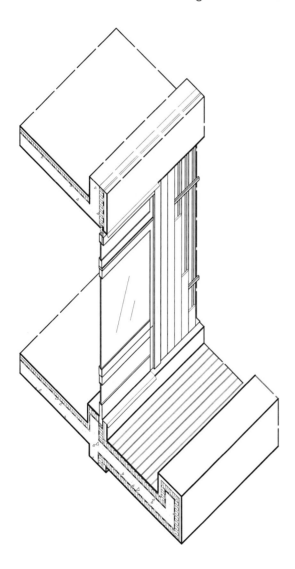

The Trellick tower retrofit was restricted to the replacement of the old single-glazed windows with high-performance double-glazed window frames, concrete envelope repairs, new lighting as well as enhancement of the entrance area. McAlston+Partners proposed a series of apartment renovations, which celebrate the building's unique design character.

It is a very sensitive intervention, which respects the building's original character. Even though the new windows reduce energy loss, cold bridges still remain, due to lack of insulation.

Sources

– Hensley, J. and Aguilar A. (2011) *Improving Energy Efficiency in Historic Buildings*.
– http://microcities.net/portfolio/the-trellick-tower-the-fall-and-rise-of-a-modern-monument/
– www.bdonline.co.uk/john-mcaslan-and-partners%E2%80%99-%C2%A317m-refurb-of-goldfinger%E2%80%99s-trellick-tower/3124613.article
– www.ringtail.co.uk/trellick-tower-kensington/
– www.rbkc.gov.uk/pdf/Trellick%20and%20Edenham%20listed%20status.pdf

◂ Figure 4.144

Trellick Tower's post-retrofit, new double-glazed window frames

◂ Figure 4.145

Trellick Tower post retrofit, west view

Westbury Estate

Original information

Location: Lambeth, South London
Address: Portslade Road
Postcode: SW8 3LE
Date of construction: 1966
No. storeys: 21
No. flats: 80
Architect: GLC Dept. of Architecture & Civic Design
Owner/client: Westbury and Mawbe Brough estates
Institutions involved: Lambeth Living

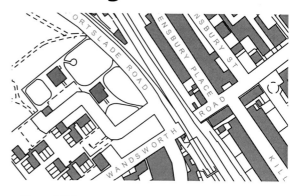

▲ Figure 4.146

Westbury Estate site plan

◀ Figure 4.147

Westbury Estate after the retrofit

Constructed in Lambeth, South London by Hunter and Partners in 1996, Westbury estate includes two residential, 21-storey towers, as well as a series of low-rise dwellings. The 62-meter-tall towers were built as an exposed reinforced concrete frame structure with a brickwork infill. The identical Westbury estate tower typology was also built in Canada Estate in South London. The Council commissioned Hunters with the towers' retrofit, completed in 2008. Furthermore, the council decided to demolish the low-rise dwellings and build new apartments, able to accommodate more people. The retrofit intervention was part of the 'Decent Home' programme launched by the UK government.

◀ Figure 4.148

Westbury Estate post retrofit, axonometric view

CHAPTER 4 Westbury Estate

◀ Figure 4.149

Durrington Tower post retrofit, north view

▶ Figure 4.150

Post-retrofit façade close-up

▼ Figure 4.151

Westbury Towers' 'twin siblings' in Canada Estate, South London

Retrofit information

Date of retrofit intervention: 2008
No. storeys: 21
No. flats: 80 per tower
Architect: Hunters
Property owner/client: London Borough of Lambeth
Contractor/developer: Apollo Group
Institutions involved: Lambeth Living, LHC
Governmental programme: Decent Homes

The retrofit focused mainly on cleaning repairing the towers' exterior brickwork walls, roof and exposed concrete structure. All exposed concrete columns and beams were coloured in light blue and white finish. The existing single-glazed windows were replaced by double-glazed aluminium frames. Low energy lighting was installed in public areas of the buildings.

The retrofit intervention practised at the Westbury estate is among the least ambitious recorded. It has improved the buildings' sustainable performance mainly through the replacement of the windows but there are still major thermal losses mainly due to the thermal bridges linked to the buildings' exposed concrete structure. Its appearance and social structure remained almost unchanged. The project was awarded by the LHC's 1st project of the year award, as a showcase of outstanding work for the ultimate benefits of residents.

Sources

– Seaborne and Mike (1998) Westbury estate from the Wandsworth Road station footbridge, No.MoL_IN37290, Museum of London
– http://ukhousing.wikia.com/wiki/Canada_Estate
– www.bettertransport.org.uk/blogs/roads/160414-westbury-bypass-success
– www.hunters.co.uk/files/3013/6689/4096/Retrofit_brochure.pdf
– www.social-life.co/project/westbury_estate/

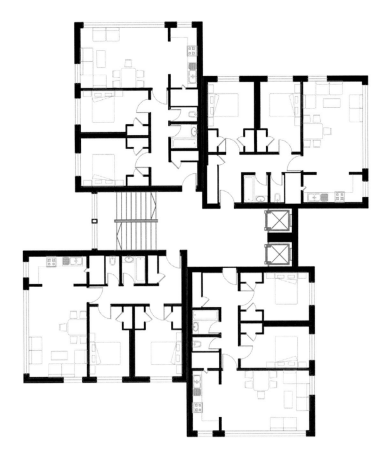

◀ Figure 4.152

Durrington Tower post-retrofit typical floor plan

Weybridge Point

Original information

Location: Wandsworth, London
Address: Culvert Road
Postcode: SW11 5AT
Date of construction: 1971
No. storeys: 16
No. flats: 61
Owner/client: Borough Council of Wandsworth

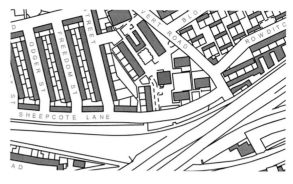

▲ Figure 4.153

Weybridge Point site plan

▲ Figure 4.154

Weybridge Point after the retrofit

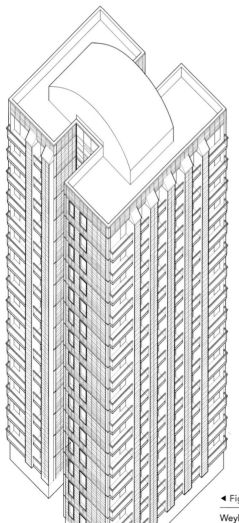

◀ Figure 4.155

Weybridge Point post-retrofit, axonometric view

▼ Figure 4.156

Weybridge Point post-retrofit, south view

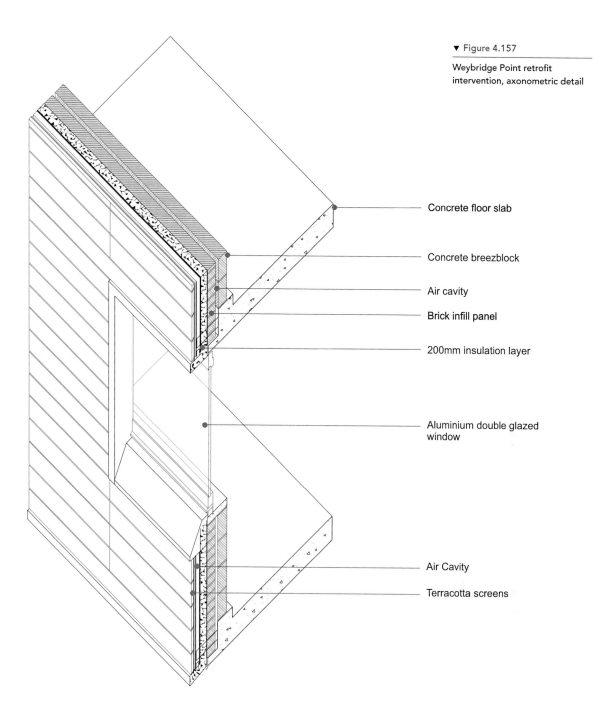

▼ Figure 4.157

Weybridge Point retrofit intervention, axonometric detail

Weybridge Point was built as a residential social housing tower by the Borough Council of Wandsworth, completed in 1971. The 17-storey concrete frame building was originally cladded by brickwork. Its continuous material and social deterioration during the 1990s initiated the building's retrofit in 2005.

CHAPTER 4 Weybridge Point

Retrofit information

Date of retrofit intervention: 2005
No. storeys: 16
No. flats: 61
Architect: AK Design Partnership
Property owner/client: Apollo London Ltd
Contractor/developer: Retrofit UK Ltd.
Institutions involved: Mark Heywood Associates
Cost: £3 million

The tower has been over-cladded mainly by insulated terracotta-faced rain-screens. In addition, aluminium polyester powder-coated panels and insulated render have been used on balcony cheeks and soffits. The original single-glazed windows were replaced by double glazing. The dark brown natural brick colour and the grey exposed concrete were covered by a light brown terracotta colour. The tower has been crowned with a rounded rooftop and based on a plastered bottom zone on the ground floor.

The tower's retrofit led to drastic improvement of its environmental performance. Its appearance changed completely, erasing its brutalist characteristics, embracing a rather post-modern aesthetic. The Borough Council sold the tower to Apollo London before the renovation. The occurring retrofit continued the trend towards privatisation and shared ownership.

▼ Figure 4.158

Weybridge Point terracotta rain-screens over-cladding

Sources

– http://akdp.moonfruit.com/weybridge-point/4536562437
– http://picssr.com/photos/proteusfaçades/interesting/page5?nsid=69349406@N08
– www.emporis.com/buildings/139575/weybridge-point-london-united-kingdom
– www.markheywood.plus.com/pages/Projects/projects.html

▼ Figure 4.159

Weybridge Point, south-east view

▼ Figure 4.160

Weybridge Point, south-west view

Chapter 5

Conversations with the architects

Interview with David Rudkin, HLP Architects (Greenfields Place (South Sefton, Liverpool), Barton Village (Salford, Manchester), Ladywell Green (Eccles, Manchester) and Blacon, The Saints and The Heights (Chester))

1. How where these projects commissioned?

   It was through a bid, a small invited competition. There is a EU procurement website on which all these calls are advertised. Architects can register there and receive notices when new projects are being advertised. Practices can submit their tender in a team with their consultants and move to the next phase according to how they have scored. The top ten, eight or six proposals can enter the framework and work for the organisation for the next four years. Sometimes projects don't go ahead, though. We went through the process for the Liverpool towers commission, 10–15 years ago.

2. Confirmation of key dates: when was the project commissioned?

   Our first high-rise housing refurbishment was Greenfields in Liverpool, working for One Vision. This first project was commissioned somewhere before 2009, Barton Village and Ladywell Green a bit before 2011, and the towers in Chester at the end of 2012.

3. When did the building works start? When were the refurbishments completed?

   Our first project started in 2009, the projects in Salford and Eccles in 2011–2012, and the one in Chester in 2013.

4. Who owns the towers?

   The Liverpool Housing Association, City West Housing Association and Sanctuary Housing.

5. What was the social, technical and architectural condition in which you found the estate when you started to work on each projects?

   Greenfields: The towers had had a thermal upgrade around 1995, which was a thermal render with adhesive and some mechanical fixings. The system failed, leading to damp problems, and that is why it was necessary to go for another upgrade which involved a more comprehensive intervention including a new layout and façades, fire protection, landscape, modernising fittings. The retrofits are about the environmental programme (comfort, low bills) as importantly as providing a nice built environment that attracts people to live in the towers.

Barton Village and Ladywell Green: The most important factor was to bring big changes in bill terms. The electric underfloor heating provided originally failed so they were using storage heating, which is a very cheap system to install but very inefficient, so they were paying a lot of money and many tenants were suffering fuel poverty. In Barton Village, bills went from £80–100/month to £20/month (£5/week). This requirement, together with subsidies coming from the government's environmental programmes, allowed us to develop a comprehensive and innovative energy-efficient strategy.

Towers in Chester: This is an ongoing retrofitting process, which was already designed when we were appointed. In this case, there were no subsidies, and the budget was very limited, so there was no scope for an innovative technical intervention, and most of the project focused on design improvements.

In terms of social structure, before the retrofit, most of the flats were rented by social housing tenants. The retrofit also brings private rented flats. Most of the people living in these towers are elderly. To avoid antisocial behaviour, the blocks get 'zoned' by age in all these schemes: a block for over 50 years old tenants, younger block, etc. The vacant towers are open to everybody, but priority is given to those who have a relative in the towers or in the neighbourhood to support family connections, what is called Local Lettings Policy. This is a trend to prioritise people within the area, and stop gentrification.

6. **How have you approached this project (design concept and methodology) in relation to the improvements that have been requested?**
    Housing associations compete for tenants to live in their stock nowadays. There are a lot of vacancies everywhere, so making the flats appealing plays an important role in the design process. For us, providing contextualisation for the estates is an important part of our design approach, where tackling the elevations of the towers and the landscape surrounding them are critical interventions.

7. **From your point of view, were there any important values in the initial design that should be preserved and or even enhanced in these projects? Were you aiming at preserving or changing their identity?**
    None of the towers we have refurbished are listed or presented special design characteristics, they were part of the numerous blocks developed in the 1960s that look all the same, lacking character or identity. Besides, some of the towers had gone through previous renovation processes that had already changed their image. For instance, in Greenfields Place,

CHAPTER 5 Conversations with the architects

213

the 1990s upgrade was done in a postmodern colouring style. These are recognisable patterns that get easily outdated. It was very important for tenants and housing associations to change the image of the blocks.

8. **Which retrofit insulation techniques did you use? Was the design intervention affected by the insulating product palette? To what degree was the colour scheme determined by it?**

Greenfields: Following the building regulations standards of the time, externally we used insulated render with extruded polystyrene that gives a better performance in a thinner layer (90 mm). The tower has brick cladding around the base, which is also insulated. We replaced the old windows with double-glazed aluminium windows. And we used aluminium panels in the infills. We have also added a heat recovery ventilation system (spider). The elevation patterns are based on function, rather than on 'fashion' patterns, and we followed a natural palette of colours, that match more easily the surroundings. It is functional because the colour pattern is generated through the building's functions, and different materials are applied to these different areas creating vertical bands: glazed living rooms, renders in bedrooms and vertical communications, etc.

Barton Village and Ladywell Green: The thermal comfort strategy is based on a new technology of thermal plant developed for these two projects, called Ecopods. Each of the towers has an Ecopod installed on the roof, so each thermal plant serves 60 flats. The thermal circuit of gas and hot water goes up and down the building, providing thermal gain to the structure. The Ecopods' enclosure is made of metal cladding, which holds 20 m^2 of PV cells on its roof that provide for a heat sink, and help the boiler to preheat the water in the circuit. Having the building's services installed on the roof frees the ground floor for a social hub. Insulation is provided by rendered insulation, as a cost-effective material strategy, where one floor is done per day. Barton Village is close to a conservation area with sandstone, so we chose the same colour in the render to match this context and the Manchester red brick. In Ladywell Green, we had a different approach: colour is used to the outside of the site, and walls are in white to the inside of the site as a backdrop to the church. The use of colour is driven by context, as in the other projects. A key design theme is the use of the Lowry colour palette based on the five colours used by the local artist – Prussian Blue, Vermilion, Yellow Ochre, Ivory Black and Flake White. The materials have been closely managed through a contextual design approach to form a sensitive backdrop to the Grade I listed St. Mary's church and the Grade II listed Lamb Hotel. The main idea is how the building is perceived from the road, and this perception changes as one moves, following a rotational movement around the towers, which is also supported by the new landscape provision. The colour scheme is again based on natural colours: sandstone for the base, terracotta for the rest of the height. Frames are made of aluminium and powdered steel using a bronze colour. Existing balconies are enclosed to provide a sunspace for each apartment, creating vertical glass towers at each corner.

Towers in Chester: In this project each tower is individually designed within a common palette of materials, otherwise they would be identified as council housing, if the same strategy was used for all schemes. In this case the design strategy is based on simpler blocks, playing with the planes to break uniformity, and with a diversified provision of views from different perspectives, so the set of towers don't look like a barrier. In this sense, the colour strategy is designed to break down the masses, appearing as interlocking blocks in which the mass of the block uses a different material. Depending on the view, you get a different picture of the group of towers.

9. **To what degree were stakeholders involved in the refurbishment process? Did they have an impact on the projects' design?**
   Absolutely, especially tenants, who had a say on layout and design strategies through consultations. It is a valuable experience for our practice; it is very rewarding to do interventions that have so much impact on so many people. For Barton Village, our first consultation happened on 21 July 2010, and we went knocking on doors to leave an invitation to the consultation event to get their views on elevations and layouts. We had lots of meetings with them, collected questionnaires, chatted about what they liked or disliked; they love physical models and full-scale mock-ups.

   Proposing community-focused designs is received very positively from housing associations. We won these projects because we involved tenants and provided the highest number of flats. Housing associations are politically well organised, and have provided an easy and good experience for our practice.

10. **What were the restrictions you faced during this refurbishment? Did they impose changes or compromises in your initial proposal?**
    Tight budgets are the biggest obstacles we have faced.

11. **These refurbishments have taken place/will take place with the towers inhabited?**
    In the four towers of Liverpool and Barton Village we used the decant strategy, because they had one complete tower empty. So as each tower is getting retrofitted, tenants are rehoused in the vacant flats in other blocks. After the retrofit, tenants are offered the chance to go back to where they lived to keep the community, but others prefer to stay in the new one. Sometimes they are offered houses in other estates that belong to the same organisation or they prefer to go somewhere else. In these cases, the vacant tower was also retrofitted and became a privately rented building, but sometimes organisations decide to demolish it because they don't need that many flats. Rents are subsidised by the housing association, so they pay half of the rent and the tenant pays the other half (around £70/week or £280/month). In the cases where vacant flats are also retrofitted and offered for private renting, there is no subsidy (around £500/month). Either way they need to make the flats appealing, so people want to live there and pay the rent.

CHAPTER 5 Conversations with the architects

For the project in Eccles, residents were kept in situ while the retrofit took place. The process took one year per block, and it took two years in total to do the three blocks, in an overlapping process.

12. **Did you benefit from any governmental refurbishment schemes? If so, did this have an impact on the project? Do these programmes need to become more specific (including renewable energy and aesthetic parameters)?**
Our projects in Salford and Eccles used CESP and CERT, as mechanisms for British Gas to give contributions to reduce carbon emissions. These programmes allowed the development and installation of the Ecopods, which included PV cells.

13. **Was the retrofit commissioned in order to meet the UK's Carbon Plan? If so, are you meeting the targets?**
We matched the Decent Homes Standards for the thermal and other aspects in the first scheme, and we definitely got a very efficient energy performance in the projects in Salford and Eccles. The project in Salford won a prize.

14. **Any post-occupancy measurements taken/or planned to be taken to actually check the tower's performance?**
No.

15. **Did the retrofit affect the towers' social structure?**
Yes, as I said, people get organised by age, and there are some flats privately rented, as I said before.

16. **Are there a limited number of contractors/manufacturers involved in most of the refurbishment projects taking place in the country?**
Due to how the tendering and commissioning process works, once you fulfilled all the requirements to be in the framework, you tend to benefit from any opportunities, and practices tend to get specialised for this and any other type of projects.

17. **For architects who changed the colour in their towers: why did you do this? Was this your own choice or was this requested by the client/ stakeholders?**
Requested by client and stakeholders, as explained.

18. **After being re-clad, do the towers lose their individuality? Which cultural or heritage-related values are more valuable?**
The intention was to provide individuality and specific character to each tower. Nothing in the original design was relevant in terms of heritage, and the towers had already being partially modified.

19. **Did the first retrofit commission lead to commissions of further refurbishments?**
Yes.

20. This is the bibliography we have about this building, could you suggest any other relevant documents that are missing from our list?
I cannot recall any at the moment, but I can provide original photographs and documents about the project.

Interview with Charles Ellis, John Robertson Architects (Great Arthur House, Golden Lane Estate, London)

1. How was this project commissioned?
In 2001, Great Arthur House went to the top of the City of London Corporation's (CLC) priority list. John Robertson Architects (JRA) decided to present a refurbishment proposal, but then the tower went down the list again and nothing happened. In 2010, CLC organised a limited competition, to which they invited five architectural practices, based on their experience refurbishing historical buildings. JRA, in particular, had experience refurbishing Grade II listed buildings in which was clear their respect and sensitivity to bring back to life the building's original design. JRA won the competition in April 2011. CLC gave two reasons for JRA winning the competition: (1) we were the only ones who had prepared a proposal in collaboration with a façade consultant and an engineering practice, so it was really well detailed and offered different fully illustrated solutions for each of the specific technical problems that needed to be resolved; and (2) we were one of the only two proposals presenting a replacement solution for the façade with the building still inhabited, and ours was the one that meant the lowest impact for the tenants.

2. Confirmation of key dates: when was the project commissioned?
JRA won the competition in April 2011.

3. When will the building works get started? When will they be completed?
Works will start in January 2016. We are expecting completion mid-2017. We are planning to replace the façade section by section, dividing it into 10 m-long strips. Each strip will be removed and built up again before moving to the following strip. That way, we will not need a scaffolding for the whole façade during a whole year. Works for each of the strips are planned to last 15 weeks. During those 15 weeks, a temporary inner wall will be provided in each flat. These are called Structurally Insulated Panels (SIPS).

4. Who owns the tower?
It is shared ownership: 60 per cent is owned by the City of London Corporation (CLC), 40 per cent is privately owned with a leasehold for 120 years. CLC maintains the right to decide about any works in the building, and all the tenants have to support those decisions. The building is still managed by CLC (concierge, maintenance, etc.).

5. **What was the social, technical and architectural condition in which you found Great Arthur House when you started to work on this project?**
The building envelope at Great Arthur House was in a bad condition, leaking badly and uninsulated. It is full of cold bridges, you can feel the wind behind the glass wall (the level of infiltration is significant), the façade leaks, many panels have been repaired and patched up, the glass cleaning system is broken down. It is technically and aesthetically decayed. The current glass façade's U-Value is 9, and the spandrel panels' (yellow colour) 7. Our target is to reduce it to below 2. The rooms are so small that we didn't want to reduce the space by adding extra thickness to the exterior walls; kitchens and bathrooms are only 2 x 1.5 m, so we were looking for the most efficient solution complying with these criteria. It is a fine balance. The boilers were all changed in 1980. In the 60 per cent of the flats owned by the council, they will be replaced by new condensing boilers. About 2 per cent of the flats are equipped now with this type of new boiler. Communal areas elsewhere on the estate, such as the pool and the gym areas got refurbished recently and are hugely popular. The roof terrace will require some repairs as well, but it is not part of the contract project. It is not in use currently due to health and safety reasons.

Overall, the building has nice design features (post and newspaper holder in the entrance door, the milk delivery cabinet), but the flats are very small. It is still very popular, so rents are extremely high, a typical symptom of gentrification.

6. **The refurbishment will take place with the tower inhabited?**
Yes, that was a key factor in our proposal.

7. **How have you approached this project (design concept and methodology) in relation to the improvements that had been requested?**
CLC commissioned several technical reports to assess the existing condition of the building, the last two were issued in 1990 and 2000. These reports indicated the necessary replacements such as for the glazed curtain wall, the windows on the north and south elevations, as well as for glazed timber balcony doors. The building needed localised external concrete repairs (also on the rooftop), and the replacement of the cleaning and maintenance system for the new façade provided. The bid emphasised the curtain wall replacement, which was the main priority. Other less important upgrades were left out due to the limited budget.

Our approach focused on a solution demanding minimum demolition, allowing tenants to remain in the building during the construction process. CLC's targets were aiming for the minimum number of changes in relation to the original design (e.g. maintaining the sliding aluminium windows, originally fabricated by Quicktho, a bus window manufacturer), which posed a great challenge for thermal performance. Two full-scale mock-ups were built and tested, trying to improve their thermal performance, implementing contemporary technology while following the original aesthetics.

Another challenge was to match the original yellow shade of the curtain wall façade panels (original Vitrolite glass), as the old manufacturer no longer exists. Samples from the façade were taken to a contemporary manufacturer, who produced several tests to find the closest yellow shade to the original panels. The window manufacturer is Fillmetalbau, an Austrian firm. They produce everything for the façade. Integrating the new façade into the structure was problematic because any new double-glazed design would be too heavy for the existing slab. The solution was to install a 12 mm x 250 mm galvanised plate to each slab edge and spanning between the concrete shear walls to which the panels are fixed. The new glazing will match the original depths of the mullions and transoms as closely as possible.

8. **From your point of view, were there any important values in the initial design that should be preserved and or even enhanced in this project? Were you aiming at preserving or changing its identity?**
People admire the elevation's Modernist clarity, the aluminium and glass curtain wall. The rooftop is a late addition to the project, it only came about 1954. It is a Grade II listed building, so the project is totally focused on preserving the building's identity.

9. **To what degree were stakeholders involved in the refurbishment process? Did they have an impact on project design?**
Stakeholders were actively involved. English Heritage was consulting us on conservation guidelines. The Twentieth Century Society was notified about the planning progress; there is a strong relationship with the council and the residents, there is a Residents Liaison Officer (one representing council tenants and one representing private owners) who attended many meetings, so they could have a say in many decisions (e.g. choice of contractor). There are many committees involved: the projects sub-committee, the finance sub-committee and the housing management sub-committee.

10. **What were the restrictions (e.g. listed building regulations, limited budget) you faced during this refurbishment? Did they impose changes or compromises in your initial proposal?**
It is a Grade II listed building. The original design has to be respected for any interior or exterior intervention. Final decisions are taken by the CLC so the budget is scrutinised and the goals are taken to the minimum decent performance.

11. **Did you benefit from any governmental refurbishment schemes? If so, did this have an impact on the project? Do these programmes need to become more specific (including renewable energy and aesthetic parameters)?**
Yes, our goal was to match the Decent Homes Standard. We tried participating in the Green Deal programme with British Gas, but it didn't work due to residents' average income being higher than allowed.

12. Was the retrofit commissioned to meet the UK's Carbon Plan? If so, are you meeting the targets?
No.

13. Did you use any renewable energy systems? If yes, which ones? Did they affect your design approach?
No. We discussed the possibility of renewable energy systems with the City planners but we soon realised that it was not a realistic possibility.

14. Any post-occupancy measurements taken/planned to be taken to actually check the tower's performance?
We are planning to monitor energy bill changes after the completion of the re-cladding project.

15. Did the retrofit affect the towers' social structure?
The social structure is changing already. The flats were originally built for city workers, so never as social housing really. There are only one-bedroom flats, so the building is pretty self-selecting in terms of the type of households. Only singles, couples or single parents choose to live there. Some of the flats have been sold for £350,000.

16. Are there a limited number of contractors/manufacturers involved in most of the refurbishment projects taking place in the country?
Our general contractor is Keepmoat; they work exclusively for local authorities. It is a £5.8 million contract. The curtain wall and windows will cost about £4 million, the remaining sum is for concrete repairs, repainting, replacing the cleaning system, and roof repairs. Eighty contractors applied to tender for the job, 14 of them entered the second round, 6 of them had actually experience in façade retrofits. It took us six months to select a contractor. It was a delicate decision since residents wanted reliable people, who could make sure that the works will not last longer than planned, and that works would proceed to a high standard.

17. For architects who didn't change the tower's colour: change of colour/materiality appears to be a primary approach followed in many of the refurbishments of these towers, as a means to change the tower's overall image. Why do you think this is happening? Do you think it is to remove the social stigma that some of these towers have, that colour is an effective vehicle to send a message to the citizens: this is a new, happier tower? The use of colourful panels and details leads to the disappearance of the material's natural colour (concrete/brick/render) or the original aesthetics of the tower. Do you think this is important to maintain the projec's original identity?
Yes, it is about looking modern, clean, etc. Many of these towers look the same, there is no singularity in their designs, so the recladding is an opportunity to add some character and brightness to the tower. Everybody wants that: the client and the residents. Usually, the architects suggest

different colour schemes and present them to the residents. They vote for the scheme they like the most.

18. **After being re-clad, do the towers lose their individuality? Which cultural or heritage-related values are more vulnerable?**
Not in the case of these really similar towers. I think they look a lot better, I agree that colour is the way to do it.

19. **Did the first retrofit commission lead to commissions of further refurbishments?**
Not yet.

20. **This is the bibliography we have about this building, could you suggest any other relevant documents that are missing from our list?**
There is a lot of material in the RIBA library and the London Metropolitan Archive. There is also an original documentary about the Golden Lane Estate. It was well published in the magazines of the time.

Interview with Andrew Mellor, PRP Architects (Crossways Estate, London)

1. **How was this project commissioned?**
I was not involved in the commissioning phase, but as far as I know, it went through an invited bid, including a master plan and the architectural proposal.

2. **Confirmation of key dates: when was the project commissioned?**
Not exactly sure.

3. **When did building works get started? When was it completed?**
Building works started in 2002, I entered the project in 2004. The project was completed around 2014–2015

4. **Who owns the tower?**
The property was sold to Swan Housing. Part of the flats are now privately owned, and partly either under shared ownership or tenanted as affordable rent apartments. The different types of properties are located in different blocks.

5. **Was this your first post-war tower block refurbishment project?**
The Crossways Estate is among the first, definitely the largest project.

6. **What was the social, technical and architectural condition in which you found the estate when you started to work on this project?**
The buildings were in a very bad condition. There were lots of social and technical problems. The complex was a hub for drugs and

CHAPTER 5 Conversations with the architects

221

criminality. Overall it was an inhospitable area, especially in relation to the footbridges, leading to the entrances. The concrete structure was damaged, the heating system in bad condition and cold bridges were everywhere.

7. How have you approached this project (design concept and methodology) in relation to the improvements that had been requested?
    We started to analyse the complex and identify the problems. We then investigated possible ways to resolve them. There was an ongoing debate about demolishing the towers. We wanted to retain the tower's main identity and characteristics. We wanted to improve the living conditions and offer different types of flats for different occupants.

8. From your point of view, were there any important values in the initial design that should be preserved and or even enhanced in this project? Were you aiming at preserving or changing its identity?
    The flats offer an amazing view of London. We wanted to retain the towers' identity but renew their image. We wanted to keep their iconic character and emphasize verticality.

9. Which retrofit insulation techniques did you use? Was the design intervention affected by the insulating product palette? Is it too simplistic? To what degree was the colour scheme determined by it?
    The concrete structure was over-clad by polyester coated aluminium panels. The old windows were replaced by triple-glazed aluminium windows. The old brickwork was over-clad using an insulated render finishing. The floor plans were changed as well. There are four flats per floor now, in different sizes (one- and two-bedroom flats). The heating system was renewed.

10. To what degree were stakeholders involved in the refurbishment process? Did they have an impact on project design?
    Stakeholders were involved, especially the residents. We wanted to involve residents as part of a greater social sustainability process.

11. What were the restrictions you faced during this refurbishment? Did they impose changes or compromises in your initial proposal?
    The biggest problem was the neighbouring railway tracks (DLR). It was difficult fitting in the cranes on the site and keeping the required distance from the rails.

12. The refurbishment has taken place with the tower inhabited?
    It was not inhabited. Occupants were decanted to the new rise complex built aside from the towers until construction works were completed. They could return to the towers afterwards.

13. Did you benefit from any governmental refurbishment schemes? If so, did this have an impact on the project? Do these programmes need to become more specific (including renewable energy and aesthetic parameters)?
Not sure about it, there might have been some support from the Greater London Authority. The retrofit was mostly funded by selling part of the flats.

14. Was the retrofit commissioned in order to meet the UK's Carbon Plan? If so, are you meeting the targets?
I am not sure about that either.

15. Did you use any renewable energy systems? If yes, which ones? Did they affect your design approach?
No.

16. Any post-occupancy measurements taken/or planned to be taken to actually check the tower's performance?
Not yet for the Crossways Estate, there are post-occupancy measurements for Trafford Towers though.

17. Did the retrofit affect the towers' social structure?
Yes, it did. Many of the old residents have left the property. Some of the leaseholders sold their property to the new owner (Swan). Many did swap their own flat to a new one, others took the money offered and left. Problematic (criminal) residents were removed by the police. There was certainly gentrification taking place.

18. Are there a limited number of contractors/manufacturers involved in most of the refurbishment projects taking place in the country?
I don't know.

19. For architects who changed the colour in their towers: why did you do this? Was this your own choice or was this requested by the client/stakeholders?
We wanted to give an identity to each of the three towers. We chose pastel colours to harmonise with the surrounding context. The actual colours were chosen by the design architect and were communicated to the residents through colour samples. They would show samples to the residents.

20. After being re-clad, did the towers lose their individuality? Which cultural or heritage-related values are more vulnerable?
No, on the contrary, individuality was further expressed. There was a real revitalisation of the ground floor zone, which was one of the initial ideas reintroduced from the original 1960s design concept.

21. Did the first retrofit commission lead to commissions of further refurbishments?
Yes, it got PRP established in tower retrofitting. It definitely contributed to getting similar commissions, such as the Trafford Towers in Manchester.

CHAPTER 5 Conversations with the architects

22. This is the bibliography we have about this building, could you suggest any other relevant documents that are missing from our list?
I would recommend the BBC series called *25 Minutes*, there is one episode about the Crossways Estate.

Interview with Roy Roberts, Falconer Chester Hall Architects (Adlington Tower, Liverpool)

1. How was this project commissioned?
It was through a bid, Arena Housing had advertised it.

2. Confirmation of key dates: when was the project commissioned?
Early 2004.

3. When did building works get started? When was it completed?
The works started in 2004, and it was completed in 2005.

4. Who owns the tower?
Arena Housing, one of the housing associations.

5. What was the social, technical and architectural condition in which you found the estate when you started to work on this project?
The building was in a bad condition, wet and cold, no insulation at all. It was not usable, to be honest. Most tenants were elderly people. No criminality issues, though.

6. Was this your first post-war tower block refurbishment project?
Not sure about that to be honest. This was my first post-war tower refurb but not sure if FCH has done any before.

7. How have you approached this project (design concept and methodology) in relation to the improvements that had been requested?
We approached the project from inside out. We wanted to improve the layout of the apartments, unifying it with the kitchen and create a large opening living area with a nice view, down the river.

8. From your point of view, were there any important values in the initial design that should be preserved and or even enhanced in this project? Were you aiming at preserving or changing its identity?
Yes, we wanted to maintain the tower's character and make it desirable. We wanted to maintain the brickwork walls and highlight them. We changed the mortar colour of the original wall and brought it back to life.

9. Which retrofit insulation techniques did you use? Was the design intervention affected by the insulating product palette? Is it too simplistic? To what degree was the colour scheme determined by it?

We insulated the cavity walls with foam, replaced the windows with double-glazed aluminium frames, enclosed the balconies and transformed them into winter gardens. The heating system was upgraded as well. Since we maintained the brickwork, we chose grey/blue window frames to achieve a vivid contrast to the brick. The living room wall panel was removed and replaced with a glazed curtain wall, thus they can enjoy a floor-to-ceiling open view to the river.

10. What were the restrictions you faced during this refurbishment? Did they impose changes or compromises in your initial proposal?

It was a value-for-money project, so keeping expenses within the budget was the biggest challenge.

11. To what degree were stakeholders involved in the refurbishment process? Did they have an impact on the project's design?

Yes, they were involved, there was a tenant representative, we had meetings every two weeks. It was an enjoyable, constructive process. Everyone was happy at the end of the project.

12. The refurbishment has taken with the tower inhabited?

All tenants were moved to the vacant flats in the neighbouring tower while retrofit works were taking place.

13. Did you benefit from any governmental refurbishment schemes? If so, did this have an impact on the project? Do these programmes need to become more specific (including renewable energy and aesthetic parameters)?

It might be that Arena Housing has received some governmental funding, but I am not sure about that.

14. Are there a limited number of contractors/manufacturers involved in most of the refurbishment projects taking place in the country?

Our contractor was Lovell who won the tender. I think they have worked on tower retrofits before.

15. Was the retrofit commissioned in order to meet the UK's Carbon Plan? If so, are you meeting the targets?

No. The budget was too low for that. We insulated as much as we could, but we did not aim for a certain accreditation.

16. Did you use any renewable energy systems? If yes, which ones? Did they affect your design approach?

No. There was no budget for that.

CHAPTER 5 Conversations with the architects

17. Any post-occupancy measurements taken/ or planned to be taken to actually check the tower's performance?
No, but the bills have improved massively.

18. Did the retrofit affect the towers' social structure?
All of the old occupants remained in the tower, however, some of the empty flats got tenanted after the refurbishment.

19. For architects who didn't change the tower's colour: change of colour/ materiality appears to be a primary approach followed in many of the refurbishments of these towers, as a means to change the tower's overall image. Why do you think this is happening? Do you think it is to remove the social stigma that some of these towers have, that colour is an effective vehicle to send a message to the citizens: this is a new, happier tower? The use of colourful panels and details leads to the disappearance of the material's natural colour (concrete/brick/render) or the original aesthetics of the tower. Do you think this is important to maintain the project's original identity?
Maintaining the brickwork was a conscious decision. We managed to revitalise its appearance just by changing the mortar colour and the window frames. This was the vehicle to maintain/revitalise the tower's architectural integrity. This was also a scheme about renewal and reuse of the main building fabric as well as the vast improvement of the habitable spaces.

20. Did the first retrofit commission lead to commissions of further refurbishments?
I am not sure if they got more commissions after I left.

21. This is the bibliography we have about this building, could you suggest any other relevant documents that are missing from our list?
FCH has a fully documented record of the scheme, with original materials.

Interview with Jonathan Falkingham, Urban Splash (Park Hill, Sheffield)

1. How was this project commissioned?
It was a long conception period, at least 10 years for sure. It was a process initiated by the Sheffield City Council. The project was launched at the Venice Biennale, eight years ago.

2. Confirmation of key dates: when was the project commissioned?
I don't remember the exact dates, it was a very long process.

3. When did the building works get started? When was it completed?
I don't remember the exact dates. It was completed in 2011.

4. **Who owns the tower?**
   About one-third of the estate is still social housing owned by the Sheffield City Council, another third has been privatised, while another third is in a shared ownership status. The ground floor area has some commercial functions as well.

5. **Was this your first post-war tower block refurbishment project?**
   It was definitely the first large-scale retrofit project we completed.

6. **What was the social, technical and architectural condition in which you found the estate when you started to work on this project?**
   The building was in a very bad condition, socially and structurally. There was vandalism everywhere, outdoor toilets, drugs, and violence. There were serious fire protection and technical issues. The heating system was in a very bad condition.

7. **How have you approached this project (design concept and methodology) in relation to the improvements that had been requested?**
   We always start by examining the building and look at the good sides of it as well as into what needs to be changed. It is a selective process. The complex was suffering from extreme social problems, such as drugs and crime. We wanted to demonstrate transformation, the change should become evident.

8. **From your point of view, were there any important values in the initial design that should be preserved and or even enhanced in this project? Were you aiming at preserving or changing its identity?**
   Yes, there were many architectural qualities worthy of being preserved, especially the 'streets in the sky' concept and the brickwork colour scheme. It is a Grade II listed building.

9. **Which retrofit insulation techniques did you use? Was the design intervention affected by the insulating product palette? Is it too simplistic? To what degree was the colour scheme determined by it?**
   We have used anodised insulated panels to over-clad the brick walls and have replaced the old windows with new, double-glazed windows. Central entrances were moved indoors. We could not insulate the concrete structure, so cold bridges still exist there. Ceiling height maximisation was preferred to insulation sometimes.
   We kept the brickwork colour scheme and transferred it to the anodised panels. Overall, we wanted to demonstrate transformation and high quality.

10. **To what degree were stakeholders involved in the refurbishment process? Did they have an impact on project design?**
    We had a very good collaboration with the stakeholders. They were real partners. There was a big working group including English Heritage,

City Council and residents. It added value. The original architect was involved too. Yes, the stakeholders did have a positive impact on various decisions.

11. **What were the restrictions you faced during this refurbishment? Did they impose changes or compromises in your initial proposal?**
All restrictions were imposed by the Grade II listing. English Heritage was observing the process. The 'streets in the sky' concept was important to us and therefore it was retained. We removed the stacked bridges, which were in a very bad condition and developed central indoor entrances, within the building volume.

12. **The refurbishment has taken place with the tower inhabited?**
The block remained inhabited, but occupants were moved to other parts of the complex for as long as the building works were affecting a certain section of the building.

13. **Did you benefit from any governmental refurbishment schemes? If so, did this have an impact on the project? Do these programmes need to become more specific (including renewable energy and aesthetic parameters)?**
No, the project was financed through the privatisation of the property.

14. **Was the retrofit commissioned in order to meet the UK's Carbon Plan? If so, are you meeting the targets?**
No, that would only have been possible by over-cladding the entire structure.

15. **Did you use any renewable energy systems? If yes, which ones? Did they affect your design approach?**
No.

16. **Any post-occupancy measurements taken/or planned to be taken to actually check the tower's performance?**
No.

17. **Did the retrofit affect the building's social structure?**
Yes, de facto. Many of the old residents have left. There is a commercial zone on the ground floor, functioning as a cultural hub, many creative businesses have settled in.

18. **Are there a limited number of contractors/manufacturers involved in most of the refurbishment projects taking place in the country?**
There are obviously some contractors which have more experience with retrofit projects, they tend to get more retrofit commissions than others.

19. For architects who changed the colour in their towers: why did you do this? Was this your own choice or was this requested by the client/stakeholders?

The colour pallet from the brick gradient was already there. We kept that principle, replacing it with more colourful, stronger tones. Eco west was the colour curator.

20. After being re-clad, do the towers lose their individuality? Which cultural or heritage-related values are more vulnerable?

That did not happen with Park Hill, the complex kept its unique character.

21. Did the first retrofit commission lead to commissions of further refurbishments?

Yes, possibly. Considering Park Hill, we have only completed phase one, so now we are continuing with the other. We have also been commissioned to do the Balfron Tower, another iconic building. We are also looking into the conversion of 1960s–1970s offices into apartments.

22. This is the bibliography we have about this building, could you suggest any other relevant documents that are missing from our list?

No, not at the moment, but you should contact us again to get original photographs and documents about the project.

Interview with Craig Bolton and Paul Swallow, West and Machell Architects (Greenhouse, Leeds)

1. How was this project commissioned?

The Council invited developers to come forward to purchase the site. The Council favoured our client's proposal for its modern, forward-thinking sustainable design.

2. Confirmation of key dates: when was the project commissioned?

In 2005, we first started looking at feasibility and sketch scheme options.

3. When did building works get started? When was it completed?

The works started in 2008, and it was completed in 2010.

4. Who owns the tower?

CITU developed the scheme into the Greenhouse. It used to be a Workers Hostel owned by Leeds City Council and was later bought by our client for development into private apartments, office and live-work units.

5. Was this your first post-war tower block refurbishment project?

It was the first large-scale 'exemplar sustainable' project for the practice, many other projects followed. We gained a lot of experience in the use of renewable energies and how best to use them in new commissions.

CHAPTER 5 Conversations with the architects

229

6. What was the social, technical and architectural condition in which you found the estate when you started to work on this project?
    The building was in a bad condition, it was abandoned around 1988. It became a real social problem within the area.

7. How have you approached this project (design concept and methodology) in relation to the improvements that had been requested?
    The building was used for hostel accommodation. The building was split into male and female sides, each side with cellular bedroom accommodation and communal washrooms within the basement. To create modern internal apartment layouts and improve density, we started by removing the four inner courtyards and creating one big internal court. We then added a new internal ring of new build around the central courtyard. We then added two additional storeys on the rooftop. The floor plates were then subdivided into a number of studio, one-, two- and three-bedroom apartments and office space. The eco-element was a significant client driver for the project. Our sustainable design starting point was to 'build tight, insulate right'. We then looked at sustainable renewable technologies.

8. From your point of view, were there any important values in the initial design that should be preserved and or even enhanced in this project? Were you aiming at preserving or changing its identity?
    The corner and five-storey vertical slot windows were the most interesting feature of the original Art Deco design. All the existing openings were maintained but we always felt it important to give the building a new identity.

9. Which retrofit insulation techniques did you use? Was the design intervention affected by the insulating product palette? Is it too simplistic? To what degree was the colour scheme determined by it?
    We over-clad the brickwork with a high performance insulated render system (130 mm). The two additional storeys were clad with a rain-screen boarding system We used materials with high U-values in both cases. The lower area was clad in a simple clean looking minimalist white. The upper two floors a dark grey and green contrasting top. The simplicity of the base with the contrasting top makes for a striking modern design.

10. To what degree were stakeholders involved in the refurbishment process? Did they have an impact on the project's design?
    There were regular meetings with CITU, discussing all matters arising.

11. What were the restrictions you faced during this refurbishment? Did they impose changes or compromises in your initial proposal?
    The combination of old and new designs coming together and including all the renewable technologies were an interesting challenge.

12. The refurbishment has taken/will take place with the building inhabited?
No, the building has been abandoned since 1988.

13. Did you benefit from any governmental refurbishment schemes? If so, did this have an impact on the project? Do these programmes need to become more specific (including renewable energy and aesthetic parameters)?
The project was privately funded but aimed for the very highest exemplary sustainable standards.

14. Was the retrofit commissioned in order to meet the UK's Carbon Plan? If so, are you meeting the targets?
Not directly, but we followed sustainable homes standards best practice.

15. Did you use any renewable energy systems? If yes, which ones? Did they affect your design approach?
Yes, there are plenty of them. There are solar panels, rainwater harvesting systems and wind turbines on the roof; we are using geothermic energy to pre-heat the water; there is an IT intelligent home system which regulates energy consumption. Occupants can monitor their energy bills, or book a pool car from the basement. One can trace where electricity is being spent. It makes green living into almost a lifestyle. The highly visible turbines act also as a symbol, they signalise the eco-friendly element of the building. Renewable/sustainable sourced materials have been specified where possible. Everything from bamboo timber kitchen worktops and floors to recycled plastic door numbers.

16. Who was the contractor involved? Did they have any previous retrofit experience?
Our contractor was Clegg Construction, they were chosen by CITU. I think they had worked on building retrofits before.

17. Did the retrofit affect the building's social structure?
Many of the occupants have an eco-friendly lifestyle, so the building became a hub for eco-friendly activities. It is fully occupied at the moment; it became a very popular property. It has its own strong community. There is a deli at the ground floor, they have eco-friendly market activities and off-site allotment schemes to grow your own food.

18. For architects who changed the colour in their buildings: why did you do this? Was this your own choice or was this requested by the client/stakeholders?
We wanted to change the building's identity. The green tones were matching the projects name, 'The Greenhouse' and added a splash of modern colour to the top of the building. The white colour took inspiration from the 1930s Art Deco-style buildings.

CHAPTER 5 Conversations with the architects

19. Did the first retrofit commission lead to commissions of further refurbishments?
    Yes, we have commissioned quite a few other projects since then.

20. This is the bibliography we have about this building, could you suggest any other relevant documents that are missing from our list?
    We can share with you original information about the building.

Chapter 6
Final discussion
Conclusions from the tower blocks analysis

Change of colour and materiality

Change of colour and materiality has been observed in almost all non-listed tower blocks. It is a trend that is evident in the stakeholders' interviews, as well as through the towers' photographic documentation. The overall need for image change translates into a change of colour and material. Concrete and brick are being left behind. Horizontality observed in most original elevations of the housing blocks is being replaced with verticality (e.g. Chalcots Estate, Figure 6.1) or geometrical patterns (e.g. Netherthorpe estate, Figure 6.2). The retrofitted buildings try to break with their past and all the negative memories they have been associated with.

▼ Figure 6.1

Verticality expressed on the Chalcot Estate's façade, London

▼ Figure 6.2

Geometrical patterns, Netherthorpe Complex, Sheffield

Choice of colour and the generic re-colouring strategy vary. This is a process which usually involves all stakeholders, including the tenants. In most estates, such as the Callow Mount (Figure 6.3), the architects have tried to harmonise the buildings with their environment, in this case, through the choice of green colour in a forest background. In other cases, as in Park Hill, the new colour is inspired by the original condition. The vertical gradient composed of different earthy brick tones is replaced by a new gradient of shiny red, orange and yellow anodised aluminium panels. In the case of the Greenhouse, the green colour was used on the rooftop extension with a symbolic purpose, associated with the building's name.

In many cases, the use of white, light grey or light pastel colours (e.g. Little Venice Towers, Bow Cross, Chalcots Estate, Edward Woods, Figure 6.4) allow the buildings to clearly break with their brick-dominated build environment. In other estates, such as the Netherthorpe Complex, colour patterns follow the *Zeitgeist* of their time, adopting symmetrical, post-modern pastel patterns.

Maintenance of the original colour and materiality is common with retrofitted listed buildings (e.g. Brunswick Centre and Trellick Tower). The original design is being respected and the character of the building remains unchanged. The case of Adlington Tower (Figure 6.5) is one of the few precedents, where an 'insignificant', common-looking council tower keeps its brick materiality and original design. As the project architect states, the brick walls received a new, darker mortar and their appearance was renewed without over-cladding or colour change.

Looking at the overall picture, one could argue that the urge for individual appearance leads to another way of unification, imposed by the predominating retrofit techniques, colour pallets and materiality. A new colourful aluminium-render look is gradually replacing brick and concrete exterior walls. There is not a common colour strategy. In some cases, architects try to harmonise with the building's surroundings, while in other cases light colours are chosen in order to break with it, as well as with the past. More colourful retrofits have been observed in the North-west of England (e.g. Park Hill, Callow Mount) rather than in London.

▲ Figure 6.3

Green colour tones used to harmonise the tower blocks with their environment, Callow Mount Complex, Sheffield

▲ Figure 6.4

Light colours used in Edward Woods Estate's façade retrofit, London

▲ Figure 6.5

Original material retained, brick walls received new mortar, Adlington Tower, Liverpool
Source: Photograph © Roy Roberts.

▲ Figure 6.6

Rooftop extension, Waybridge Point, London

Retrofit strategies

Insulating the housing block is the architects' main concern. The combination of the 'wrap it' and 'replace it' techniques offers by far the most common retrofit strategies recorded. Most of the estates receive a new insulated over-cladding and are having their old single-glazed windows replaced by new, high performance double- or triple-glazed frames. Insulated render or aluminium rainscreen systems are the predominant techniques applied, imposing an entirely new aesthetics on the blocks. Most of the listed buildings (e.g. Trellick Tower) receive only minor skin repairs and window replacement, leaving the buildings exposed to cold bridges and energy loss. The 'add in' strategy has been only partly applied to Keeling House, as the old windows were not replaced and leaseholders installed secondary glazing systems from the inside of the apartments. The 'add-on' strategy is commonly observed, as most of the towers receive new entrances, additional rooftop floors (e.g. Weybridge Point, Figure 6.6) or even additions to their inner courtyards (e.g. Greenhouse).

Almost all the towers recorded in this sample have received electrical and mechanical upgrades, such as a new heating system, boiler, lighting and kitchen replacement. These measures are often subsidised by governmental schemes (e.g. 'Decent Homes' scheme).

Design quality and innovation

The quality of design and the drive for innovative solutions observed in this sample are rather limited. In most cases, as stated by the interviewed architects, design intentions are driven by pragmatic parameters, such as the budget and technical or environmental issues. In many cases, such as Greenhouse, the Bow Cross complex or Adlington Tower, space planning improvements associated with accessibility, and floor plan extension are the main design drivers. The limited budget seems to reduce design ambitions to colour change and balcony enclosure (e.g. Callow Mount Complex). Both interventions eliminate the 'brutalist' horizontality dominating the towers' appearance, replacing it with a base, middle and top order (e.g. Parsons House, Figure 6.7).

In some housing blocks (e.g. Little Venice Towers, Greenhouse) the initial design is maintained as in its original state, despite the complete materiality change. Only in a few tower blocks, can a clear, ambitious design intention be identified. The Parsons House retrofit with its characteristic, red vertical rails is one of the first which took place. It completely transforms the original tower, emphasising its verticality, creating a high-tech style 'crown top'. The 3 Towers' intervention is probably the most dramatic image change observed. The new façade introduces a completely different, irregular design rhythm, changing the building's proportions by embedding the balconies within the massing and adding a colourful top ending addition. Similar elements can be also observed in the Tamworth Towers retrofit, including glazed balconies, newly introduced horizontal façade elements and a colourful topping addition.

However, more radical, innovative solutions such as the Tour Bois-le-Prêtre (Figure 6.8) retrofit in Paris have not been observed in our sample.[1] The 1960s tower block was completely transformed by retrofit architects Druot, Lacaton & Vassal. All floor slabs were extended outwards increasing the room sizes and creating new conservatories and balconies (Figure 6.9). A new façade of corrugated aluminium over-cladded the new exterior of the tower, adding new large windows and glazed balconies. Floor-to-ceiling glass separates the apartments from the new terraces to let more natural light into each residence. Besides an entirely new appearance, the building was transformed entirely in its substance, receiving an additional winter garden buffer zone, increasing its overall surface by 3,560 sq m. The project was awarded the 2013 'Designs of the Year Award' offering a precedent for future retrofit interventions.

The Marriot Tower retrofit in Frankfurt (Figure 6.10) is another case of extraordinary design innovation.[2] The 160 m-tall hotel tower, design by Just. Burgeff Architekten & Agkathidis adopted emerging technologies in its anodised aluminium panel over cladding design. The folded insulated panels form a moiré pattern on the building's façade, allowing it to change its appearance according to daylight changes or different points of view. The tower achieved green building status and was awarded the Eurosolar Prize 2011.

Another innovative retrofit intervention has been realised in Bordeaux. The Lormont urban development project consists of three former brutalist

▲ Figure 6.7

Base, middle and top order on Parsons House retrofit, London

▲ Figure 6.8

Tour Bois-le-Prêtre, extended floor slabs retrofit, Paris

▲ Figure 6.9

Tour Bois-le-Prêtre, interior view of winter gardens

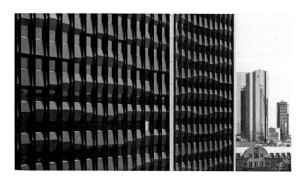

▲ Figure 6.10

Marriott Tower retrofit with folded aluminium panels, Frankfurt-upon-Main

housing blocks, which were recladded with translucent, sliding polycarbonate windows, creating an ever-changing façade.[3] The additional skin layer has increased the living space, while thermally insulating the towers and offered them a unique contemporary identity. The loggia spaces are accessed through sliding doors from the living rooms in each apartment. The polycarbonate surfaces that cover the previously open sections of the balconies are fitted to tracks, allowing them to slide between open and closed, as LAN architects describe.

One cannot claim that it is not just budget-related issues, which enabled innovative design solutions, as none of these projects was particularly expensive. It appears to be related to different ambitions, the design culture and the project's environment, which allowed architects to go beyond the corporate, standardised retrofit solutions as commonly practised.

Renewable energies

Only nine of the 39 estates examined in this sample (23 per cent) have received some form of renewable energy appliance. Photovoltaic panels have been installed in all of them. In some cases, such as in Edwards Woods and Ferrier Point, the panels are integrated into the façades, becoming an actual design element, demonstrating the new eco-friendly image of the building. Edward Woods and Greenhouse use wind turbines on their rooftops. Greenhouse is the most advanced housing block in terms of renewable energy utilisation. Besides solar and wind power, the building applies geothermic energy to preheat the water to be used for heating, as well as various smart technology systems minimising energy consumption. According to the project's architect, Craig Bolton, the building has managed to become attractive to tenants by advertising an eco-friendly lifestyle. The energy produced by those systems is consumed in the estate's communal spaces.

According to the interviewed architects, the high cost of renewable energies in combination with the relatively small power produced and the long payoff period makes their use less attractive to developers and owners. They are often considered more of an image maker, an advertisement for what the building stands for.

CHAPTER 6 Final discussion

Listed buildings

The sample of housing blocks presented in this book includes a total of eight Grade II listed buildings. Seven of them are located in Greater London and one in Sheffield. They are all characteristic examples of the 1960s and 1970s modern-brutalist architecture and have often become real city icons (e.g. Trellick Tower, Brunswick Centre, Balfron Tower, Park Hill). Due to the restrictions imposed by their listed status, all buildings have been retrofitted with great respect to their original design, only replacing the old single-glazed windows and repairing the damaged concrete or brick outer skin. Park Hill is the only retrofit to be awarded a RIBA award, making it the best-published retrofit recorded. However, respect for aesthetics is directly linked to compromises in performance, as all of them maintain cold bridges, exposed floor slabs and lack adequate thermal insulation. Keeling House is the most extreme case, as no insulation measure has been taken, while Trellick, Balfron and Brunswick Centre received only double glazing. Park Hill (Figure 6.11) and Golden Lane Estate received new insulated panels, but their concrete structure remained exposed.

▲ Figure 6.11

Park Hill, insulated anodised aluminium panels retrofit, Sheffield

Social sustainability

Social sustainability is a critical and highly complex issue, in all of the housing blocks examined. While all of them suffered physical decline during the late 1980s and 1990s, their pre-retrofit social status varies. In Bow Cross, for instance, the social structure had already collapsed, the towers were highly unpopular, stigmatised by very high crime rates. In other cases, such as Greenhouse, the buildings were abandoned or uninhabitable. Other estates, such as Golden Lane or Balfron Tower managed to maintain affordable rents in combination with a 'healthy' social structure. Thus, the post-retrofit impact on their social composition differs. However, by looking at the overall picture of the sample presented here, the trend towards a second wave of privatisation, following the 'right to buy' wave in the 1980s, becomes evident. Many of the pre-retrofit residents leave, and property prices rise.

In Park Hill, for instance, as stated by Urban Splash director Jonathan Franklin, only one-third of the apartments remain social housing, while one-third is fully privatised, and the remaining one-third is in shared ownership status, thus partly privatised. Part of the former apartments on the ground floor have been converted into working spaces, attracting young creative businesses as residents. The post-retrofit status of Great Arthur House is the same, with the three ownership types replacing the majority of the former council-owned apartments.

▲ Figure 6.12

Balfron Tower, in uninhabited condition, November 2016

In the case of Greenhouse, where the property was fully abandoned for years, the building was privatised before being retrofitted. According to its project architect, Craig Bolton, the building is fully inhabited now, contributing to the revitalisation of the entire neighbourhood.

Looking at Balfron Tower (Figure 6.12), we can observe a different situation. According to the building residents' online archive,[4] the large majority of the flats (99 out of 146) were in ownership of the council and only about one-third on leasehold until the property's ownership was transferred from the council to Poplar HARCA in 2007, under the condition of bringing all flats up to the Decent Homes Standard. Since then, the tower has been designated with 'decant status', thus all occupants had to abandon the building, in preparation for its refurbishment. Only a few leaseholders able to contribute to the refurbishment cost were able to maintain their leasehold status, while all remaining tenants will not be able to return. It is notable that these figures were never announced by Poplar HARCA. The refurbished apartments will be sold under 'Balfron Tower Developments', and all pre-retrofit social rents will be lost. Similar incidents have been reported in many other estates. The trend towards complete privatisation is much stronger in the Greater London Area, where property prices are much higher than in the rest of the country. It is obvious that local and central governments have to realise that if affordable housing is to be maintained in Greater London, further funding for retrofits and housing associations is necessary. Ongoing privatisation and gentrification of council estates lead to a massive decrease in social sustainability.

In contrast, the ownership status in the post-retrofit Adlington Tower in Liverpool did not change, as the property remains majority council-owned. Most old tenants have returned to the building, while the retrofit intervention managed to attract additional new tenants, who occupied pre-retrofit empty flats. This is a different situation in the North-west, where partial retrofitting of unoccupied properties can attract new tenants and contribute to social sustainability.

Talking to the architects

The interviews with the architects reveal many common approaches, but also differences. Starting with their design approach, the urge for image renewal is common to almost all of them. With the exemption of JRA, who clearly wanted to keep Great Arthur House's design identity as pure as possible, all the other offices aimed to demonstrate change in one way or another. Nobody stated any clear conceptual approach, linked to a design philosophy or manifesto. It is mostly pragmatic drivers playing a role, such as attracting new tenants, improving the floor plan layout, minimising costs and demolitions.

All the interviewees, except JRA, adopted colour or materiality change as a means of identity change. Colours are chosen by creative directors or teams, often in collaboration with clients and stakeholders. Contextual coherence is a common aim.

The commission process is described similarly in all the interviews. HLP give the most detailed description. Commissions take place through a small invited competition advertised online, accessible to the common EU market. Practices can submit their tender in a team with their consultants and proceed to the next phase according to their score.

All interviewees confirm the very poor pre-retrofit condition of the properties. Criminality is mentioned as a major problem by PRP and Urban Splash. Physical decay and damage were a common problem, making some of the buildings uninhabitable (Greenhouse) or threatening them with demolition (Bow Cross).

Looking at the sustainable interventions, all the architects try to insulate in the best possible way, according to the given design framework. West and Machell Architects are the only ones who used an extensive variety of renewable energies, including wind turbines, geothermal and photovoltaic technologies, followed by HLP who used eco-pods and photovoltaic panels in some of their projects. None of the architects stated the UK's Carbon Plan as a target they were directly aiming for, but are confident that their interventions have contributed towards that aim.

All the architects describe collaboration with stakeholders as productive, positive and important for the project's development. Landlords, tenants, housing associations are the common stakeholders, while in listed buildings, the Twentieth Century Society and English Heritage are mentioned as key contributors to the process. Regular consultation meetings were a common method of communication.

The retrofits had a substantial impact on the towers' social sustainability, as all the architects confirmed. In almost all cases, many of the old tenants have left their apartments, the ownership status of the apartments is changing. In some cases (Greenhouse and Park Hill), non-residential functions are being introduced as well. Gentrification is more intense in London, as described by JRA. Adlington Tower in Liverpool appears to be an exception, as all tenants returned to their refurbished apartments, as project architect Roy Roberts stated.

As to the major obstacles and restrictions, they vary from project to project. In some cases, it is the very tight budget and the extremely bad condition of the property, in other cases, the integration of sustainable technologies, the tight conditions on site or the regulations set by the Grade II listing.

Prospects: energy efficiency, heritage and social sustainability

If 80 per cent of the building stock will still be with us in 2050, how well will it meet our needs, that is, what is required in 2050? Which aspects and in which ways do these buildings need to be adapted or renewed? What are the key parameters that will determine a successful adaptation, to obtain buildings that will efficiently cater for our needs? We can look at this problem from different perspectives. There are factors related to local cultural and social morphology, and factors that are purely related to the physical description of the building, such as form, construction techniques, maintenance, infrastructure of services, landscape/site and urban context. Buildings not only have to be assessed in terms of their state of repair, but also in terms of how successfully this built environment responds to future needs: new types of households, new activities developed at home, climate change, environmental performance . . .

In this final section, we have identified several critical topics, for which we are providing some insights. We do not intend to cover each of these very complex problems in depth, but rather point out what we believe are key issues in any strategy to improve future plans and interventions. Our intention is to use this chapter both as a showcase of some of the most promising initiatives, and as a catalyst to trigger a more extensive discussion.

The demolition vs refurbishment debate

There is a growing body of research evidencing that extending the lifecycle of buildings through refurbishment is preferable to demolition in terms of economic, ecological and social impacts. Diverse examples demonstrate that even hard-to-treat structures can be retrofitted to achieve the same high energy efficiency standards found in new construction, especially when the retrofit work is planned so that residents can stay in their homes, thus avoiding the negative economic and emotional impact of being decanted during the process. It has also been proven that retrofitting existing buildings can provide income-generating opportunities. Despite these facts, the discussion around demolition versus refurbishment is still open. At the beginning of 2016 the government was determined to demolish 100 tower blocks[5] (Figure 6.13).

▶ Figure 6.13

Demolition of tower block, Manchester, UK

The argument in favour of demolition is based on the speed and efficiency of our current decarbonisation strategy. The government calculates that in order to meet the 2050 target, 5,000 homes need to be refurbished per day.[6] According to their modelling results, the Average Standard Assessment Procedure rating can only improve from 44 (1996) to 66 (2050), so the only way to decarbonise the UK is to increase the demolition rates, from the current 20,000 homes/day to 80,000 homes/day, to get rid of all the worst performing buildings.[7] This estimate doesn't include important considerations, and these actually form the base for those in favour of refurbishing:

- The heritage and sociocultural value of the evaluated properties.
- The energy and capital invested: properties in the public sector are currently less likely to be the worst performing stock, with many of them having gone through improvements over the years, they are more likely to have higher embodied carbon and more energy-efficient measures installed.
- The urban systems and infrastructure currently serving these properties.
- Demolition costs estimated £50,000 per home.[8] In addition to this, there is a waste impact: the construction and demolition sector contributes 35 per cent of all waste in the UK, with more than 4 million tonnes of waste to landfill each year.[9] Although 73 per cent of the waste is recycled, refurbishing still provides a lower impact on the environment since demolition waste and new construction impacts are avoided.
- Refurbishing delivers better performance housing at a faster rate than demolishing and building anew, and permits retention of social housing stock, that is continuously shrinking.
- Rehousing process costs and well-being impact on tenants: involving the use of the private rented sector, with higher housing benefit bills and even homelessness. The reduction in council stock also implies that displaced families can end up in houses in worst conditions than the ones they left.
- During the demolishing and rebuilding process there are a number of negative impacts on the community living in the block and their vicinity to take into consideration:
  - Emptying a large estate is a process that takes between 5–10 years, meaning that many properties will be empty for long periods while some neighbours still live in the estate. A large number of empty properties increases the probabilities of crime and vandalism incidents, endangering the remaining tenants. This situation also seriously affects the communal services (i.e. shops or schools), to the point they can even be forced to close, leaving the community without these services.[10]
  - Another negative consequence is the tendency to lose housing capacity in the estates during this process, with a loss of up to 500 homes a year. This, together with the problem that the replacement homes might no longer be affordable to social tenants due to construction costs and benefit cuts (above all, in London), leaves low-income families in a very weak position to access a decent home.[11]

Despite all this evidence, each building needs to be assessed on an individual basis. In order to cope with the different factors and complex variables involved in this evaluation, there are several technical models that work, based on building performance, mostly related to energy, environmental and economic performance. These mathematical models are based on numerous assumptions, for instance, in relation to consumption patterns, weather patterns, standards, occupants' behaviour (i.e. comfort preference, knowledge to make good use of environmental measures), building resilience and ageing capability, etc. This is a very time-consuming, subjective and complex calculation, that shows great scope for improvement in different aspects, most obviously the actual modelling techniques. Undertaking this calculation also reveals that retrofitting is still an incipient discipline, in need of a more robust structure to support it, requiring:

- Research on the design, installation and operation of energy-efficiency upgrades.
- Development of the retrofitting market regarding skills, knowledge and increased supply of sustainable construction techniques and materials. There is still a higher risk in taking less instructed labour in these subjects due to a lack of regulations in this area, and using less conventional, established and even bespoke materials that usually implies higher capital costs.
- Finance mechanisms are less well established than for new construction.
- Management capacity to understand and undertake retrofits. This involves access to qualified information, public policies, incentives, standards, and finance as well as having the ability to judge, make informed decisions involving long-term scenarios, and being inclined to invest. Social landlords are in a more supported position than individual owner-occupiers to develop this capacity, thanks to the existing network of stakeholders involved in any decisions, and therefore this makes the retrofit of social towers an easier enterprise to plan. The typical cost of low carbon measures is £5,000–£12,000 per flat. The incentives provided and the obligations imposed on the public sector, together with the fact that individual owners prefer to invest in decoration (i.e. renovating the bathroom or the kitchen) rather than insulating their houses, have led to a much bigger proportion of energy efficiency measures installed in social housing than in housing stock in the private sector.
- Establishing standards that regulate the level of retrofit to be attained. A study developed by the Energy Savings Trust entitled 'Roadmap to 60%: eco-refurbishment of 1960s flats',[12] categorises energy-efficient refurbishment as being of low, middle, and high cost. This report states that a '60% reduction in CO_2 emissions by 2050 can only be achieved by "deep retrofit" measures', meaning extensive work to the building fabric, a complex mixture of technologies, customised design, structural changes, user engagement to ensure levels of savings are achieved and a capital cost of £10,000 per flat.[13] Deep retrofitting also implies six to eight weeks of works in the building, and supplementary costs if the residents must be relocated.

However, some individual initiatives challenge these facts using creative proposals. In line with Druot, Lacaton & Vassal's approach in Bois-le-Prêtre, Savills estate agents, in a report to the Cabinet Office in January 2016, argued for restoring London's street patterns by 'regenerating and intensifying' large housing estates, adding 50 per cent more homes.[14] Addressing housing renovation means working with the city on strategies that embrace private and public space. For that, it is necessary to identify unplanned interstices, space opportunities and energy flows. Equally, it entails the responsibility of looking for and interpreting new forms of order, as opposed to consuming new land. The focus should be on the optimisation of space, awareness of orientation, geographic and environmental conditions, transforming from the inside towards the outside. City growth is not about size, but about social quality. And, finally, it is critical to claim locality: form and materiality generated within the local culture, rather than importing from other cultural realities. In Druot, Lacaton & Vassal's words: 'Never demolish, never remove or replace, always add, transform and reuse!'[15]

Savills' fundamental proposal of 'long-term investment in low-cost renting' allows existing tenants to remain in the community mixed with new neighbours through a process of densification and upgrading, rather than demolition, thus fitting more homes into existing estates. Many of these modernist estates are designed in ways that do not maximise land use. Savills' proposal focuses on the use of infill building to create denser street frontages within the estate, following traditional street patterns. The main goal would be to enliven the ground floor-level experience by replacing empty spaces with housing and services. They suggest that density could be increased by at least 50 per cent, most easily in estates that have a stable community and well-maintained facilities, but even more challenging cases can benefit from more intensive designed street levels, by modifying or getting rid of outdated or disused landscape and circulation elements typical of those years. In some of the examples studied they found out that roads, pavements and car parks occupied more space than anything else in the estates. They proposed operations such as to increase the land take for buildings, preserve open space, give space over to private gardens, include commercial units, open new roads to re-knit the site into surrounding streets improving accessibility and permeability, and offer quieter back streets and mews-like enclaves. By providing commercial routes and well-connected streets, they offer the opportunity to landowners to diversify risk away from residential property and increase the real estate value.

An example of this strategy successfully developed is the Edward Woods Estate (Figure 6.14), achieved during its energy-efficiency refurbishment in 2012–2014, which combined the existing high- and medium-rise blocks' upgrades with the construction of new housing. This arrangement granted the retention

▲ Figure 6.14

Edward Woods Estate, combination of refurbishment with additional housing units

of the nearly 2,000 almost entirely low-income council tenants while using the new housing as a key opportunity for income generation to pay the works and as an instrument to increase the social mix in the estate.[16] The same principle can be used at both dwelling and estate level: working with the interstices, the spaces between housing units and blocks, to form street and city. The tools are assembling, dismantling, adding, modifying, conserving/minimising demolition, expanding, reordering, collage, densifying, flexibility, accessibility, and diversity of space and use.

Engaging householders to take up low carbon retrofits

Even though refurbishment could be the best way forward for most of the buildings, engaging householders to embrace what can be a long and hassling process is a very challenging task (Figure 6.15). Either decanted or kept *in situ*, comprehensive energy-efficient retrofit works can be a very stressful process for residents, in most cases entailing a three-year period of noise, dust, intrusion and services disruption. This is an obvious obstacle for engagement, which together with other factors such as financial affordability, and access to knowledge and advice about the right type of retrofit measures, present a key barrier that needs to be addressed. Many of the incentives launched by the government try to overcome these obstacles and present attractive vehicles to create demand for energy-efficiency improvements: 'low hassle measures that achieve big energy savings at a highly subsidised price (often for free)'.[17]

Despite all the attempts to make things easy, the uptake is not only still low, but most importantly, not enough to achieve the climate change targets. There is no doubt about the potential benefits of these incentives, but the key issue is to make appropriate use of them. An independent study developed by

▶ Figure 6.15

Engaging the tenants in the design process, Ladywell Green estate, Greater Manchester

CHAPTER 6 Final discussion

the UK Green Building Council in 2013, after analysing all the existing incentives and several other options, suggested three additional measures to the existing policy framework to boost the number of homeowners engaged in retrofitting: (1) Stamp Duty Land Tax; (2) Council Tax; and (3) an Energy Efficiency Feed-in-Tariff.[18] The main goal of this study is to show that there is a number of feasible tools for creating a long-term driver for retrofit, each with its unique set of benefits and challenges and that more diversity, information and publicity are needed to reach the main agents in this process.

The proposed incentives have not been implemented, and there is no evidence of to what extent these or any other independent proposals have been evaluated by any governmental agencies. Ideally, industry should work with the government to evaluate these proposals in accordance with objectives, political and economic context, feasibility, and urgency to boost efficiency in uptake.

This is a crucial aspect of the retrofit process that would require higher transparency and more detailed information: how is the strategy to create demand devised? Why is it not solidly informed by the actual users and professionals who should supervise the quality of the work?

Lack of institutional holistic strategy: fire safety

There is a considerable concern to meet carbon reduction targets, which are obviously an urgent mission where incentives are instrumental, but we believe that we are missing the opportunity to have a more holistic programme coordinating these interventions.

This can clearly be done at a technical level to ensure minimum quality and safety standards are met. A challenge in considering an existing block for refurbishment is to discover what the construction is and whether any over-cladding has taken place since it can hide the construction, especially if the building used a large panel system. The current teams making decisions in local authorities might not know how the original buildings were built or, in many cases, altered over the years.

An example of this lack of control was evident during the fatal fire that occurred at Lakanal House in Southwark (Figure 6.16), London, in 2009, which took the lives of six people. Unfortunately, as we were ending this last chapter, tragedy struck again on 14 June 2017: a horrendous fire at Grenfell Tower (Figure 6.17), North Kensington, destroyed 151 homes and caused 80 deaths,[19] generating a whole new level of public interest and concern around fire safety in buildings, and especially in tower blocks. Since then, the focus has moved radically from energy: the media and public opinion are now almost entirely concentrated on fire safety

▲ Figure 6.16

Lakanal House repaired, after the fire

in high-rise housing, and the strong suspicion that some failure either in the design, the specification or the installation of external cladding played a major part in the disaster. Research into the tragic incident at Grenfell Tower is moving fast, both in terms of the inquiry and producing abundant professional discussion. For this reason, we have decided to further develop this section and respond as best we can to the situation as we go to press.

At the time, the Lakanal House fire was referred to in the news as the worst ever tower block fire, and urgent recommendations intended to prevent similar events in the future. Unfortunately, eight years later, we are witnessing an even worse tragedy at the Grenfell Tower in Kensington. Reflecting on this new tragedy has understandably prompted questions that were already asked not long ago during the Lakanal House inquiry, which took place between 2009 and 2013.

Lakanal House consisted of 98 flats in 14 storeys on top of a two-storey podium, all built of *in situ* reinforced concrete. Over the years, a great number of improvements had been carried out, and a couple of years before the fire, a full refurbishment made the flats weathertight and thermally insulated, but the whole intervention did not account for fire protection. Originally built as a Section 20 building under the London Building Acts in 1959, it should have had a one-hour fire resistance between tenancies. The former timber window frames were replaced with two-piece aluminium frames, where the outer frame was separated from the inner one by a plastic insert to prevent cold bridges. The spandrel panels were replaced with TRESPA panels, which together with the double-glazing and aluminium frames, amply fulfilled the thermal problems. The fire broke out in Flat 65 on the ninth floor, and within ten minutes the flames were already two floors above, with window frames and panes of glass falling from the building.[20]

▲ Figure 6.17

Burned-out Grenfell Tower

The Grenfell Tower retrofit was designed by Studio E Architects and retrofitted by the contractor firm Roydon for a budget of £8.6 million.[21] The 24-storey building was built in 1974 by the Kensington City Council. Studio E Architects specified an insulation system comprising Celotex FR5000 insulation board attached to a timber backing. The drawings also specified a Reynobond aluminium composite material rain-screen panel to be installed 50 mm in front of the insulation. Rain-screen cladding panels can come with either a polyethylene core or a slightly more expensive, honeycombed mineral core, which is more fire-resistant. The panels used on the Grenfell Tower were the cheaper, more flammable version.[22]

The police officially confirmed that the devastating fire was started by a Hotpoint FF175BP fridge-freezer explosion, which took place inside one of the fourth-floor flats.[23] When the fire broke out, around 1 a.m., 350 people are thought to have lived in the tower's 129 flats.[24] The blast escalated rapidly, engulfing the entire building from the fourth floor upwards, killing at least 80 inhabitants. What happened inside the building remains unclear. However, many of the survivors report that the fire alarm could not be heard within the flats, smoke engulfed the tower's core as the fire spread all through the cladding. Many residents were told to stay in their flats, which proved to be fatal. Many eyewitnesses reported that they hardly managed to find the fire escape, because of the smoke in the corridors and the staircase.[25] Many of the 255 survivors suffered from smoke inhalation injuries and cyanide poisoning, as a result of burning polyisocyanurate, present in both furniture foam and insulation. The University of Leeds estimates that the burning 18 tonnes of insulation and 8 tonnes of cladding panels should have generated temperatures around 1,000°C.[26]

Research into the Lakanal House's tragedy already had evidenced a number of issues that required further consideration in fire safety design. After the devastating fire at Grenfell Tower, the same issues are manifested, being currently frantically debated by different experts. We have grouped them into five areas of discussion: (1) supervision, regulation and prevention; (2) cladding; (3) sprinklers; (4) compartmentation and layout; and (5) signage and information.

Supervision, regulation and prevention

The Lakanal House inquiry revealed that the information available regarding fire safety was ambiguous or confusing in different aspects. For starters, there is no clear legal definition of what a high-rise building is. When the London Borough of Southwark had to respond to the recommendations made by Frances Kirkham CBE, Assistant Deputy Coroner (the Coroner's Court) in 2013, they decided that her recommendation would apply to 'blocks above 30 metres, equating to those of 10 storeys and above', as specified in Code of Practice BS9991: 2011 related to the installation of sprinklers in new buildings,[27] and they also decided to apply them to 'any lower height but complex blocks, i.e. those with more than one means of escape, along with the council's sheltered housing schemes and temporary accommodation hostels which house our most vulnerable residents'[28] In specialised academic and policy-related literature, a building is considered to be high risk if it has a minimum of five or six storeys, which will require the installation of lifts. According to Section 12 of Approved Document B, Vol. 2, which covers the design of external walls for fire safety and includes specific requirements for tall buildings, they are considered as such when they are above 18 m tall.

Consequently, after the Grenfell Tower disaster, the Department for Communities and Local Government (DCLG) asked local authorities, housing associations and private owners to check residential blocks over 18 metres in height, which moves the number of storeys back to six for current checking purposes, but still no official definition of high rise has been set out yet.

Documents related to fire safety regulations for the design and construction of buildings have also elicited profuse comments from different fronts. Fire safety in UK buildings is governed by part B of the Building Regulations, which has not been reviewed in depth since 2006. Many experts claim that the document is outdated and in urgent need of a substantial renovation, focusing on evacuating people which is good, but presuming that the fire can be contained and will not spread through the façade and ingress from outside.[29] Non-combustible design choices are critical, and current regulations are not enforcing these choices.

The coroner in the Lakanal House case also called for a review of part B, requesting 'clear guidance (regulations) and expressed in words and format that are intelligible to the wide range of people and bodies engaged in construction, maintenance and refurbishment of buildings'. In this document, the Coroner corroborates that

> [the] current Approved Document B (Building Regulations) is a most difficult document to use, and it is necessary to refer to additional documents in order to find an answer to relatively straightforward questions concerning the fire protection properties of materials to be incorporated into the fabric of a building.[30]

The formal review of Approved Document B was first proposed by the Secretary of State for Communities and Local Government in 2013 in response to the Coroner's Rule 43 letter following the inquest into the deaths resulting from the 2009 fire at Lakanal House, but this still has not happened, and the official response from DCLG is not published.

After the Grenfell Tower blaze, the government created an independent advisory panel to organise the support that tower block residents need during current checks in the many existing tower blocks around the country.[31] The panel, which met for the first time at the end of June, was headed by Ken Knight, the ex-London Fire Commissioner and former government Chief Fire and Rescue Adviser, and also included Peter Bonfield, Chief Executive of the BRE; Roy Wilsher, Chair of the National Fire Chiefs Council; and Amanda Clack, President of the Royal Institution of Chartered Surveyors (RICS). Although the panel said it would 'draw in wider technical expertise as necessary to inform their advice', there is currently no representation from the RIBA or the building construction industry,[32] which has prompted comments of discontent from the architectural profession.

In the RIBA Statement on Design for Fire Safety, sent to all RIBA members on 22 June 2017, the professional body tried to give a clear message on their main concerns in relation to the regulatory and procurement regime for buildings. Their concerns are as follows:[33]

1. Delays to the review of Approved Document B, particularly with regard to the relationship of the Building Regulations to changing approaches in the design and construction of the external envelopes of buildings.
2. An Approved Document which together with related British Standards provides a very comprehensive but highly complicated regulatory framework.
3. The impact of the Regulatory Reform (Fire Safety) Order 2005, in particular, the introduction of a regime of fire risk self-assessment and the repeal of fire certificate legislation with oversight by the local fire authority.

CHAPTER 6 Final discussion

4. Developments in building procurement approaches which mean that the Lead Designer (architect or engineer) is no longer responsible for oversight of the design and the specification of materials and products from inception to completion of the project, with design responsibility often transferred to the contractor and sub-contractors, and no single point of responsibility.
5. The virtual disappearance of the role of the clerk of works or site architect and the loss of independent oversight of construction and workmanship on behalf of the client.

With this document, the RIBA urged the government to undertake an immediate review of fire safety regulations, not only for high rise but also other types of buildings, such as schools. The document also tried to provide some guidance on the use of the current regulatory framework, with a focus on cladding specification and the correct design of external walls for fire safety, which, from the beginning, have been key issues in the recent tragic events. But we believe that points 4 and 5 are also crucial aspects of this discussion, and represent a previous stage in the fire safety design process: who is responsible for the oversight of fire safety checks, and supervising that any refurbishment works or alterations in buildings are properly executed?

Deon Lombard, architect and former project director at TP Bennett, who has worked on many retrofit projects on residential towers, describes similar concerns regarding the current fire safety approval process and the spread of responsibility throughout the different parties. He claims that architects often specify materials during the planning phase, which are then replaced by alternative materials selected by the developers, contractors or sub-contractors. 'With architects now seldom having the authority to insist on specific products being used, there is a tendency to go for cheaper materials, without necessarily understanding the impact or potential knock-on effect.'[34] The role of the architect seems to be declining, giving space to other parties taking crucial decisions, often neglecting health and safety regulations. In addition, the privatisation of public safety controls and inspection is increasing the problem. Local authorities are the rightful places for independent inspections, working independently of the planning function and the private sector. Specification of materials should be brought back to a single point of responsibility under the architect or engineer, who is responsible for the specification of materials, working with building control and the fire officer. 'Allow the experts to do what they know best without interference from politicians or those who tend to take shortcuts or the cheapest option. Look where that has got us.'[35]

During the investigation of the Lakanal House fire, it was revealed that the property had not been put through any fire safety checks, even though there were numerous opportunities to assess whether the level of fire protection at the building was adequate. The building had undergone different refurbishment and material alterations: the pipework for the heating system was installed in the ceiling cavity above the communal corridors in the 1980s, providing an opportunity to ensure that the fire stopping around pipes leading into flats, and segmentation within the ceiling itself, offered adequate protection from fire; during the major refurbishment of 2006/7, the Health and Safety advisors to the London Borough of Southwark proactively advised on this issue, but the Council's housing department did not prioritise carrying out fire risk assessments in all of its properties; and there was evidence of approved individual alterations in flats, such as in Flat 79 which eliminated partition walls to create open plan spaces, that might have negatively contributed to the spread of smoke, that also represents a missed opportunity to consider the adequacy of fire protection. As the report states, by 3 July 2009, Lakanal House had not been assessed. Nonetheless, in the inquest, it was determined that if that had happened, it still would not have made a significant difference to the results, due to the non-invasive nature of fire risk assessments, but it would have been beneficial to highlight aspects of the building that needed further investigation.

Due to a similar situation, at the time of this report Scotland Yard investigations into the Grenfell disaster state that there are 'reasonable grounds' to suspect that the Royal Borough of Kensington and Chelsea, as well as the Chelsea Tenant Management Organisation are guilty of corporate manslaughter.[36] In this respect, the RIBA suggested that a new regulatory framework should be created, informed by the specialist fire safety expertise coming from professional organisations like the Building Research Establishment (BRE), the Fire Protection Association, the Fire Safety Federation, the Institute of Fire Engineers, the Association of Specialist Fire Protection and the All Party Parliamentary Fire and Rescue Group, in coordination with the building construction industry.

Finally, among the most radical solutions proposed to regulate the problem, is their demolition, as Mayor Khan stated in the *Observer*: 'It may well be the defining outcome of this tragedy that the worst mistakes of the 1960s and 1970s are systematically torn down.'[37] This phenomenally drastic solution might seem a rational way of tackling the problem straight at its source. However, all these tower blocks offer a substantial affordable refuge to thousands of households, contributing to social balance in an increasingly gentrified housing market. What would happen to all the tenants? What would replace the tower blocks? Most probably, more of the typical corporate, high-end apartment blocks with much higher rents. It is evident through this survey in this book, that many towers have been successfully retrofitted, proving the demolition argument wrong. In support of this argument, 18 staff from University College London, including the Bartlett Dean Alan Penn, claim in a common letter to the Mayor of London, that the residential tower blocks have a large role to play in tackling the housing crisis. They suggest that the Grenfell disaster should lead to improved standards for tower block refurbishment, rather than their demolition.[38] Retrofitted tower blocks, can if done correctly, ensure high-quality standards in combination with low carbon emissions, affordable rents and fire safety (e.g. Greenhouse Leeds). The Grenfell disaster opens the way for high standards in safety, environmental and social sustainability, rather than further investment in profit-oriented tower gentrification or demolition.

CHAPTER 6 Final discussion

Cladding standards and fire safety checks following Grenfell Tower
At Lakanal House the fire spread up through the façade panels. The aluminium window frames were distorted by the flames originating in Flat 65, creating gaps through which the curtains of the flat above caught alight. These gaps also helped smoke to spread under and through floorboards.[39] The requirement was for composite panels in window sets to be Class 0 (although they were not), but not fire-resistant to 60 minutes (FR60).[40]

According to Dr Sarah Colwell, currently Director of Fire Suppression Testing & Certification at BRE:

> Fires within buildings have the potential to spread externally by breaking out through windows, travelling over or through the cladding system and then breaking back into the building at another level, so by-passing the internal compartmentation for the structure and thus potentially placing residents and building users at risk. Flames can extend over 2m above the window opening from which they break out, regardless of the type of cladding materials used. This can lead to a potential of secondary fires developing if the fire performance characteristics of the external cladding system are not fully assessed. The mechanisms by which fire can spread externally include combustible materials and cavities – either as part of a system, or those created by delamination of the system or material loss during the fire. Once flames enter a cavity, they have the potential to travel significant distances, giving rise to the risk of unseen fire spread within the cladding systems.[41]

The demand for improved thermal performance has resulted in an increased amount of thermal insulation incorporated into the building's envelope. This has led to the production of a wide range of cladding systems on offer, that try to combine different performance needs, replacing traditional building techniques, often introduced on the back of the sustainability agenda. The needs of one provision can sometimes conflict with the needs of another, the challenge for designers is to provide performance compliance without compromising the building's safety. And in this regard, it is crucial not to use thermal insulation products that are combustible (such as flammable polyurethane and polystyrene), and to use materials of limited combustibility for all components of the cladding system below and above 18 metres of height, because, otherwise, the potential combustible fire load within the envelope can significantly increase. To be on the safe side, this includes every layer of the cladding panel (insulation, internal lining board and the external cladding panel) as well as the small gasket parts. When looking at the classification and specifications of insulating materials, it is critical to understand the difference between surface spread of flame classification (which only measures the spread of a flame across the material surface) and actual combustibility, clarified in the product's Declaration of Performance. Designing with non-combustible products is the safest option for architects, but if the designer wants to propose a façade insulation system, it will need to be assessed against the acceptance criteria set out in BR135 Fire Performance of External Thermal Insulation for Walls of Multi-storey Buildings.

How well fire tests can actually predict a product's fire performance is another issue, that needs continued research. Sarah Colwell says:

> Since the overall fire performance of the system is reliant on the interaction of all the elements within the cladding system, small-scale component testing cannot always reflect the overall fire performance of the complete system when installed in a real building.[42]

Another critical opinion comes from Dr Tsavdaris, Associate Professor at the University of Leeds,[43] who believes that the way building components are being tested in terms of their fire resistance performance is totally outdated. Cladding products are tested individually in the UK, rather than in combination with other materials, as they occur in reality. Often it is the material system which could create a chimney effect, as he believes happened in the Grenfell Tower disaster. He proposes a testing system similar to what happens in the United Arab Emirates, where building components are tested as material systems.

The fire spread at the Lakanal House was unexpectedly fast in every direction, trapping people inside the building, with the exterior cladding panels burning through in just four and a half minutes.[44] Before any work is carried out, it is necessary to check the original construction and discover any conflict between new thermal materials that may affect the fire integrity of the building. This applies to all refurbishments where thermal insulation is upgraded, to avoid the dangers of fire spread, and there are many other structural and technical concerns.

As Arnold Tarling, chartered surveyor at Hindwoods, points out, the issue is that under building regulations, only the surface of the cladding has to be fire-proofed to Class 0, which is about surface spread, but not the internal layers of the panel assembly, which are the ones that were burning at the Grenfell Tower.[45]

At the time we are writing this section, there is much public concern and comment about potential flaws in the cladding that was on Grenfell Tower, but the exact reasons for the speed of the spread of fire have not been determined yet. In its last refurbishment, the Grenfell Tower was clad with ACM cassette rain-screen panels, an aluminium composite material with the thermal insulation panels assembled inside. The reason this specific cladding product was used on the Grenfell Tower, despite opposing current regulations, will be one of the key issues of the running investigations. German construction companies have been banned from using plastic-filled cladding panels (e.g. Raynobond PE), on buildings taller than 22 metres since the 1980s, as is the situation in the USA, where similar panels cannot be used on buildings taller than 15 m. The panels are also banned in the UAE.[46]

The Department for Communities and Local Government sent a letter to Local Authorities and Housing Associations on 18 June 2017, and to owners, landlords and managers of private residential blocks in England, on 20 June 2017, communicating that owners and managers of residential tower

CHAPTER 6 Final discussion

blocks need to urgently carry out fire safety checks to ensure that appropriate safety and response measures are in place, and in particular, asking them to identify whether any panels used in new build or refurbishment are a particular type of cladding made of aluminium composite material. They put in place a testing process for samples of at least 250 × 250 mm in size, which are to be sent to a testing facility at BRE at no cost. They prioritise buildings over six storeys or 18 metres high. The offer is for the initial testing only and the cost of any remedial action will be the responsibility of the owner of the building.[47] The definition provided to identify aluminium composite material (ACM) describes it as a type of flat panel that consists of two thin aluminium sheets bonded to a non-aluminium core, typically between 3 and 7 mm thick, with a painted or metallic finish. It can be differentiated from a solid aluminium sheet by looking at a cut edge wherein the different layers are visible.

Government authorities started an immediate investigation into the materials used in other tower retrofits across the country, including councils in London, Sheffield, Leeds, Manchester, Glasgow, Aberdeen and Dundee. So did many architecture practices, which started reviewing their designs for tower blocks and the building materials used. So far, numbers keep rising, revealing that numerous tower blocks are clad with flammable panels. A few weeks after the tragic blaze, 120 tower blocks across 25 local authorities are known to have failed a combustibility test.[48] As a consequence, the 650 properties in Chalcots Estate, Camden (Figure 6.18), were evacuated, causing a chaotic situation for residents and the City Council.[49] Besides the use of a similar cladding material to the one used on Grenfell Tower, there were reports of fire doors not complying with current safety standards. According to the BBC, the cladding is to be removed on 11 tower blocks, including Chalcots Estate.[50] The newly established governmental programme through the Building Research Establishment (BRE) will continue its assessments to thousands of towers across the country until a certain degree of safety has been restored. While the BRE is state-funded, there is no certainty about who will carry the cost of affected refurbished towers and about what will happen to tenants and leaseholders of this towers until the problem has been resolved.

Sprinklers

The coroner in the Lakanal House investigation clearly highlighted the need for retrofitting of sprinklers in high-rise buildings in her recommendations to both the London Borough of Southwark and the Secretary of State for Communities and Local Government. This measure has also been repeatedly requested by other coroners and fire and rescue services, but no legal enforcement has compelled social housing providers to do so. Although there is no

▲ Figure 6.18

Chalcots Estate, Camden, had to be evacuated after the Grenfell disaster due to fire safety concerns

doubt about the benefits of sprinklers, their installation is recurrently considered either not practical or economically viable.

DCLG says they presented their views on sprinklers in a letter sent to social housing providers, but this letter has not been published, and to date, there is no clear indication of what action the government is taking to these calls to install sprinkler systems in high-rise housing buildings. Currently, only buildings built after 2007 and more than 30 metres high are required to integrate sprinkler systems. Some social landlords have retrofitted sprinklers in their tower blocks, and after the Grenfell Tower blaze, many are confirming that they will take this action on all their high-rise properties (i.e. in Sheffield, which will affect some of the buildings studied in this book), but no government statements have announced any plans to enforce the provision of sprinklers in these buildings. The London Borough of Southwark's response to the Rule 43 letter states that they sought advice from the government on this issue, but they did not get any:

> The social housing sector has looked to government for guidance on the retrofitting of sprinklers, but the response from the Department of Communities and Local Government (DCLG), to the Southampton Rule 43 letter suggests that, instead of taking a view on behalf of all social housing landlords, DCLG considers that decisions regarding the retrofitting or not of sprinkler systems to high rise building is for landlords to consider themselves.[51]

There are current discussions about the main obstacles to their installation. One obvious one is cost, but many experts say that it has become significantly more affordable, although estimates give highly variable values: for instance, the British Automatic Fire Sprinkler Association estimates that the cost of fitting a system in Grenfell Tower would have been around £200,000, but fitting a system to 47 flats in Callow Mount, a 13-storey block in Sheffield, came to £55,000 or £1,150 per flat.[52]

The London Borough of Southwark surveyed three of the council's typical high-rise blocks and identified different issues. One was that the council had no right of access to leasehold properties, meaning that they could not either assess or consider the fitting of sprinklers in those areas, leaving their installation up to the discretion of the actual leaseholders, expecting they would fund this work for the sake of benefitting their own properties. The effectiveness of the sprinkler system relies on covering the whole building, leaving no areas unprotected, so it is critical that all individual properties have the system installed (with leasehold properties being up to 50 per cent of the properties in some cases). This situation led the council to focus the fire safety measures on communal areas, which, obviously, is not enough. In addition to this, the installation of the system requires proper integration into the building's fabric. The system requires a structural engineering report for a water storage tank and core drilling for services; the design and installation of general routing for the pipework throughout the building (communal areas and dwellings), housed behind fireproof covings or partitions as well as water storage tank and 60-minute fire rated service hatch to each dwelling for service and monitoring (builders work); fire signal cabling, a

CHAPTER 6 Final discussion

255

sprinkler monitoring panel, a bespoke addressable fire alarm, and pump power supplies (electrical work); certified fire stopping for all branches formed in construction during the works, after all the piping and cabling is complete; plastering and decoration (paint).[53] The installation of the sprinkler system, therefore, requires a full feasibility study that takes into consideration the design intent and construction and structural complexities of each building, as well as the existing fire protection measures already in place.

The RIBA also recommends their installation, but other opinions consider that compartmentation and other appropriate fire stopping and early warning systems, such as heat and smoke detection, might be enough.

Compartmentation and layout

By looking at Grenfell Tower's basic floor plan (Figure 6.19), one can quickly realise that the tower has only one fire escape, the main staircase, which is not adequate for a 24-storey building with hundreds of residents. In addition, there are no fire doors defining fire compartments within the building's core, which explains why the smoke coming from the apartments managed to cover the entire building core so quickly, adding an additional obstacle to escaping residents. One really wonders how such major fire safety problems have been totally ignored in a building which has been retrofitted recently.

In previous inquests, it is clear that compromising the compartmentation of the building during refurbishment or material alterations in the building plays a critical role in the risk of fire spread. That was a determining cause for fire and smoke spread, leading to life risk, in the Lakanal House fire. The design of the cladding system and any other works in the building require the incorporation of fire stops in every floor plate and party wall around each individual property within the high-rise block, to prevent the spread of fire. There are regulations defining how to grant compartmentalization, they only need to be followed, and the works to be supervised to ensure they are properly executed on site, especially when upgrading works are undertaken in existing blocks, to ensure that a compartmentation is maintained.[54] Requirements for compartment floors, compartment walls and protected shafts (for stairs, lifts, chutes, ducts and pipes) are set out in Section 8 of Approved Document B, Vol. 2.

As with the installation of sprinklers, the letter from the Lakanal House inquest's coroner to the Secretary of State for Communities and Local Government drew attention to the 'uncertainty about the scope of inspection for fire risk assessment purposes which should be undertaken in high rise residential buildings' since 'evidence was adduced

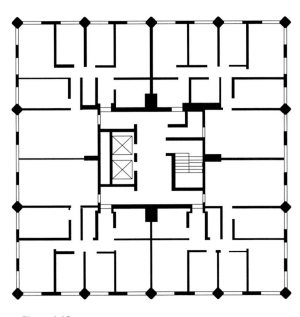

▲ Figure 6.19

Grenfell Tower, typical floor plan

which indicated that inspection of the interior of flats or maisonettes in high rise buildings was necessary to enable an assessor to identify possible breaches of the compartment', and for that, recommended clear guidance on 'the definition of "common parts" of buildings containing multiple domestic premises; inspection of a maisonette or flat which has been modified internally to determine whether compartmentation has been breached'.[55]

Signage and information

A final issue is how well fire safety information is provided to all relevant parties: not only designers but most importantly to residents and fire rescue services. During the inquiry of the Lakanal House fire, it was revealed that the fire brigade found it really difficult to find where specific flats were within the estate, which was a major obstacle in allowing them to reach the victims in time. Likewise, there was confusion about which escapes residents should use, in which circumstances they have to use them, and how to use them.

The coroner requested the London Borough of Southwark should provide efficient fire safety features information to all residents, including 'walking residents through relevant features such as escape balconies, and demonstrating how to open fire exit doors and where these lead'. Guidance should also be provided regarding how to react to fire, as well as planning of the different means to disseminate information to residents. In the same way, clear signage for evacuation procedures, including layout clarity to assist the emergency services to understand the building and its surroundings, should be provided. However, as with the installation of sprinklers, the council found difficult to assess (gas checks, conditions of the property), non-tenanted properties for which they do not have the right of access.

Information supplied by the emergency services to those residents at risk seems also to be a crucial issue since it seems clear that those residents who disregarded the advice to stay put and decided to go down the fire escape saved their lives, whereas those who followed that advice and stayed died. This happened at Lakanal House and seems to have happened again at Grenfell Tower. Although this issue is beyond the scope of this book, since it is not directly connected to refurbishment design, it helps to clarify part of the situation, and reinforces the idea that more holistic, consistent and clear information for all tower blocks, at both the technical and the user level, should be in place.

Lack of institutional holistic strategy: design

In addition to the obvious need to grant technically reliable interventions, there is crucial scope for design reflection. The Modern movement brought the opportunity to revise living standards, introduce new technologies, embrace the concepts of comfort and convenience, and investigate new social arrangements and structures. Despite their failures, there was an enormous investment in design exploration supported by public agencies, with a significant number of architects actively contributing and putting their efforts into the national housing programme. The actual central and local government endeavour to produce better houses for all not only generated the necessary regulatory and physical frameworks, it also engaged in the organisation of trips to visit exemplary pioneering developments in other countries, importing innovative construction and organisational techniques, developing design guidelines, etc. All that resourceful and instrumental wealth is not present in the equally large-scale endeavour of retrofitting the existing stock. There is a lack of perspective: refurbishment is regarded as the cheapest way of fixing a problem, rather than as an opportunity for redesigning our built environment.

At present, success is measured in numbers of insulated walls and lofts, or of PV cells installed, but what is the actual quality of those insulation and PV cells installations? To what extent are we using this opportunity to introduce cutting-edge technology (i.e. the new generation of solar cells), materials or design strategies?

The economic restriction is a critical issue in most of the towers investigated, and therefore the retrofits are driven by meeting minimum standards, left to the skills of the architects' team to optimise the limited funding to a maximum output. Examples such as the renovation of the Bois-le-Prêtre tower in Paris (built in 1959–1964, retrofitted 2005–2010) by Druot, Lacaton & Vassal should be extended across Europe. The renovation of this tower was approached as a competition organised by Paris-Habitat, France's largest public utility social housing company, with the aim of show that renovating is better than demolishing and building anew. The winning entry establishes a very clear connection between energy and living quality upgrading. In a previous refurbishment that took place in 1990, the tower's new image related to the postmodern patterns covering the buildings of those years, similar to the many renovation results that took place in the UK's high-rise blocks. The universality of those patterns, as a representative image of that particular period, provided the same anonymity and placelessness criticised in the modern buildings, again considering the tower as a global decontextualised object. The approach used by Druot, Lacaton & Vassal works from the inside towards the outside, focusing on maximising the human experience, at both dwelling and neighbourhood scales. Each flat is extended between 22–60 square metres by adding a 3-m-deep band of glazed winter gardens (2 m deep) and balconies (1 m deep) covering the full height of each long side of the block. The design of this extension includes two floor-to-ceiling, fully operable and transparent enclosures: one replacing the original façade, and the other between sunrooms and balconies, allowing flexibility to expand or reduce the living area (indoors-outdoors) according to use.

The design keeps the existing robust concrete structure and the same idea of the light façade, but in combination with a thermal buffer created by attaching the sunrooms to the living areas. With this strategy, they aimed to reduce 50 per cent of the heating consumption. This project successfully evidenced the potential to evolve from heritage at a lower cost: demolishing and rebuilding each flat would have cost €170,000 per flat, whereas the renovation work cost €100,000 per flat.

▲ Figure 6.20

EcoPod in Enfield by David Rudkin Architects

We are in the middle of a well-advanced initiative to exhaustively retrofit the UK building stock, and no institutional body is supervising, coordinating, or supporting the design of these interventions. No organisation provides design research, guidelines, good practice sharing, etc. There are good punctual efforts in many places, but there is no central platform from which to get advice about up-to-date techniques, materials, technologies, publications, etc. How can a practice based in the south of England know about the EcoPod (Figure 6.20) developed in the Northwest? How can we be aware of the research developed in multiple universities across the country? Even, how can we be aware of the programmes, incentives and funding opportunities launched by the government? The tendering process is also limiting, leading to the specialisation of certain architectural offices since it is easier to access the same type of job once you are in the framework. Additionally, renowned architects don't seem to be engaged in this process, which is again a great contradiction: the retrofit operation has a similar magnitude to that of erecting all the post-war buildings, and at that time many progressive architects and urban planners were keen on working for the councils. Druot, Lacaton & Vassal's retrofit also serves as an example of world-renowned architects emphasising the importance of engaging in this process: there is a need for design-intensive input to make this investment meaningful.

Here in the UK, the Retrofit for the Future[56] programme from UK Innovate (Technology Strategy Board), in collaboration with the RIBA, could be this referential platform. Unfortunately, the Retrofit for the Future was a one-off programme; in addition to this, explorations were based on efficiency only, without actually having a design impact. It aimed to explore retrofit techniques, provide the opportunity to improve strategies and explore new collaboration ways to use less energy, cut carbon emissions and save costs. None of the case studies in this programme are high-rise flats, the funding and the characteristics of the programme (directed to the improvement of individual households) made that impractical.

We agree that this programme offered a key starting point to encourage collaboration between housing providers, designers, contractors and researchers, and has helped to stimulate new business opportunities in the retrofit market. Although this work generated a guide accessible to the public, offering useful information for any organisation considering a retrofit project, it nonetheless represents a closed process. The source of information should be active, continuously fed and evolving. As suggested above, a government programme related to technology and innovation in close collaboration with the RIBA could definitely provide the necessary dynamic framework to coordinate the country's retrofit endeavour. That way, the government not only provides subsidies to undertake ecological upgrades but also controls the quality of those upgrades in design terms.

Meeting the minimum decent requirements was obviously not only a great concern, but also an obligation, which therefore triggered the active response from stakeholders. The same thing will happen with Energy Efficiency Standards. We need these policies. The moment they became mandatory, different mechanisms were created and deployed to reach those targets (ALMOs, stock transfer, etc.), involving the whole of the society more deeply and globally: everybody becomes a stakeholder. The ecological retrofit becomes a vehicle for citizens, organisations and local authorities to be aware of a problem, and work on it together. This is a critical step in the process: being aware that decarbonisation starts with each of us individually, it is not only the government's responsibility, something far away from us. We have not only a say in the way we can achieve it, but also an opportunity to improve our own neighbourhoods and lives.

Once the minimum has been reached, a second stage in the process should target the next level of quality. The mechanisms and structure are all in place now (housing associations, tenants' organisations, ALMOs, boards, architects familiar with retrofitting techniques, consultation processes, and so on). This structure required a huge human and intellectual investment, and should not be lost.

The building construction industry plan: where does refurbishment sit in that context?

The construction industry is a major indicator of a country's economic growth. The UK's construction industry contributes £110 billion per annum (7 per cent of GDP) to the national economy. Out of the total construction output in the UK, approximately 25 per cent is public sector; in terms of type of construction, 60 per cent is new construction and 40 per cent is refurbishments and maintenance.[57] Low carbon construction is a key part of any developmental programme in the construction industry, due to both the environmental requirements set in domestic and foreign regulatory frameworks as well as an increased societal demand for greener products, which opens new commercial opportunities and will drive future markets.

The sustainable building industry was forecast to grow at an annual rate of 22.8 per cent until 2017.[58] To achieve a 'resource-efficient, modern and globally competitive economy', the government established three strategic priorities: (1) smart construction and digital design; (2) low carbon and sustainable construction; and (3) improved trade performance. The UK Vision for construction in 2025, led by the Construction Leadership Council established for this purpose in 2013, is set out in a report called *Construction 2025-Industrial Strategy: Government and Industry in* Partnership,[59] which laid out the following specific green targets:

- 50 per cent reduction in overall time from inception to completion for new build and refurbished assets;
- 50 per cent reduction in greenhouse gas emissions in the built environment;

260   CHAPTER 6 Final discussion

- to consolidate a strong structure of specialised supply chains and commercial relationships;
- to lead the world in research and innovation by fully embracing advanced materials, new technologies, digital design and smart construction;
- investment in achieving a skilled, motivated and diverse workforce;
- to promote local production and social sustainability – reducing carbon due to transportation, and supporting local craftsmanship and knowledge. The UK imports £12 billion of construction products annually, and exports £6 billion. The government's target is a 50 per cent reduction in the trade gap between total exports and total imports of construction products and materials.[60]

Different organisations contribute to the development of the government's strategy, its vision and ambitions, and the delivery of its commitments: the Construction Industry Council, the Construction Leadership Council, Constructing Excellence in the Built Environment, and Construction Products Innovation. The low carbon construction industry in particular, is supported by the Technology Strategy Board (the UK's Innovation Agency) and the Green Construction Board. The former created the Low Impact Buildings Innovation Platform, as the main instrument to provide programmes and tools designed to accelerate innovation to improve sustainability in the built environment. The latter was established in October 2011 as a consultative forum for government and the UK design, construction, property and infrastructure industry. At first, its priority was to provide focus, direction and clarity to the business and growth opportunities generated by the shift to a green economy. In the longer term, the objective was to develop and implement a strategic framework for the promotion of innovation and sustainable growth in this sector.

Looking at what all these different organisms say about the future of construction, none of them makes special mention of retrofitting. While the industry is clearly identified as following a direction committed to environmental concerns, there are no explicit intentions or criteria within the strategic framework related to refurbishing: it might be included in the general estimations, but still it is not considered to require specific considerations in the national plan. In other words, it is not identified as an area with specific demands. However, some sectors are clearly benefitting from the green retrofit process, such as the visible growth experienced by the thermal insulation sector across Europe. In the UK's *Construction Sector Infographic*, published in 2013, it was a highlight, predicting that it would support 60,000 jobs by 2015.[61] As thermal insulation is one of the major demands to achieve thermal comfort that meets both Decent Homes Standard and the decarbonisation of the UK, the sector's growth must have been significantly impacted by the implementation of the government programmes of this period (the Green Deal and ECO). The demand for the delivery of thermal insulation to existing buildings has generated a high diversification of products and techniques, related to issues such as improved technical performance, accessibility of the building fabric, building's protection status or a new individualised image for the building. These factors should inform the construction industry's strategic plan for the immediate and long-term future, so that the retrofit area can be better supported.

CHAPTER 6 Final discussion

Sustainability challenges for tower blocks

A recent report developed by the Green Alliance, which examined the challenges faced by residents of high-rise housing in trying to live greener lifestyles, exposes how existing policies are actually 'largely designed with street level properties in mind and therefore fail to support and incentivise sustainable living for high-rise residents'.[62] They draw attention to the fact that many of these policies increasingly leave to the individual householder the decision to take environmental actions forward, which is clearly more challenging for tower block residents since they have less control over the different building and management systems around them. An additional problem is that many of them live on low incomes or benefits that can barely cover their own basic needs. This poor condition puts these householders in a very disadvantaged position to develop a responsible attitude towards our natural resources. Therefore, a critical conclusion from this study is the imperative need for policies that consider the specific context of high-rise housing, to ensure that all UK residents have equal accessibility to green and comfortable living standards.

Greening the UK is not only about reducing CO_2 emissions, there are other important parameters involved that also contribute to global sustainability. In its investigation, this report has identified seven areas in which high-rise blocks offer unique opportunities to meet low carbon targets and social well-being by appropriately using: (1) smart meters; (2) minimum energy efficiency standards; (3) energy self-sufficiency; (4) waste management; (5) water management; (6) green areas; and (7) sustainable transportation. We fully second their argument to better support these seven areas for more resilient and healthier high-rise housing environments:

- *Smart meters.* The government established a central change programme to deliver the roll-out of 53 million gas and electricity smart meters to all homes and small businesses in Great Britain by the end of 2020.[63] The main phase of this project, where most households will have smart meters installed by their energy company, will take place between 2015 and 2020. Evidence shows that smart metering enables the users to better manage their energy use, save money and reduce emissions. Tower blocks present advantages and challenges to the installation of smart metering. On the one hand, the installation can be more easily coordinated since most of them are run by housing associations and therefore all flats have the same energy supplier, which minimises time and costs. On the other, the technology has presented some communication issues due to all the meters being installed in the basement, which needs a proper solution to allow tower block residents to benefit from smart meters like any other UK householder.
- *Minimum Energy Efficiency Standards.* With the Minimum Energy Efficiency Standard (MEES), from 2018, tenants in the private sector will have the right to demand energy-efficiency improvements in their properties, whereas tenants in the public sector will not enjoy an equivalent right or level of empowerment. Tower blocks should have specific incentives to address their contextual characteristics, coordinated with housing providers and energy

suppliers. As previously discussed, they present a unique opportunity to easily tackle many hard-to-treat homes at one go, and therefore should be a clear goal in the national ecological upgrade programme. Either creating a specific programme for them, or extending the MEES to social housing tenants, would allow those blocks that are in most need to access improvements, or for those that were very basically renovated to get a better level on the scale.

- *Increasing energy self-sufficiency.* Given the compactness of tower block estates, and their scale to both generate and use heat, they should be more extensively supported to create low-carbon heat networks or to be integrated into district heating schemes, making use of excess heat generated by a central heat source. Replacing inefficient systems can achieve carbon savings at a lower cost than retrofitting flats, which is even maximised by the fact that the existing pipe networks in the blocks can be reused for the new systems, therefore minimising disruption to residents. Decarbonising the heating system is key to achieving the government's target since heating accounts for half of the residential greenhouse emissions. Biomass centres based on wood pellets seem to be successfully installed in many tower blocks across the UK (Merseyside, Newcastle, the Midlands, London), which, in combination with renewable sources of energy, could make tower blocks independent from the grid, managing their own energy production and consumption.

- *Waste management.* There is an EU target for the UK to recycle at least 50 per cent of waste generated by households by 2020. The England 'waste from households' recycling rate was 43.9 per cent in 2015. This is a decrease of 0.9 percentage points, from 44.8 per cent in 2014. Recycling rates had previously been increasing each year. This is the first time the 'waste from households' recycling rate has been lower than 44 per cent since 2011.[64] The average recycling rate for England is 43.9 per cent, for Wales 66 per cent,[65] and for Scotland 44.2 per cent,[66] but high-rise housing presents some challenges to achieve these targets: according to DEFRA, the logistics of collecting materials for recycling is likely to be more challenging in flats than in areas of street-level housing.[67] Again, a tailored service is necessary for high-rise blocks: doorstep collection is expensive because it is less accessible; collection at the bottom of the block is the common practice, but means lower recycling rates; rubbish chutes don't help: in most cases they are for general waste, this weakens the incentive to recycle, as general waste disposal is so much easier, and even where chutes have been converted to recycling chutes, there are problems with correct usage; provision of recycling capacity is often inadequate for the number of households served, leading to overflowing recycling bins and untidy bin stores. Recycling in flats requires previous information about the block to provide the right recycling facilities at a reasonable cost, as well as a designed recycling plan. This is particularly critical for those local authorities with housing stock where a higher proportion of dwellings are flats, if they are to meet the recycling targets.

- *Water.* As with gas and electricity meters, there is evidence that installing water meters can save water by more than 10 per cent.[68] Water meters allow residents to be aware of how much water they are using, enabling a wiser

CHAPTER 6 Final discussion   **263**

use of water (for instance, installing water-saving devices) that will, in turn, reduce their bills (water bills, but also gas or electricity bills from heating water). Meters might not be suitable for tower blocks if they have access to communal facilities or a shared hot water supply. At the moment, water companies can refuse to install meters based on these or other issues (cost, access to space, etc.), leaving the most vulnerable population (those on a low income) unprotected. This would not happen if the government established a compulsory water metering scheme, and devised a specific plan for high-rise housing to exploit their opportunities, rather than seeing this housing typology as an obstacle.

- *Green spaces*. Most high-rise housing has green or open space within their estates, but the way it is used varies greatly from one to another. A study from 2010 found that less than 1 per cent of people living in social housing use the green space in their estate.[69] In some instances, these spaces are neglected, becoming unsafe, and subject to becoming car parking space or ground for new construction. Green spaces can generate a very beneficial environment, promoting health, wildlife, social cohesion, well-being and recreational uses for the neighbours, such as playgrounds, gardens or allotments. Open spaces are a very efficient vehicle to enhance the social sustainability of the estate, bringing neighbours together from different blocks or even nearby estates, which should be supported by social landlords. We have seen that this was a clear instrument for success in Greenhouse, in Leeds (Figure 6.21).

◀ Figure 6.21

Food beds for herb cultivation in the Greenhouse, Leeds

- *Sustainable transport.* Frequently blocks suffer from poor access to shops, post offices and other amenities, as well as poor connection to public transport. With the opportunity to influence the travel behaviour of large numbers of people at once, the government should involve tower block residents in consultations to plan greener local transport strategies. To promote biking and walking, the renovation works should include secure bike and storage space; well-lit, signed and safe paths around estates, bike lanes, and access routes to estates.

Measuring the efficiency of the retrofits

After engaging all the stakeholders and completing the renovations works, the next question to ask is: how effective are the implemented measures in meeting their original purpose? And, what is the level of satisfaction of the residents?

The best vehicle to measure the real impact of the energy-efficient improvements is through the production of post-retrofit reports containing objectively measured data as well as subjective data. This again should be centrally controlled, as a critical instrument to provide feedback about: success in the use of energy-saving incentives (to obtain a realistic perception of depth of engagement), quality of the implemented work, and performance results of the measures installed. This post-occupancy monitoring should be done after at least one year, to allow for time to collect energy bills, as well as subjective evidence, such as the occupants' experience in relation to environmental comfort and convenience of use in all four different seasons.

This type of assessment has been successfully done in several estates, in most cases carried out by independent research bodies.[70] These studies reveal that keeping residents informed needs constant effort, with still many of them unaware of the main reason behind the renovation works even after the refurbishment is completed. This is not only important because efficient communication between all parties is always needed to fruitfully advance any project, but also because a great part of the success in providing greener buildings significantly depends on the users: their understanding of the measures installed, and their willingness and responsibility to be efficient. Good communication involves understanding that the individual benefits and the community benefits depending on how the different resources are used. In many cases, residents seem to be more concerned about the associated products of the renovation projects, such as the provision of a concierge service and the quality of internal redecoration, than about energy efficiency, even though fuel poverty is usually a critical issue for many of the inhabitants of these blocks.

In general, the outcome confirms the expected results: the overall energy use is reduced after the retrofit, normally with some of the apartments experiencing better cost savings due to specificities such as position in the block, layout or type of treatment. The decrease in energy consumption does not directly imply lower energy bills, due to the average 10 per cent increase in energy price rises experienced in recent years across the major energy supply companies. In the Edward Woods Estate, where bills were examined before

CHAPTER 6 Final discussion

265

and after the refurbishment, despite the impact of this increase the installed measures still provide a positive output (with savings higher than the energy price rises), leading to residents paying either the same or lower bills than before.[71]

However, post-occupancy studies also show performance gaps, that is, mild-to-serious differences between the predicted performance (the energy savings expected from the energy-efficiency upgrade) and the real savings achieved in practice (how much energy is consumed by the building post-retrofit). This difference between the designed and simulated data, and the real data, can range from low to dramatically high, and depends on two successive factors: first, the efficiency in the organisation and delivery of the different building production processes (design, procurement, construction), alongside the level of skilled labour involved in these processes; second, the user's behaviour after the energy-efficiency programme has been implemented (the rebound effect).[72]

To mitigate the first issue affecting performance gaps means optimising the production processes, and requires a technical approach: improving modelling tools, providing training to labour, optimising project management strategies, and so on. However, tackling the second issue requires social strategies. In some instances, the increase in energy consumption is related to positive access to environmental comfort: homes that could not afford to be warmed before the retrofit can be adequately heated when energy is more accessible, reducing fuel poverty and improving the residents' health. But in other cases, savings from energy bills might lead to consuming energy in other ways, related to a change in lifestyle: allowing occupants to travel more, having access to additional domestic appliances or electronic devices, etc. Additionally, there is also an increased use of energy that is not intentional, and it is produced by losses in low-quality equipment or by a poor understanding of how to use the environmental control systems. In this sense, there is an urgent need to educate and encourage people to use their new systems in a responsible and well-informed way.

In the wider context, the issue of performance gaps is currently a key research concern. Findings from different studies have revealed very different results from the predicted scenarios, with energy consumption in buildings being two times higher than the modelled calculations,[73] or even five times higher in the case of in-use energy consumption.

There are positive trends towards improving energy efficiency, such as advances in technology, but it needs to be understood that real efficiency only occurs when the whole building has been designed holistically: it is not just a question of adding a new boiler or lighting system, but of making all the different energy-efficient measures work in synergy. This thinking is well rooted within the design community (architects and engineers), but needs to be more emphatically transmitted to the rest of the sectors: there is need for more integrated and active institutional arrangements for strategic management of the retrofit process.

There are also some new trends that negatively affect our energy performance: there is an increased use of air conditioning, electronics and appliances at home, as well as some services as they become more affordable or give a sense of being ecological (e.g. low consumption light or heating). The use of renewable energy sources play a key role to counteract user's behaviour. In this direction, there is a clear demand for continued investment in research on power generation technologies and their requirements (i.e. batteries), to make them more efficient, accessible and affordable.

The implementation of low or zero carbon sources of energy is a critical first step to reduce the emissions coming from building use. In some of the tower blocks inspected in this book, we have seen that the installation of renewables, in addition to the production of energy, might have other values in mind: the aim might be to provide a flagship example, not only to cut costs but also to renew the image of the estate. Sometimes, that desire to convey a message of modernisation is delivered at the expense of the technology's performance: we have seen photovoltaic cells installed in canopies or building façades that prioritised visual exposure, compromising the maximisation of solar radiation exposure, and therefore yielding an inferior output. We agree with the necessity for this message, but think that it should be channelled using other design means that would also more actively contribute to the quality of the living experience at ground levels, such as materiality, lighting, landscape or spatial opportunities for the community to engage in activities.

UK retrofits in context

As in the UK, European research in the past two decades was focused on better understanding the housing stock, through an extensive inspection and survey of properties: collecting, organising and analysing different types of data. EU research projects such as OPET Building, SUREURO, LOCOSOC and *High-Rise Refurbishment* (2002–2006) funded by the International Energy Agency and EuroAce, which involved 28 countries, reported on similar issues, trends and challenges across Europe.[74] To meet carbon reduction targets, it was necessary to identify which barriers tend to prevent refurbishment, and what mechanisms could be deployed to motivate and engage stakeholders (for both short- and long-term occupants), promote capital investment, and support the most disadvantaged population. These projects have set a fundamental structure across Europe to attain an accurate picture of the state of high-rise housing buildings, reclaiming that best practice applied to the refurbishment of the high-rise stock is crucial to gain the highest energy savings, and identify the regions with the highest potential for improvement.

Analysis from a demographic point of view shows that there has been a clear change in family structures, which is a critical factor in how the housing stock needs to accommodate new forms of inhabiting. Although married or civil partner couple families are still the most common type of family, statistics show a substantial housing demand from single persons (both old and young, women being the majority), as well as other increasing patterns: dual career households, dual career commuter couples, serial cohabitation, the return of young adults living with their parents or collective living.[75] A general increasing trend is the

CHAPTER 6 Final discussion

267

integration of new functions in old spaces, either to adapt or extend the existing standard family house to accommodate these new family structures, or due to other changes, such as the growth in higher-level non-manual occupations, which, together with the spread of flexible employment patterns and development of communication technology, allows the use of the house in different times and ways. Another issue to consider for the future of our existing housing stock, is to be up to date with how people tend to change their houses, what makes them invest in specific renovations, based on cultural and social trends: for instance, the need for an extension or the flat's layout modification due to change in family composition or usage pattern, such as including a work-related facility, a utility room, a conservatory or urban agriculture.

The energy efficiency of homes has been steadily improving, aiming equally at repairing and providing modern facilities, services and especially thermal comfort. At the European level, there is common agreement on confirming that it is easier to access information from and keep track of the evolution of the social housing sector, than the private housing sector. However, it is difficult to locate information on key patterns such as usage, lifestyle, maintenance or the priorities that underpin people's vision for future improvements in their homes. In addition to this, in the UK, the mechanisms in place for compiling information are not equally set in all the country's regions. The statistical outline of the housing stock is more detailed in England (Housing Survey) than in the rest of the UK (Wales, Northern Ireland and Scotland).

While there is a clear improvement in terms of thermal comfort, progress in overall environmental performance is not as evident, and much more arduous to quantify. Therefore, the most recent European research has shifted focus. Now that we understand our social high-rise housing stock needs and we are well immersed in comprehensive retrofitting activity in most countries, it is time for assessment: monitoring, mapping and modelling the refurbishment process and our future environmental impact. Projects like *TABULA* and *EPISCOPE* (2009–2012 and 2013–2016 respectively), supported by the European Commission in the framework of the Intelligent Energy Europe programme involving 20 European countries, set out as the main target to make these processes transparent and effective. This entailed the design of actions to attain climate change targets. The UK representative in this project was BRE (British Research Establishment), originally a government-funded research laboratory, currently an independent multi-disciplinary building science centre. The first project tracked the implementation of energy-saving measures and their effect, creating a critical pool of energy-related data useful to learn from each other about successful energy-saving strategies, as well as providing a framework for cross-country comparisons of building features, measures and energy performance.[76] One of the main goals was to establish a set of energy performance indicators (e.g. building insulation, heat supply system, heat generation system, special systems (photovoltaics)), so all refurbishment processes in the different countries are assessed using the same criteria. These indicators were set to allow evaluators and stakeholders to produce high-quality interventions, comply with existing regulations, and monitor and manage the refurbishment process efficiently in terms of cost and energy savings measuring. Currently,

268   CHAPTER 6 Final discussion

the majority of these post-occupancy studies are punctual initiatives, funded and produced by individual research projects from academic environments or non-governmental, independent organisations. A broader European initiative such as *TABULA* and *EPISCOPE* provides the opportunity to develop a more comprehensive strategy, installing solid bottom-up building stock monitoring procedures for all countries using different instruments: energy certificate databases, surveys, census, energy bills, strategic asset development, and energy management.

While the need for energy efficiency and thermal comfort is well assimilated and absorbs a good deal of attention, there is a less clear vision about what climate change as a global phenomenon might demand from buildings in the coming years. We should not forget that new conditions (e.g. floods) might generate other urgent actions to be tackled socially and technically.

Final comments

The national UK Carbon Plan has established ambitious targets, impossible to meet without a comprehensive strategic vision for the existing UK's housing stock. This new vision must be based on a radical restructure of the way the housing stock is managed and renovated, and most definitely needs new financial instruments to promote and make investment viable, as well as an efficient coordination of all the parties involved in this process: householders, landlords, designers, developers and lenders. Equally, effective laws, codes of performance and procedures (fiscal incentives, obligations) are fundamental to accomplish this endeavour.

We understand the urgent necessity to address energy efficiency, but we would like to emphasise in our final words that it is important to look at these buildings from other points of view too, such as their substantial embodied socio-cultural value, and their potential for new forms of understanding heritage and identity. The energy upgrading process is seen as a convenient vehicle to assess, improve or incorporate other design needs, which happens in the best of cases, but our view is that these other aspects need attention on their own right.

Current European efforts are devoted to assessing, monitoring, evaluating, and being more efficient environmentally, but what comes after that? Aren't we missing the opportunity to evaluate other aspects in depth once we are altering high-rise housing estates physically and at many other levels (e.g. life-usage, social environment, safety, sense of place, sense of belonging, sense of pride, people's aspirations and needs)?

We believe that changes in buildings' form and structure have a critical impact on the social and cultural values that both occupants and surrounding neighbours experience, and their future depends on providing a successful environment, defined by a continuous flow of activity, a clear cultural identity and planned maintenance mechanisms.

We have mentioned different initiatives that try to bring this holistic perspective to the refurbishment process, offering concrete and in most cases well-analysed strategies supported by case studies. We hope that this book becomes a catalyst to spark this kind of discussion, bring more visibility to existing initiatives, and trigger the development of many more in the near future.

Notes

1 Ilka Ruby and Andreas Ruby, *Druot, Lacaton & Vassal – Tour Bois Le Prêtre* (Berlin: Ruby Press, 2013).

2 Lara Menzel (ed.) *Facades, Design Construction and Technology* (Salenstein: Braun Publishers, 2012).

3 LAN Architects (2015). Available at: www.lan-paris.com/en/projects/lormont

4 Available at: balfrontower.org, 2015.

5 Anne Power, Professor of Social Policy and Head of LSE Housing and Communities, blog. Available at: http://blogs.lse.ac.uk/politicsandpolicy/sink-estates-demolition/ (accessed 4 March 2016):

6 BRE, Energy Saving Trust, *Refurbishing the Nation: Gathering the Evidence* (Watford: BRE, 2012).

7 Kate Crawford, Charlotte Johnson, Felicity Davies, Sunyoung Joo, and Sarah Bell, *Demolition or Refurbishment of Social Housing? A Review of the Evidence* (London: UCL Urban Lab and Engineering Exchange for Just Space and the London Tenants Federation, 2014), p. 4.

8 Power, blog, op. cit.

9 Crawford, *et al.* op. cit., p. 4.

10 Power, blog, op. cit.

11 Ibid.

12 Energy Savings Trust, Mears Groups and Travis Perkins, *Roadmap to 60%: Eco-refurbishment of 1960s Flats* (August 2008). Available at: http://tools.energysavingtrust.org.uk/cym/Publications2/Housing-professionals/Refurbishment/Roadmap-to-60-eco-refurbishment-of-1960s-flats-2008-edition

13 Ibid, p. 47.

14 Savills Research Report to the Cabinet Office, Completing London's Streets. How the regeneration and intensification of housing estates could increase London's supply of homes and benefit residents (7 January 2016). Available at: http://pdf.euro.savills.co.uk/uk/residential---other/completing-london-s-streets-080116.pdf

15 Anne Lacaton and Jean-Philippe Vassal at the 'Tower, Slab, Superblock: Social Housing Legacies and Futures' forum, 10 December 2016.

16 Power, blog, op. cit.

17 UK Green Building Council, *Retrofit Incentives: Boosting Take-Up of Energy Efficiency Measures in Domestic Properties*, Campaign for a Sustainable Built Environment. Task Group Report, July 2013. Available at: www.ukgbc.org/sites/default/files/130705%2520Retrofit%2520Incentives%2520Task%2520Group%2520-%2520Report%2520FINAL_1.pdf

18 Ibid.

19 According to different media, by the end of June 2017 the death toll had reached 80, with different authorities stating it was likely that this number would rise above a hundred.

20 Sam Webb, email conversation with Sam Webb (15–16 October 2014). Webb was involved in the surveys of Ronan Point to prepare evidence of the structural conditions of the building for the 1968 Public Enquiry. Since then, Webb has been a researcher and tenants' advisor for other large panel system tower blocks, as well as expert witness for the families in the Lakanal House Fire Inquest 2009.

21 Richard Waite, Will Hurst, and Ella Braidwood, 'News analysis: Five questions about Grenfell Tower that must be answered', *The Architects Journal* 20 June 2017. Available at: www.architectsjournal.co.uk/news/news-analy sis-five-questions-about-grenfell-tower-that-must-be-answered/10020900. article?v=1

22 R. Davies, K. Connolly, and I. Sample, Cladding for Grenfell Tower was cheaper, more flammable option", *The Guardian*, 16 June 2017. Available at: www.theguardian.com/uk-news/2017/jun/16/manufacturer-of-cladding-on-grenfell-tower-identified-as-omnis-exteriors

23 Angela Monaghan, 'Grenfell Tower fire: MP says public must be told to stop using Hotpoint model', *The Guardian*, 27 June 2017. Available at: www. theguardian.com/uk-news/2017/jun/27/grenfell-tower-fire-hotpoint-fridge-freezer-mp-andy-slaughter

24 Jan-Carlos Kucharek, 'Analysis of a tragedy', *RIBA Journal* 21 July 2017. Available at: www.ribaj.com/intelligence/grenfell-tower-tragedy-london

25 Nicole Morley, 'Witnesses describe the horror of Grenfell Tower fire', *Metro News* 14 June 2017. Available at: http://metro.co.uk/2017/06/14/witnesses-describe-the-horror-of-grenfell-tower-fire-6706961/?ito=cbshare

26 Kucharek, 'Analysis', op. cit.

27 BS9991:2011. Fire Safety in the design, management and use of residential buildings. Code of Practice: 'All buildings with a floor higher than 30m above ground should be fitted with sprinklers.'

28 London Borough of Southwark response to Rule 43 letter (23 May 2013. Available at: www.lambeth.gov.uk/sites/default/files/ec-london-borough-southwark-letter-response-to-rule-43-23May2013.pdf

29 Sam Webb, cited in Oliver Wainwright and Peter Walker, '"Disaster waiting to happen": fire expert slams UK tower blocks', *The Guardian*, 14 June 2017 Available at: www.theguardian.com/uk-news/2017/jun/14/disaster-waiting-to-happen-fire-expert-slams-uk-tower-blocks

30 The Coroner's Court, letter to Rt Hon. Eric Pickles, MP Secretary of State for Communities and Local Government, 20 May 2013.

31 Gov.UK (27 June 2017) Communities Secretary Sajid Javid announcement, 'Expert panel appointed to advise on immediate safety action following Grenfell fire'. Available at: www.gov.uk/government/news/expert-panel-appointed-to-advise-on-immediate-safety-action-following-grenfell-fire

32 Richard Waite, 'Anger at absence of architects on Grenfell fire expert panel', *The Architects Journal* 29 June 2017. Available at: www.architects-journal.co.uk/10021209.article?utm_source=newsletter&utm_medium=

email&utm_campaign=AJ_EditorialNewsletters.Reg:%20Send%20-%20
Daily%20bulletin&mkt_tok=eyJpIjoiWmpVeE5XTTBPRGsyTURZdyIsInQi
OiJ2XC9KUDBFenB3WEF2cXU0RW9tZ25SNzhhOVo0N05Lak95RTFJYIRH
TzFjMFI0THNuRlBkZjJvMmlOVDhwcnBESzZsQzJnUFIndFpTdW5MaW1EM
WdseHFPWTc3ancyaG44S0pwbVVwRU8yTlwvUXA5YTdFT0I2bUdZSkZudW
wyWXAwln0%3D

33 Royal Institute of British Architects (RIBA), *Statement on Design for Fire Safety*, circulated to all RIBA members by email on 22 June 2017.

34 Deon Lombard, 'Architects like me know Grenfell Tower fire was an avoidable tragedy', *The Guardian*, 17 June 2017. Available at: www.theguardian.com/public-leaders-network/2017/jun/17/architects-grenfell-tower-fire-was-an-avoidable-tragedy

35 Ibid.

36 Vikram Dodd and Harriet Sherwood, 'Grenfell council "may have committed corporate manslaughter" – Met police', *The Guardian*, 28 July 2017. Available at: www.theguardian.com/uk-news/2017/jul/27/met-says-grenfell-council-may-have-committed-corporate-manslaughter?CMP=fb_gu

37 Press Association, ' "Tower blocks could be torn down" – Sadiq Khan', *The Telegraph News*, 18 June 2017. Available at: www.telegraph.co.uk/news/2017/06/18/tower-blocks-could-torn-sadiq-khan/

38 Collin Mars, 'Academics: "Don't use Grenfell Tower tragedy to justify high-rise demolitions"', *The Architect's Journal*, 4 July 2017. Available at: www.architectsjournal.co.uk/news/academics-dont-use-grenfell-tower-tragedy-to-justify-high-rise-demolitions/10021325.article?blocktitle=election&contentID=18880

39 Lakanal House Coroner Inquest (14 January–28 March 2013). Available at: www.lambeth.gov.uk/elections-and-council/lakanal-house-coroner-inquest

40 Class 0 is not a classification defined by a British Standard, rather it is defined in Approved Document B as a sample that achieves Class 1 in a surface spread of flame test and achieves an index of performance (I) not exceeding 12 and a sub index (i1) not exceeding six in the fire propagation test.

41 Sarah Colwell, 'External fire spread – the testing of building cladding systems', presentation at the BRE Trust conference on fire engineering projects: November 2008. Available at: www.ifsecglobal.com/external-fire-spread-the-testing-of-building-cladding-systems/

42 Ibid.

43 Alexi Mostrous, 'Call for fire regulations to be overhauled after Grenfell tragedy', *The Times*, 19 June 2017. Available at: www.thetimes.co.uk/article/call-for-fire-regulations-to-be-overhauled-after-grenfell-tragedy-zbtczhhjp

44 Webb, '"Disaster"', op. cit.

45 Arnold Tarling, cited in Oliver Wainwright and Peter Walker, ' "Disaster waiting to happen": fire expert slams UK tower blocks', *The Guardian*: 14 June 2017. Available at: www.theguardian.com/uk-news/2017/jun/14/disaster-waiting-to-happen-fire-expert-slams-uk-tower-blocks

46 Rob Davies, Kate Connolly, and Ian Sample, 'Cladding for Grenfell Tower was cheaper, more flammable option', *The Guardian*, 16 June 2017. Available at:

www.theguardian.com/uk-news/2017/jun/16/manufacturer-of-cladding-on-grenfell-tower-identified-as-omnis-exteriors

47 Letter from DCLG to local authorities and housing associations. Available at: www.gov.uk/government/publications/safety-checks-following-the-grenfell-tower-fire:

> On buildings with a floor over 18m above ground level, where ACM panels are identified, it is necessary to establish whether the panels are of a type that complies with the Building Regulations guidance ie the core material should be a material of limited combustibility or Class A2 (Material of Limited combustibility as described in Table A7 of Approved Document B (vol. 2). Class A2-s3, d2 or better in accordance with BS EN 13501-1).

48 Kevin Rawlinson, 'Sixty towers across England found to have unsafe cladding', *The Guardian*, 25 June 2017. Available at: https://www.theguardian.com/uk-news/2017/jun/25/revealed-60-towers-across-england-found-to-have-unsafe-cladding

49 Robert Booth, 'London council that evacuated building knew of fire door problem five years ago', *The Guardian*, 28 June 2017. Available at: www.theguardian.com/uk-news/2017/jun/28/london-council-that-evacuated-building-knew-of-fire-door-problem-five-years-ago

50 BBC News, 'Cladding to be removed from 11 London tower blocks', 24 June 2017. Available at: www.bbc.co.uk/news/uk-england-london-40381643

51 London Borough of Southwark, op. cit.

52 Ian Cobain, 'Fire safety: repeated calls for retrofitting sprinklers to high-rises were ignored', *The Guardian*, 18 June 2017. Available at: www.theguardian.com/uk-news/2017/jun/18/fire-safety-repeated-calls-for-retrofitting-sprinklers-grenfell-towers-to-high-rises-were-ignored.

53 London Borough of Southwark, op. cit.

54 Scott Sanderson, in Oliver Wainwright and Peter Walker, '"Disaster waiting to happen": fire expert slams UK tower blocks', *The Guardian*, 14 June 2017. Available at: www.theguardian.com/uk-news/2017/jun/14/disaster-waiting-to-happen-fire-expert-slams-uk-tower-blocks

55 The Coroner's Court, op. cit.

56 *Retrofit for the Future* was a £17 million programme launched in 2009. It catalysed the retrofit of over 100 homes across the UK, with an ambition of achieving an 80 per cent reduction in the in-use CO_2 emissions of each property. See https://retrofit.innovateuk.org/documents/1524978/2138994/Retrofit%20for%20the%20future%20-%20A%20guide%20to%20making%20retrofit%20work%20-%202014

57 Cabinet Office, May 2011. *Government Construction Strategy*. Available at: www.gov.uk/government/uploads/system/uploads/attachment_data/file/61152/Government-Construction-Strategy_0.pdf

58 HM Government, *Construction 2025. Industrial Strategy: Government and Industry in Partnership*, July 2013. p.10. Available at: www.constructionleadershipcouncil.co.uk/wp-content/uploads/2016/10/bis-13-955-construction-2025-industrial-strategy.pdf

59 See www.nationalplatform.org.uk/map.jsp?id=20; www.gov.uk/government/uploads/system/uploads/attachment_data/file/210099/bis-13-955-construction-2025-industrial-strategy.pdf

60 Office for National Statistics (ONS) *Monthly Statistics of Building Materials and Components* (March 2017). Available at: www.gov.uk/government/collections/building-materials-and-components-monthly-statistics-2012#publications

61 See www.gov.uk/government/uploads/system/uploads/attachment_data/file/229339/construction-sector-infographic.pdf

62 H. Kirke-Smith, Green Alliance, *Towering Ambitions: Transforming High Rise Housing into Sustainable Homes.* December 2012. Available at: www.green-alliance.org.uk/resources/Towering%20ambitions.pdf

63 Department for Business, Energy & Industrial Strategy. Available at: www.gov.uk/guidance/smart-meters-how-they-work

64 Department for Environment, Food and Rural Affairs (DEFRA), 'Statistics on waste managed by local authorities in England in 2015/16'(15 December 2016). Available at: www.gov.uk/government/uploads/system/uploads/attachment_data/file/664594/LACW_mgt_annual_Stats_Notice_Dec_2017.pdf

65 Statistics and Research (September 2016). Available at: gov.wales/statistics-and-research/local-authority-municipal-waste-management/?lang=en

66 SEPA, 7 November 2016. Available at: www.sepa.org.uk/media/219489/2015-household-waste-summary-data-with-commentary.pdf

67 DEFRA, Waste Implementation Programme, Local Authority Support Unit (WIP LASU). The research has been carried out by Waste Watch and the Safe Neighbourhoods Unit. Waste Watch is the UK's leading national environmental organisation promoting sustainable resource management in the UK. The Safe Neighbourhoods Unit (SNU) is a not-for-profit research and development body with charitable status specialising in community development, community safety, regeneration and environmental improvement work in disadvantaged communities.

68 Ofwat (The Water Services Regulation Authority) (December 2013). Available at: www.ofwat.gov.uk/wp-content/uploads/2015/11/prs_lft_101117meters.pdf

69 CABE, *Community Green: Using Local Spaces to Tackle Inequality and Improve Health* (London: CABE, 2010).

70 For instance, L. Lane, A. Power and B. Provan, *Case Study: Edward Woods Estate. High Rise Hope Revisited. The Social Implications of Upgrading Large Estates.* LSE Housing and Communities, October 2014.

71 Ibid.

72 Crawford, *et al.*, *Demolition or Refurbishment of Social Housing?* op. cit. pp. 3, 43.

73 See, for instance, studies from PROBE (Post Occupancy Review of Buildings and their Engineering), the Carbon Trust's Low Carbon Buildings Accelerator and the Low Carbon Buildings Programme. Available at: www.cibse.org/knowledge/building-services-case-studies/probe-post-occupancy-studies; www.zerocarbonhub.org/sites/default/files/resources/reports/Closing_the_Gap_Between_Design_and_As-Built_Performance-Evidence_Review

_Report_0.pdf and www.carbontrust.com/media/81361/ctg047-closing-the-gap-low-carbon-building-design.pdf

74 P. Waide (November 2006), *High-Rise Refurbishment: The Energy-Efficient Upgrade of Multi-Story Residences in the European Union.* International Energy Agency and European Alliance of companies for Energy Efficiency (EuroACE).

75 Office for National Statistics (4 November 2016). *Families and Households in the UK: 2016.* Available at: www.ons.gov.uk/peoplepopulationandcommunity/birthsdeathsandmarriages/families/bulletins/familiesandhouseholds/2016

76 T. Loga, B. Stein and N. Diefenbach, 'TABULA building typologies in 20 European countries: Making energy-related features of residential building stocks comparable'. *Energy and Buildings* 132 (2016): 4–12.

Figure credits

Figure 1.1 Photograph © Thomas Annan and William Young. Courtesy of British Library.
Figure 1.2 Photograph © Simon Pepper, 1980.
Figure 1.3 Photograph © Fox Photos/Getty Images.
Figure 1.4 Photographs © Liverpool Record Office, Liverpool Libraries.
Figure 1.5 Photograph © Architectural Press Archive/RIBA Collections, 1961.
Figure 1.6 Photograph © Authors, 2014.
Figure 1.7 Photograph © John Maltby/RIBA Collections.
Figure 1.8 Image © Authors.
Figure 1.9 Drawing © Authors.
Figure 1.10 Photographs © John Claridge.
Figure 1.11 Photographs © Robert Blomfield.
Figure 1.12 Image © Authors.
Figure 1.13 Photograph © Getty Images.
Figure 1.14 Photograph © Lotte Grønkjær.
Figure 2.1 Department of Energy and Climate Change, 31 March 2016.
Image © Authors.
Figure 2.2 Department of Energy & Climate Change, 31 March 2016.
Image © Authors.
Figure 2.3 Image © Authors.
Figure 2.4 Based on chart published by the National Audit Office, 2016. Produced by
authors.
Figure 3.1 Image © Authors.
Figure 3.2 Image © Authors.
Figure 3.3 Photograph © Authors.
Figure 3.4 Photograph © Authors.
Figure 3.5 Image © Authors.
Figure 3.6 Image © Authors.
Figure 3.7 Drawing © University of Liverpool.
Figure 3.8 Photograph © Authors.
Figure 3.9 Photograph © Authors.
Figure 3.10 Image © Authors.
Figure 3.11 Image © Authors.
Figure 3.12 Image © Authors.
Figure 3.13 Image © Authors.
Figure 3.14 Photograph © Authors.
Figure 3.15 Image © Authors.
Figure 3.16 Photograph © Authors.
Figure 3.17 Photograph © Authors.
Figure 3.18 Image © Authors.
Figure 3.19 Image © Authors.
Figure 3.20 Image © Authors.
Figure 3.21 Image © Authors.
Figure 3.22 Image © Authors.

Figure 3.23 Image © Authors.
Figure 3.24 Image © Authors.
Figure 3.25 Image © Authors.
Figure 3.26 Image © Authors.
Figure 3.27 Image © Authors.
Figure 3.28 Image © Authors.
Figure 3.29 Image © Authors.
Figure 3.30 Image © Authors.
Figure 4.1 Drawing © Authors.
Figure 4.2 Drawing © University of Liverpool.
Figure 4.3 Photograph © Authors.
Figure 4.4 Photograph © Authors.
Figure 4.5 Drawing © University of Liverpool.
Figure 4.6 Photograph © Authors.
Figure 4.7 Photograph © Authors.
Figure 4.8 Photograph © Authors.
Figure 4.9 Photograph © Authors.
Figure 4.10 Drawing © Authors.
Figure 4.11 Drawing © Authors.
Figure 4.12 Photograph © RIBA Collections, 1968.
Figure 4.13 Photograph © Authors.
Figure 4.14 Drawing © University of Liverpool.
Figure 4.15 Photograph © Authors.
Figure 4.16 Photograph © Authors.
Figure 4.17 Drawing © Authors.
Figure 4.18 Photograph © RIBA Collections, 1965.
Figure 4.19 Drawing © Authors.
Figure 4.20 Photograph © Authors.
Figure 4.21 Drawing © University of Liverpool.
Figure 4.22 Photograph © Authors.
Figure 4.23 Photograph © Authors.
Figure 4.24 Drawing © Authors.
Figure 4.25 Photograph © PRP Architects.
Figure 4.26 Photograph © Authors.
Figure 4.27 Photograph © Authors.
Figure 4.28 Photograph © Authors.
Figure 4.29 Drawing © University of Liverpool.
Figure 4.30 Photograph © Authors.
Figure 4.31 Drawing © PRP Architects.
Figure 4.32 Photograph © PRP Architects.
Figure 4.33 Photograph © PRP Architects.
Figure 4.34 Drawing © Authors.
Figure 4.35 Photograph © RIBA Collections, 1976.
Figure 4.36 Drawing © University of Liverpool.
Figure 4.37 Photograph © Authors.
Figure 4.38 Drawing © Authors.
Figure 4.39 Photograph e © Authors.
Figure 4.40 Photograph © Authors.
Figure 4.41 Photograph © Authors.
Figure 4.42 Drawing © Authors.
Figure 4.43 Photograph © Albert Coe, Myra Coe, 1962.

Figure 4.44 Drawing © University of Liverpool.
Figure 4.45 Photograph © Authors.
Figure 4.46 Drawing © University of Liverpool.
Figure 4.47 Photograph © Authors.
Figure 4.48 Drawing © University of Liverpool.
Figure 4.49 Photograph © Authors.
Figure 4.50 Drawing © Authors.
Figure 4.51 Photograph © RIBA Collections, 1969.
Figure 4.52 Drawing © University of Liverpool.
Figure 4.53 Photograph © Authors.
Figure 4.54 Drawing © University of Liverpool.
Figure 4.55 Photograph © Authors.
Figure 4.56 Drawing © University of Liverpool.
Figure 4.57 Drawing © Authors.
Figure 4.58 Photograph © Authors.
Figure 4.59 Drawing © University of Liverpool.
Figure 4.60 Photograph © Authors.
Figure 4.61 Photograph © Authors.
Figure 4.62 Drawing © University of Liverpool.
Figure 4.63 Photograph © Authors.
Figure 4.64 Drawing © Authors.
Figure 4.65 Photograph © Authors.
Figure 4.66 Drawing © University of Liverpool.
Figure 4.67 Photograph © Authors.
Figure 4.68 Drawing © Authors.
Figure 4.69 Photograph © Authors.
Figure 4.70 Photograph © Authors.
Figure 4.71 Drawing © Authors.
Figure 4.72 Photograph © JRA.
Figure 4.73 Drawing © University of Liverpool.
Figure 4.74 Photograph © Authors.
Figure 4.75 Drawing © Authors.
Figure 4.76 Drawing © JRA.
Figure 4.77 Photograph © Authors.
Figure 4.78 Photograph © Authors.
Figure 4.79 Photograph © Authors.
Figure 4.80 Photograph © Authors.
Figure 4.81 Drawing © Authors.
Figure 4.82 Photograph © West & Machell Architects.
Figure 4.83 Drawing © University of Liverpool.
Figure 4.84 Photograph © Authors.
Figure 4.85 Drawing © University of Liverpool.
Figure 4.86 Photograph © Authors.
Figure 4.87 Photograph © West & Machell Architects.
Figure 4.88 Drawing © West & Machell Architects.
Figure 4.89 Photograph © West & Machell Architects.
Figure 4.90 Drawing © West & Machell Architects.
Figure 4.91 Drawing © Authors.
Figure 4.92 Photograph © RIBA Collections.
Figure 4.93 Drawing © University of Liverpool.
Figure 4.94 Photograph © Authors.

Figure 4.95 Drawing © University of Liverpool.
Figure 4.96 Photograph © Authors.
Figure 4.97 Photograph © Authors.
Figure 4.98 Drawing © University of Liverpool.
Figure 4.99 Drawing © Authors.
Figure 4.100 Drawing © University of Liverpool.
Figure 4.101 Photograph © Authors.
Figure 4.102 Drawing © University of Liverpool.
Figure 4.103 Photograph © Authors.
Figure 4.104 Photograph © Authors.
Figure 4.105 Drawing © Authors.
Figure 4.106 Photograph © Robert Blomfield.
Figure 4.107 Drawing © University of Liverpool.
Figure 4.108 Photograph © Authors.
Figure 4.109 Photograph © Authors.
Figure 4.110 Photograph © Authors.
Figure 4.111 Drawing © Authors.
Figure 4.112 Photograph © Authors.
Figure 4.113 Photograph © Authors.
Figure 4.114 Drawing © University of Liverpool.
Figure 4.115 Photograph © Authors.
Figure 4.116 Drawing © University of Liverpool.
Figure 4.117 Photograph © Authors.
Figure 4.118 Drawing © Urban Splash.
Figure 4.119 Photograph © Authors.
Figure 4.120 Drawing © Urban Splash.
Figure 4.121 Drawing © Urban Splash.
Figure 4.122 Drawing © Authors.
Figure 4.123 Drawing © University of Liverpool.
Figure 4.124 Photograph © Authors.
Figure 4.125 Photograph © Authors.
Figure 4.126 Drawing © University of Liverpool.
Figure 4.127 Drawing © Authors.
Figure 4.128 Drawing © University of Liverpool.
Figure 4.129 Photograph © Authors.
Figure 4.130 Photograph © Authors.
Figure 4.131 Drawing © University of Liverpool.
Figure 4.132 Drawing © Authors.
Figure 4.133 Photograph © Alamy.
Figure 4.134 Drawing © University of Liverpool.
Figure 4.135 Photograph © Authors.
Figure 4.136 Drawing © University of Liverpool.
Figure 4.137 Photograph © Authors.
Figure 4.138 Photograph © Authors.
Figure 4.139 Drawing © University of Liverpool.
Figure 4.140 Drawing © Authors.
Figure 4.141 Drawing © University of Liverpool.
Figure 4.142 Photograph © Authors.
Figure 4.143 Drawing © University of Liverpool.
Figure 4.144 Photograph © Authors.
Figure 4.145 Photograph © Authors.

Figure 4.146 Drawing © Authors.

Figure 4.147 Drawing © University of Liverpool.

Figure 4.148 Drawing © University of Liverpool.

Figure 4.149 Photograph © Authors.

Figure 4.150 Photograph © Authors.

Figure 4.151 Photograph © Authors.

Figure 4.152 Drawing © University of Liverpool.

Figure 4.153 Drawing © Authors.

Figure 4.154 Photograph © Authors.

Figure 4.155 Drawing © University of Liverpool.

Figure 4.156 Photograph © Authors.

Figure 4.157 Drawing © University of Liverpool.

Figure 4.158 Photograph © Authors.

Figure 4.159 Photograph © Authors.

Figure 4.160 Drawing © University of Liverpool.

Figure 6.1 Photograph © Authors.

Figure 6.2 Photograph © Authors.

Figure 6.3 Photograph © Authors.

Figure 6.4 Photograph © Authors.

Figure 6.5 Photograph © Roy Roberts.

Figure 6.6 Photograph © Authors.

Figure 6.7 Photograph © Authors.

Figure 6.8 Photograph © Philippe Ruault, 2017.

Figure 6.9 Photograph © Phillipe Ruault, 2017.

Figure 6.10 Photograph © Eibe Soennecken

Figure 6.11 Photograph © Authors.

Figure 6.12 Photograph © Authors.

Figure 6.13 Photograph © Beate Paland, freeimages.com

Figure 6.14 Photograph © Authors.

Figure 6.15 Photograph © HLP Architects. Courtesy of David Rudkin.

Figure 6.16 Photograph © Authors.

Figure 6.17 Photograph © Authors.

Figure 6.18 Photograph © Authors.

Figure 6.19 Drawing © Authors

Figure 6.20 Photograph © HLP Architects. Courtesy of David Rudkin.

Figure 6.21 Photograph © Authors.

Index

AAB Afdeling *16*, 43
accessibility 55, 262
ACM (aluminium composite material) 253, 254
Action for Sustainable Living 197
add-in strategy 41, 42
add-on strategy 41, 42, 235
Adlington Tower: architects for 224–6; gentrification of 240; maintenance of colour/materiality 234, *235*
AK Design Partnership 210
Allied London 124
ALMOs (arm's-length management organisations) 28
Alumet Systems Ltd & Alumet Renewable Technologies Ltd 130
aluminium composite material (ACM) 253, 254
Apollo Group 205
Apollo London Ltd 210
Aragon Tower *39, 77, 108*; architects *82, 83*; building extension 55, *60*; changes to *47, 84, 91*, 108–12; colour change 67, *71*; façade of 43
Architects' Journal Retrofit 2013 Award for Housing 195
Arena Housing 224
arm's-length management organisations (ALMOs) 28
Art Deco style 157, 231
Arup, Ove 8
assessment, of tower blocks 15, 18, 241–3
Average Standard Assessment Procedure rating 242
awards: Architects' Journal Retrofit 2013 Award for Housing 195; Designs of the Year Award 236; Eurosolar Prize 236; for Greenhouse 160; for Keeling House 167; for Marriott Tower 236; for Park Hill 178, 238; RIBA Stirling Prize 2013 178; for Tamworth Towers 195; for Tour Bois-le-Prêtre 236

Axis Architecture 130
Aylesbury Estate *39, 74*: changes to 57, *84, 91*

balconies 42, 44, 55, *102, 123, 125, 126, 131*; escape, 257
Balfron Tower *114, 115, 239*; architects *82, 83*; changes to *58, 85, 91*, 113–5; electrical/mechanical upgrades 55; lack of change 67; listed status 238; retrofit completion *75*; social structure of 238, *239*. *See also* Carradale House
Barbican Estate *10*
Barton Village 31, 212–7
BBC 224
Belem Tower *40, 81*: changes to *48, 95, 97*; electrical/mechanical upgrades 55; renewable energy in 61, *65*
Bell, Peter 189
Berkeley Homes 108, 110
Bethnal Green and East London Housing Association 6, *6*
Bickerdike Court *40, 80*: changes to *48, 95, 98*; colour change *69*; electrical/mechanical upgrades 55; renewable energy in 61, *64*
Bieber 200
biomass centres 263
Birmingham, as Green Deal Low Carbon City 30
Bispham Towers *40*
Blacon 212–7
Bois-le-Prêtre 243–4, 258
Bolton, Craig 229–32, 237, 239
Bon, Christoph 150
Bonfield, Peter 249
Bow City Council 116
Bow Cross Estate *75*, 116–21; architects *83*; changes to *51, 85, 91*, 116–21, 235; colour of *70*, 234; conditions in 240; social structure of 238
box frame 38

BR135 Fire Performance of External Thermal Insulation for Walls of Multi-storey Buildings 253

Brandon Estate *39, 76*: changes to *50, 86, 91*; colour change *72*

BRE (Building Research Establishment) 26, 252, 254, 268

Breyer Group 140, 141

Bristol, as Green Deal Low Carbon City 30

British Automatic Fire Sprinkler Association 255

British Gas 140, 141, 219

British Heritage 227, 228

British Housing Act of 1949 11

Brook Hill complex 176. *See also* Netherthorpe Complex

Brownfield estate *39*, 114

Brunswick Centre *39, 77, 122–7, 122–6*, 238; changes to *59, 86, 92*; lack of change 67; listed status 234, 238

Brutalist style 114, 237, 238

building regulations, fire safety and 248–9, 253

Building Regulations, part B 248–9

Building Research Establishment (BRE) 26, 252, 254, 268

Callow Mount Complex *40, 80, 128–33*; changes to *49, 95, 98*, 128–33, 235; colour of *67, 68*, 234, *234*; electrical/mechanical upgrades 55; functional conversions 55

Camden, London Borough of 134, 136

Camden City Council 124, 134, 254

Canada Estate 203, *205*

Candia and Crete *40, 80*: changes to *98, 99*; colour change *68*

Canning Town 145

carbon emissions reduction 23–34, 263; from buildings 22; compared to target *23*; Carbon Emission Reduction Target (CERT) *27, 29*; Community Energy Saving Programme) *27, 29, 36n24*; Decent Homes Standard 26–8, 32–3, *32, 36n18*; environmental context, 22–5; government energy-efficiency retrofit programmes 25–30; Green Deal Policy (GD) *27, 29*–30, 33; reducing 1, 22, 24–5; refurbishing and 22–3; by sector *24*; timelines, *27*; UK Carbon Plan 22, 28, 216, 240, 269

Carbon Emission Reduction Target (CERT) *27, 29*, 216

Carbon Plan (UK Carbon Plan) 22, 28, 216, 240, 269

Carradale House *114*; architects *83*; changes to *58, 85, 91*, 113–5; lack of change 67. *See also* Balfron Tower

Caryl Gardens 6

CERT (Carbon Emission Reduction Target) *27, 29*, 216

CESP (Community Energy Saving Programme) *27, 29, 36n24*, 197, 216

Chalcots Estate *39, 74, 134–8*, 254; changes to *46, 86, 92*, 134–8; colour of *71*, 234; electrical/mechanical upgrades 55; evacuation of 254; façade 233, *233*

Chamberlin, Peter 150

Chamberlin Powell & Bon 14, 150

Chartist House *40, 79*: changes to *96, 99*; electrical/mechanical upgrades 55; renewable energy in 61, *65*

Chelsea Tenant Management Organisation 251

cities, growth of 3

CITU 157, 229, 230

City of London Corporation (CLC) 217

City West Homes 170

City West Housing Association 212

Clack, Amanda 249

cladding. *See* insulation; over-cladding

class 11. *See also* social structure

CLC (City of London Corporation) 217

Clegg Construction 157, 231

climate change 22, 269

Climate Change Act of 2008 22

Climate Change Committee 26

Coates, Wells 8

collective social housing 3. *See also* estates; housing stock; public housing; tower blocks

Colne and Mersea House *39, 74*; architects *82, 83*; changes to *50, 87, 92*; colour change *72*; electrical/mechanical upgrades 55; renewable energy in 61, *62*

colour 66–73; changing 216, 220–1, 223, 231, 233–4; in London *70–3*; maintaining 226, 229, 234; in North-west England *66–7, 67, 68–9, 73*

Colwell, Sarah 252, 253

comfort, in post-war period 2. *See also* insulation

commercial use. *See* working spaces

commission process 240

communal living 3

communication, energy efficiency and 265

Community Energy Saving Programme (CESP) *27*, 29, 36n24, 197, 216

conditions, physical: of Adlington Tower 224; of Crossways Estate 221–2; of Great Arthur House 218; of Greenhouse 230; of Park Hill 227; before retrofits 240

conditions, social. *See* social conditions; social structure

construction industry 11, *14*, 249, 251, 260–1

Construction Leadership Council 260

construction technology 9, 11, 38

Copenhagen *16*

Corlett Street flats 6

cottage model 5, 9

Cottingley Towers *40, 78, 66, 96, 99*

council housing. *See* estates; housing stock; public housing; tower blocks

Countryside Properties 119

courtyards *7, 12*, 42, 230

Cranbrook Estate *39, 75*; changes to *50, 87, 92*; electrical/mechanical upgrades 55

Crescent Grange Sheltered Housing 45

criminality 240

cross-wall 38

Crossways Estate: architects *83*, 221–4; techniques used on 44, 54–5

cyanide poisoning 248

David Bernstein Architects 122, 124

David Rudkin Architects 212–7, 259m

DCLG (Department for Communities and Local Government) 248, 249, 253, 255

decanting 222

decarbonisation: Average Standard Assessment Procedure rating 242; insulation and 261. *See also* UK Carbon Plan

Decent Homes Plus standard 28, 137

Decent Homes Standard 26–9, 32–3, *32*, 36n18, 136, 170, 171, 203, 205, 216, 219, 235, 239, 261

DEFRA 263

demolition 15–6, *16*, 241–5, *241*

Dennis Lennon & Partners 134

Department for Communities and Local Government (DCLG) 248, 249, 253, 255

design approaches 107, 239–40; lack of holistic 257–60; quality/innovation 235–7

Designs of the Year Award 236

developers/contractors/manufacturers 216, 218–9; Allied London 124; Alumet Systems Ltd & Alumet Renewable Technologies Ltd 130; Apollo Group 205; Berkeley Homes 108; Bieber 200; Clegg Construction 157, 231; Falkingham, Jonathan 226–9; Henry Boot 177, 188; Keepmoat 220; Lincoln Holdings 164, 165; Lovell Partnership 130, 225; Retrofit UK Ltd 119, 210; Rydon Construction Limited 136, 147, 247; Seddon Construction 197; Urban Splash Ltd *82, 83*, 102, 104, 113, 114, 178, 180, 226–9, 238, 240; Wates Living Space 168, 171

disasters. *See* Grenfell Tower; Lakanal House

Domestic Renewable Heat Incentive (DRHI) *27*, 31–2

Dovercroft Towers *40, 79*

Draper Estate *39*; changes to *56, 87, 92*

DRHI (Domestic Renewable Heat Incentive) *27*, 31–2

Druot, Lacaton & Vassal 236, 243–4, 258, 259

ECD Architects *83*, 140, 148, 192

ECO (Energy Company Obligation) *27*, 30–1, 33, 261

economies of scale, retrofitting and 24–5

EcoPods 31, 214, 216, 240, 259, *259*

Edward Woods Estate *39, 74*, 139–44, *139, 140, 141, 142, 143*, 244; architects *83*; changes to *46, 87*; colour of 71, 234, *234*; electrical/mechanical upgrades 55; energy bills 265–6; renewable energy in 61, *63*, 237; retrofit strategies for 244–5

EEC (Energy Efficiency Commitment) 26, *27*

EESoP (Energy Efficiency Standards of Performance) 26, *27*, 260

INDEX   **283**

electrical upgrades 55
electricity, clean 31–2
Ellis, Charles 217
energy, domestic 31
energy, renewable *61, 144,* 237; application of 61–5; in Ferrier Point *61,* 149; in Greenhouse 231; in London *62–3*; in North-west England *64–5*; programmes for 31–2; in retrofits 41; use of 240; user behavior and 267. *See also* EcoPods
Energy Act 2011 29
Energy and Climate Change, Department of 30
Energy Company Obligation (ECO) *27,* 30–1, 261
Energy Conscious Design Architects 141, 147
energy efficiency 33, 35n12, 24; challenges for tower blocks 262–5; measuring 265–7; rating (SAP09), 24; regulations 29; research on 267–9; self-sufficiency, 263
Energy Efficiency Commitment (EEC) 26, 27, *27*
Energy Efficiency Standards of Performance (EESoP) 26, *27,* 260
Energy Performance Certificate (EPC) 29
Energy Savings Trust 31, 243
energy suppliers/generators 29, 30, 31, 32
England, North-west. *See* North-west England
English Heritage 113, 124, 151, 155, 165, 180, 200, 219, 240
English Housing Survey: HOMES 2010 18
English Partnership's First Time Buyers Initiative 104
environmental issues, 2, 18, 23, 262–5
EPC (Energy Performance Certificate) 29
EPISCOPE 268, 269
estates: origins of 2–18; use of term 19n11. *See also* public housing; tower blocks
EuroAce 267
Europe, Eastern 11
Eurosolar Prize 236
extensions 42, 55; Aragon Tower *60, 109*; Weybridge Point *235*

façades *41*; materials of 54; original 38–41; retrofitting strategies 41–2. *See also* over-cladding

Falconer Chester Hall Architects 224–6
Falkingham, Jonathan 226–9
family 213, 267–8
Feed-in Tariffs (FIT) *27,* 31, 32
Ferrier Point *39, 74, 15, 145–8*; architects *83*; changes to *47, 88, 93,* 145–9; colour of *71*; electrical/mechanical upgrades 55; renewable energy in 61, *61, 62,* 237
fire safety 246–57; checks, 252–4; cladding standard 252; compartmentation/layout 256–7; signage/information 257; sprinklers 254–6; supervision/regulation/prevention 248–52
FIT (Feed-in Tariffs) *27,* 31, 32
flats 5–8, 17. *See also* tower blocks
floor plans 55, 235, 256–7
France: Lormont urban development project 236–7, *237*; Tour Bois-le-Prêtre 236, *236,* 243–4, 258
Franklin, Jonathan 238
fuel poverty 33, 213, 265, 266
functional conversions 55, 60, 181. *See also* working spaces

gentrification 17, 213, 240; of Crossways Estate 223; of Great Arthur House 218. *See also* social structure
geothermic energy 61, 237
GER (Government Electricity Rebate) *27,* 31
Gerard Gardens 6
Germany 236, *237*
Glasgow 14
Glastonbury House *39, 76*; changes to *88, 93*; electrical/mechanical upgrades 55; functional conversions 55; renewable energy in 61, *62*
GLC (Greater London Council) 113, 114, 200, 201
GLC Dept. of Architecture & Civic Design 203
Golden Lane Estate *39, 75, 10, 150–4,* 238; architect for 217–21; changes to *56, 88, 93,* 150–5; electrical/mechanical upgrades 55; lack of change 67; listed status 14; social structure of 238. *See also* Great Arthur House
Goldfinger, Erno 14, 113, 114, 200, 201
Government Electricity Rebate (GER) *27,* 31

government programmes. *See* programmes, government

Grange Court Tower *39*

Grant Associates Landscape Architects 180

Great Arthur House *10*, *151–4*, 217–21; façade of 38, *41*; identity of 239; listed status 151; social structure of 238. *See also* Golden Lane Estate

Greater London Council (GLC) 113, 114, 200, 201

Green Alliance 33, 262

Green Building Council 246

Green Construction Board 261

Green Deal Home Improvement Fund 29–30, 33, 219, 261

Green Deal Low Carbon Cities 30

Green Deal Policy (GD) *27*, 29–30, 33, 219, 261

Greenfields Place 212–7

Greenhouse, Leeds *40*, *79*, 44, *156–61*, 251; architects for 229–32; building extension 55; changes to *53*, *96*, *99*, 156–61, 235; colour of *67*; conditions in 240; electrical/mechanical upgrades 55; functions 60, 240; green spaces in 264, *264*; renewable energy in 61, *64*, 237; social structure of 238, 239

greenhouse gas emissions. *See* carbon emissions reduction

green spaces 264

Grenfell Tower 1, 246–57, *247*, *256*

grey water 61, 158

Hammersmith and Fulham Council 140

Hammersmith and Fulham London Borough 139, 141

Harpenmead Point *39*; changes to *46*, *88*, *93*; colour of *70*

Hawkins/Brown 178, 180

health 2–3, 266. *See also* fire safety

heating: clean heat, 31; Domestic Renewable Heat Incentive (DRHI) *27*, 31–2; emissions and 22; greenhouse gas emissions and 263; in post-war construction 38. *See also* energy efficiency

heights 11

Heights, The 212–7

Henry Boot 177, 188

Herdings Complex *40*, *78*; changes to *49*, *97*, *99*; colour of *66*

heritage 216, 221, 223, 229, 242, 258, 269

HHSRS (Housing Health and Safety Rating System) 33

Highpoint One flats 8

High-Rise Refurbishment (research project) 267

historic context: high-rise social housing, ascent of 8–14, *11–14*; Modern Movement/Modernism 5, 8, *11*, 14, 21n35; modernity 2–3, 9, *11*; origins of public housing 2–8, *4*, *6–8*

HLP Architects 212–7, 240

Hodgkinson, Patrick 122, 123, 124

holistic strategy, lack of, 269; design 257–60; fire safety 246–57

Hollamby, Ted 108

Homes and Communities Agency 180

Housing Act of 1930 5

Housing Act of 1980 16

housing associations 16, 28, 215

Housing Corporation 180

Housing Health and Safety Rating System (HHSRS) 33

housing shortage, in interwar years 3–5

housing stock: conditions of 28; energy efficiency and 23–4; inspecting/appraising 23; management of 16; maximising value of 23; types, 5. *See also* public housing; tower blocks

Hughes, John 6

Hunter and Partners 203, 205

Hunt Thomson Architects 136

identity 219, 222, 231, 239–40, 269

image renewal 214, 239. *See also* perception

individuality of tower blocks 215, 216; of Crossways Estate 223; maintaining 221; of Park Hill 229

industrialisation 2–3

infilling 38, *41*

insulation 29, 30–1, 33, 41, 214, 240; of Adlington Tower 225; of Crossways Estate 222; fire safety and 248, 252; of Greenhouse 230; of Park Hill 227; in post-war construction 38. *See also* over-cladding

Intelligent Energy Europe 268

International Energy Agency 267

Islington City Council 190

Isokon Building 8

John Gray and Partners 190, 192
John McAslan & Partners 200
John Robertson Architects (JRA) 151,
    217–21, 239, 240
Judd, Rolfe 130
Just/Burgeff Architekten & Agkathidis 236

K&C Tenant Management Organisation
    200
Keeling House 39, 76, 54, 162–6, 238;
    building extension and improvements
    55; changes to 59, 67, 89, 93, 162–7;
    colour of 73; listed status 164;
    ownership changes 60
Keepmoat 220
Kemp Muir Wealleands (KMW) 171, 172
Kensington and Chelsea, Royal Borough
    of 200, 251
Kensington City Council. 247
Khan, Sadiq 251
King, Samuel 145
Kirkham, Frances 248
Knight, Ken 249

Ladywell Green 212–7, 245
Lakanal House 1, 246–57, 246
Lambeth, London Borough of 205
Lambeth Living 203, 205
landmarks 9, 14. See also listed buildings
landscape interventions 55, 105
Lasdun, Denys 162, 164
Le Corbusier 2
Leeds 6; as Green Deal Low Carbon City
    30; retrofits in 40; slum clearance in 5.
    See also Greenhouse, Leeds; North-
    west England; individual tower blocks
Leeds City Council 156, 157, 229
Lenig House 39, 77
Leverton Gardens TARA (Tenants and
    Residents Association) 130
LHC 205, 206
lifts subsidy 9, 19n16
lighting optimisation 29
Lincoln Holdings 164, 165
listed buildings 14; aesthetic demands of
    155; Balfron Tower 114, 238; Brunswick
    Centre 124, 238; Carradale House
    114; colour change and 67; Golden
    Lane Estate 14; Great Arthur House
    151; Keeling House 164; maintenance
    of colour/materiality 234; Park Hill 14,

178, 227, 228, 238, 238; restrictions
    on retrofits 238, 240; retrofits for 54;
    techniques and 42; Trellick Tower 14,
    238
Little Venice Towers 39, 77, 169, 170, 171,
    172; changes to 47, 89, 94, 168–73,
    235; colour of 67, 70, 234
Liverpool: central flats in 5–8; Central
    Redevelopment Area 6; as Green Deal
    Low Carbon City 30; Myrtle Gardens
    7–8; retrofits in 40; slum clearance in 5.
    See also North-west England
Liverpool Housing Association 212
Livett, Alfred Hardwick 6
Local Lettings Policy 213
LOCOSOC 267
Lombard, Deon 250
London, City of 150, 151
London, Greater 14; buildings with
    over-cladding 46–7, 50–1; central
    flats in 5–8; colour change in 67,
    70–3; completed retrofits per year
    76; renewable energy in 62; retrofit
    completion timeline 74–7; retrofitted
    tower blocks in 39, 84–94; retrofit types
    in 43; slum clearance in 5. See also
    individual boroughs and tower blocks
London Building Acts 247
London County Council (LCC) 5, 108, 114,
    118
London County Council Architects
    Department 11
London Development Agency 141
London School of Economics (LSE) 141
Lormont urban development project
    236–7, 237
Lovell Partnership 130, 225
Low Impact Buildings Innovation Platform
    261
Lubetkin, Berthold 8
Lynn, Jack 14, 178

Manchester: Barton Village 31; as Green
    Deal Low Carbon City 30; retrofits
    in 40; slum clearance in 5. See also
    North-west England; individual tower
    blocks
Manchester City Council 102
manslaughter, corporate 251
Marchmont Properties Ltd 122
Mark Heywood Associates 210

Marriott Tower 236, *237*
Marshall, Linda *15*
materiality: changing 67–73, 105, 233–4; of façades 43, 54; maintenance of 234; in post-war construction 41; reasons for changing 220–1
McAlston+Partners 201
mechanical upgrades 55
MEES (Minimum Energy Efficiency Standard) 262–3
Mellor, Andrew 221–4
meters, smart 262
Metro Central Heights *39*; lack of change 67
Minimum Energy Efficiency Standard (MEES) 262–3
Ministry of Housing 15
modernisation 24, 33
modernity 2–3, 9, *11*
Modern Movement/Modernism 5, 8, *11*, 14, 21n35, 157, 164, 219, 238, 257
Mumford, Lewis 2–3
Munkenbeck + Marshall 164, 165, 167
Myrtle Gardens 6, *7–8*

National Building Agency 11
National Tower Block Network 20n32
Netherthorpe Complex *13, 40, 78, 175, 176, 177*; changes to *48, 98,* 100, 174–7; colour of *66,* 234; façade 233, *233*
Newcastle, as Green Deal Low Carbon City 30
Newham, London Borough of 145, 147
North-west England 14; buildings with over-cladding *48–9, 52*; colour change *66–7, 67, 68–9, 73*; completed retrofits per year *81*; renewable energy in *64–5*; retrofit completion timeline *78–81*; retrofitted tower blocks in *40, 95. See also individual cities and tower blocks*
Nottingham, as Green Deal Low Carbon City 30
Nu-Heat company 141

Office of Gas and Electricity Markets (Ofgem) 36n24
Old Trafford 195
Old Trafford City Council 195
OPET Building 267
Ossulston Estate 5, *6*

outdoor spaces 55
over-cladding 38, 42, *104, 106, 107*; of Aragon Tower *110, 111, 112*; fire safety and 248; in North-west England *48–9*; of Park Hill *45,* 67; removal of 254; standard for 252; techniques of 54; on towers in London *46–7, 50–51*; use of 41, 44. *See also* insulation
ownership 60; of Bow Cross *118, 119*; of Park Hill 185; of Tamworth Towers 199; types of 221; of Weybridge Point 210. *See also* privatisation; right-to-buy law

Paris-Habitat 258
Park Hill *9, 40, 178, 179, 180–5,* 238; architects *82, 83*; awards for 178; changes to *49,* 55, *97,* 100, 178–85; colour of *67, 68,* 234; developer for 226–9; façade of *41*; functions 55, 240; listed status 14, 178, 227, 228, 238, *238*; materials in 41, 67; ownership changes 60; rain-screen panels *45*; retrofit completion *80*; RIBA award for 238; social structure of 238
Parsons House *39, 76, 187, 188, 189*; changes to *46, 89, 94,* 186–9; colour change *72*; design quality/innovation 236, *236*
Peabody Donation Fund 192
Peabody Towers/Estate *39, 77, 190, 191–3*; architects *83*; changes to *50, 89, 94,* 190–3; colour change *73*; electrical/mechanical upgrades and safety improvements 55; renewable energy in 61, *62*; techniques used on 44
Peabody town 192
Peabody Trust 162, 190, 192
Penn, Alan 251
Pepys Estate 108. *See also* Aragon Tower
perception: colour and 214; of tower blocks 14–5, 105. *See also* image renewal
performance gaps 266
PFI (Private Finance Initiative) 27–8
photovoltaic panels (PV) 32, 61, 144, 149, 237, 240
Places for People 178, 180
point blocks 11, *12*
poor, organising 17, 21n35
Poplar HARCA 113, 114, 239

post-war period: construction during *14*; demand for public housing during 2, 9; reconstruction during 145, 150, 192; rehousing after 129

Powell, Geoffry 150

prefabrication building techniques 9, 38

preservation. *See* listed buildings

Private Finance Initiative (PFI) 27–8

private investment, in public sector 28

private property, programmes for 30

private sector: building flats and 6, 8, 11; energy efficiency ratings for 29

privatisation 111, 127; of Edward Woods Estate 144; effects of 114; of Ferrier Point 149; funding and 228; interventions and 107; of Keeling House 167; of Park Hill 185, 227; of Parsons House 189; of Tamworth Towers 199; of Weybridge Point 210

programmes, government 25–34, *27*; financing for 27–8; impact of *32*, 33, 36n21; for private property 30; renewable technology incentives 31–2; take-up of 30. *See also individual programmes*

protection status. *See* listed buildings

PRP Architects *83*, 113, 114, 119, 195, 197, 221–4, 240

public housing: creation of 3; demand for 2, 16; energy efficiency ratings 24; in interwar years 19n6; origins of 2–18; output in Britain *14*; in post-war years 2, 9; types of 9; in welfare state 8. *See also* estates; housing stock; tower blocks

public sector, private investment in 28

quality of life 8

Quarry Hill 6

rain screen panel systems 42, *44, 45*

rainwater collection 61, 158

recycling rates 263

refurbishment 1; vs. demolition 15–6, 241–5; emissions reduction and 22–3; new urban lifestyles and 17; opportunities provided by 16–7; research on 33–4. *See also* retrofits; *individual tower blocks*

regulations, energy efficiency 29

rehousing 5. *See also* public housing; tower blocks

Renewable Heat Premium Payment (RHPP) *27*, 31

renewable technology incentives 31–2

replace strategy 41, 42

research, European 267–8

restrictions, economic 219, 258

restrictions on retrofits 215, 240; budgets 225; at Crossways Estate 222; on Greenhouse 230; at Park Hill 228. *See also* listed buildings

Retrofit for the Future 259

retrofits 1; completion timeline *74–81*; economic opportunities of 26; goals of 25; in London 39, *84–94*; measuring energy efficiency of 265–7; need for 24; in North-west England 40, *95–100*; types/techniques 38–100, *43*, 235. *See also* techniques of retrofits

Retrofit UK Ltd 119, 210

RHPP (Renewable Heat Premium Payment) *27*, 31

RIBA (Royal Institute of British Architects) 251, 256, 259

RIBA awards: for Keeling House 167; for Park Hill 178, 238; RIBA Stirling Prize 2013 178

RIBA Statement on Design for Fire Safety 249–50

right-to-buy law 16, 127, 150, 189

Robb, George C. 156

Roberts, Roy 224–6, 240

Robin Hood Garden 14

Rockwool 140

Ronan Point 15, 20n29

Rule 43 letter 255

Rydon Construction Ltd 136, 147, 247

safety 3, 15, 55. *See also* fire safety

St. Andrew's Gardens 6

Saints, The 212–7

Sanctuary Housing 212

SAP (Standard Assessment Procedure) 35n12

Savills estate agents 243–4

Second World War. *See* post-war period

Seddon Construction 197

Shaftesbury House 157. *See also* Greenhouse, Leeds

Sheffield 5, 30, *40. See also* North-west England; *individual towers*
Sheffield City Council 128, 130, 157, 174, 176, 177, 178, 180, 226, 227, 228
Sheffield Homes 130
sheltered housing 17
Sir Thomas White Gardens 6
skin repairs 54, *56*
slab block system 38
slums 3–5, *4*, 11, *13*, 18n2
smart meters 262
smart technologies 158
Smith, Ivor 14, 178
Smithson, Alison 14
Smithson, Peter 14
smoke inhalation injuries 248
social conditions 4–5, 16–7; in Adlington Tower 224; in Crossways Estate 221–2; in Great Arthur House 218; in Park Hill 227; before retrofits 240. *See also* social structure
social housing. *See* estates; public housing; tower blocks
social structure 238–9; of Aragon Tower 111; of Balfron Tower and Carradale House 114; of Brunswick Centre 123, 127; of Crossways Estate 223; of Edward Woods Estate 144; family connections 213; of Ferrier Point 149; of Great Arthur House 220; of Greenhouse 160, 231; of Keeling House 167; maintaining community 215; maintenance of 226; mixing of classes 11; of Park Hill 185, 228; of Parsons House 189; retrofits and 213, 216, 240; of Tamworth Towers 199; of tower blocks 17; of Westbury Estate 206; of Weybridge Point 210. *See also* gentrification; social conditions
solar photovoltaic (PV) 32
Southwark, London Borough of 248, 251, 254, 255, 257
sprinklers 254–6
Sprunt Architects *82, 83*, 110
stakeholders: collaboration with 240; engagement of 215, 219, 222, 225, 227–8, 230. *See also* tenants
Standard Assessment Procedure (SAP) 35n12
standardisation, in construction technology 38

Stepney, Metropolitan Borough of 5–6
stock transfer 28
Studio E Architects 247
Studio Egret West 178, 180
sunlight exposure 6, 14
SUREURO 267
sustainability, environmental 23, 262–5
Swallow, Paul 229–32
Swan Housing Association 118, 119, 221
system building method 38

TABULA 268, 269
Tamworth Towers *40, 81, 195–9*; architects *83*; changes to *52, 98*, 100, 194–9; colour change *69*; design quality/ innovation 236; over-cladding 54
Tarling, Arnold 253
Technics and Civilization (Mumford) 2–3
techniques of retrofits 38–100; add-in strategy 41, 42; add-on strategy 41, 42; application of renewable energies 61–5; common 42, 54; cover-it strategy 41, 42; electrical upgrades 55; extensions and functional conversion 55, 60; for façades 38, 41–2; floor plan improvements 55; functional conversions 55, 60; for insulation 41; mechanical upgrades 55; renewable energies 61; replace strategy 41, 42; skin repair and windows 54; wrap-it strategy 41, 42. *See also* over-cladding; *individual tower blocks*
Technology Strategy Board 259, 261
tenants 17, 240, 265–6; competition for 213; engagement of 20n32, 215, 225, 245–6; during refurbishment 215–6, 218, 222, 225, 228. *See also* stakeholders
terraced housing 123, 176
Terrassenhäuser 123
texture, of façades 41, 43, 67
Thatcher, Margaret 127, 150, 189
thermal comfort 33, 214, 261, 268–9. *See also* insulation; over-cladding
3 Towers Complex *40*, 81; architects *82, 83*; changes to *48, 95, 97, 102–7, 102–7*; colour change *66*; design quality/innovation 236; façade 43; functional conversions 55; site plan *102*

Tour Bois-le-Prêtre 236, *236*
tower blocks: ascent of 8–14, *11, 12, 13*; assessment of 15, 18, 241–3; attitudes toward 14–5, 16, 105; conditions of 25; decline of 14–6; environmental footprint of 24–5; modernity in design of 5, *8*, 9, 11; number of 18, 20n23; social profile of 17. *See also* conditions, physical; estates; housing stock; public housing; *individual tower blocks*
tower cranes 9, 14
Tower Hamlets, Borough of 119
Tower Hamlets Council 114, 162, 165
TP Bennett 186, 250
Trafford Council 194, 195
Trafford Housing Trust 195, 197, 199
Trafford Towers 223
Transform South Yorkshire 180
Trellick Tower *39, 75*, 114, *200, 201, 202*; changes to *58, 90, 94*, 200–2, 235; lack of change 67; listed status 14, 234, 238; windows replacement *54*
Tsavdaris, Dr. 253
Twentieth Century Society 113, 124, 151, 155, 165, 200, 219, 240
25 Minutes (documentary) 224

UK Carbon Plan 22, 28, 216, 240, 269
UK Green Building Council 33
Union North Architects 104
United House London 134, 136
urbanscape 2
Urban Splash Ltd 104, 113, 114, 178, 180, 226–9, 238, 240; retrofit projects *82, 83*; 3 Towers Complex 102

View 146 *40, 52, 79*
Ville Radieuse (Le Corbusier) 2

Wandsworth, Borough Council of 207, 209
Warm Home Discount (WHD) *27*, 31
Warwick Gardens 6
waste management 263
water meters 263–4
Wates Living Space 168, 171
welfare state 3, 8, 21n35
West & Machell Architects 157, 229–32, 240
Westbury and Mawbey Brough estates 203
Westbury Estate *39, 77*, 54, *203–6*; changes to *56, 90, 94, 203–6*; colour change *73*; electrical/mechanical upgrades 55
West Midlands 14
Westminster, City of 168, 186, 188
Westminster City Council 171, 188
Westminster City Planning and Development Planning Department 186
Westminster Homes 171
Weybridge Point *39, 76, 207, 208–11*; changes to *47, 90, 94*, 207–11, 235; colour change *72*; extensions *235*; façade of 43
WHD (Warm Home Discount) *27*, 31
Wilsher, Roy 249
window replacements 54, *56*
wind power 32
Womersley, John Lewis *9*, 128, 129
Woods Environmental 157
workers, rehousing of 5–8
workers hostel 229, 230. *See also* Greenhouse, Leeds
working spaces 181, 185; addition of 55, 60; in houses 268
wrap-it strategy 41, 42

Zeilenbau layout 6, 11, *12*

290   INDEX

PGMO 07/09/2018